AF540273

Methodology of Social Research and Survey

Methodology of SOCIAL RESEARCH AND SURVEY

S.N. Dixit

CENTRUM PRESS
NEW DELHI-110002 (INDIA)

CENTRUM PRESS
H.O.: 4360/4, Ansari Road, Daryaganj,
New Delhi-110002 (India)
Tel: 23278000, 23261597, 23255577, 23286875
B.O.: No. 1015, Ist Main Road, BSK IIIrd Stage,
IIIrd Phase, IIIrd Block, Bengaluru-560085 (INDIA)
Tel: 080-41723429
Email: centrumpress@gmail.com
Visit us at: www.centrumpress.com

Methodology of Social Research and Survey

First Edition, 2011

ISBN 978-93-81293-55-3

PRINTED IN INDIA

Printed at Suman Printers, Jagatpuri Extn., Delhi

Contents

Preface

The effective, efficiency and benefit of the research are based on research method. There are several research methods, such as action research and phenomenography, qualitative research method and quantitative research method. The research methods can be divided in to several ways. But main methods are qualitative and quantitative. Quantitative research is natural science to study natural observed. It may be questionnaire, survey, experiment and numerical method such as mathematical modelling. Qualitative research is much focused on the collection and analysis of numerical data and statistics. Qualitative research method is developing in the social science and it provides researchers to study social and cultural observation. Qualitative research is described about the interview, participant and observation data. It is explain about social observable fact. Also it can be case study research, action research and ethnography.

The research deals with the broad range of human behaviour which affect by diverse influences like environmental, biological, physchological, sociological, etc. In other words, new knowledge is like a new born baby which holds great potential of growth as well as development. Like new born-child, research gives us pleasure. It also gives us satisfaction of knowing unknown that a scientist is self-justifying goodness of scientific knowledge which may be small or big.

Social research thus attempts to create or validate theories through data collection and data analysis, and its goal is exploration, description and explanation. It should never lead or be mistaken with philosophy or belief. Social research aims to find social patterns of regularity in social life and usually deals with social groups (aggregates of individuals), not individuals themselves (although science of psychology is an exception here). Research can also be divided into pure research and applied research. Pure research has no application on real life, whereas applied research attempts to influence the real world.

Research can be defined as the search for knowledge, or as any systematic investigation, with an open mind, to establish novel facts, usually using a scientific method. The primary purpose for applied research (as opposed to basic research) is discovering, interpreting, and the development of methods and systems for the advancement of human knowledge on a wide variety of scientific matters of our world and the universe.

The book attempts to recast the research process into a different and useful perspective (i) detailing the impact of theory upon social research and (ii) examining the impact of researcher upon each step of the research process.

—*Editor*

1

Social Research Theories and Methodology

During the 19th century, philosophers and others advocated the scientific study of human society. It was during that time that many thinkers developed theories about society, followed later by methodologies for testing theories and developing new ones. Theory and methodology go hand in hand when studying patterns of life in human society.

History

The 19th century French philosopher Auguste Comte was an important early figure in the development of social science theories. He believed society could be studied scientifically and objectively at a time when most societal changes were explained in religious terms.

Function

Theory helps social scientists make sense of patterns observed in everyday society. It also helps keep researchers from being taken in by patterns that could just be flukes. Theory also helps shape social research and gives it direction. In this way, theory acts as a guide, pointing researchers to the most interesting issues of society, including its politics, economics and other interactions.

Finally, theory helps researchers understand social phenomena in such a way that can suggest actions. For example, a theory that explains why teenagers drop out of high school can provide a basis for programs and interventions aimed at reducing dropout rates.

Types

Two types of approaches to the relationship between theory and research include the deductive and inductive methods. The deductive method argues from the general to the specific. Under a deductive methodology, a researcher begins with a hypothesis, then makes observations or collects data to test that hypothesis. Based on empirical evidence from the study, the researcher then decides whether to accept or reject the hypothesis. The deductive methodology, in short, tests theories and hypotheses. The inductive method, in contrast, goes from the specific to the general. Under this methodology, social scientists observe social phenomena, identify patterns and then analyse them to reach broad conclusions and develop new theories, based on research findings.

Features

To study social, political and economic phenomena, social scientists use a variety of research designs and methodologies. Research designs include single-group case studies and quasi-experimental designs comparing two groups of subjects. Measurement methods include observations, surveys, interviews, documents, and data from other sources, such as government agencies. To compensate for the inability to randomly assign subjects to treatment and control groups, many social researchers must conduct more in-depth statistical analysis to control for differences between groups of subjects. Research methodologies include qualitative and quantitative methods. Many quantitative studies follow a deductive approach, while many qualitative studies are more inductive.

Considerations

Because social science research occurs within society itself, rather than in the controlled laboratory settings used by the natural sciences, social research methodologies have some limitations that the natural sciences do not. The main limitation is that social researchers usually cannot perform the controlled experiments with random assignment to treatment and control groups. This is usually for ethical and other reasons. A group of social scientists could not, for example, randomly assign academically low-performing children to an experiment in which one group would receive a new instructional intervention and one group would not.

RESEARCH METHODOLOGY AND METHODS

The effective, efficiency and benefit of the research are based on research method. There are several research methods, such as action research and phenomenography, qualitative research method and quantitative research method.

QUALITATIVE RESEARCH AND QUANTITATIVE RESEARCH

The research methods can be divided in to several ways. But main methods are qualitative and quantitative. Quantitative research is natural science to study natural observed. It may be questionnaire, survey, experiment and numerical method such as mathematical modelling. Qualitative research is much focused on the collection and analysis of numerical data and statistics. Qualitative research method is developing in the social science and it provides researchers to study social and cultural observation. Qualitative research is described about the interview, participant and observation data. It is explain about social observable fact. Also it can be case study research, action research and ethnography.

Philosophical Perspectives

Every Research can be qualitative or quantitative. These two ways depend on the assumption, Components and which research method will be appropriate, so when we evaluate qualitative research, we need to know about theses assumptions. One of them suggests as "paradigms" for qualitative research. They are positivism, post-positivism, critical theory and constructivism.. Other suggests got three categories, based on the underlying research "epistemology". They are positivist, interpretive and critical.

Positivist research generally describes by the measurable properties and it does not depend on researcher and his/her instrument. It is generally test theory. It can be evidence of hypothesis testing, observation from sample population and countable measure of variables. "Interpretive researchers start out with the assumption that access to reality (given or socially constructed) is only through social constructions such as language, consciousness and shared meanings. The philosophical base of interpretive research is hermeneutics and phenomenology." "Critical researchers assume that social reality is historically constituted and that it is produced and reproduced by people. Although people can consciously act to change their social and economic circumstances, critical researchers recognize that their ability to do so is constrained by various forms of social, cultural and political domination ".

QUALITATIVE RESEARCH METHODS

Action Research

There are lot of definition of action research method. Action method is solving problem with using practical or experiment things. If you're research is based on "How to" then action research is very appropriate. I+ is also very important when we wish to built collaboration between with various kind of group. We can define action research in following way. "Action research aims to contribute both to the practical concerns of people in an immediate problematic situation and to the goals of social science by joint collaboration within a mutually acceptable ethical framework " The action research is tried to enlarge the stock of knowledge about the social science community.. This is consists with social changes. Kurt Lewin, a Prussian psychologist. He is most often credited with coining the term 'action-research'. He said about action research as "proceeds in a spiral of steps each of which is composed of a circle of planning, action and fact-finding about the result of the action". Spiral level based on many action research method. There are many advantages with action research. They are:

- It is based on practise, so it's avoiding problem of needing to be implements.

- It improves individual and collectives, because it encourages professional workers to recollect and use their strengths.
- It uses validity criteria and validation process based on contributes with practical situation.

Ethnography

Ethnographic research comes from the discipline of social and cultural societies. Ethnographer is needed to spend more about time on the filed. Ethnographers immerse themselves in the lives of the people they study and seek to place the phenomena studied in their social and cultural context. Ethnography now widely used in information system organisation.

GROUNDED THEORY

Grounded theory is theory grounded in experiences. However, it is often cited as a rather loose and unstructured way of approaching observed experience, which then provides grounding of the development theories. According to Martin and Turner (1986), grounded theory is "an inductive, theory discovery methodology that allows the researcher to develop a theoretical account of the general features of a topic while simultaneously grounding the account in empirical observations or data It has specific approach to built the theories, so it's different with other methods. The ground theory suggests there must be reciprocal action among data collection and analysis. This approach is increasing among IS research literature, because the method is extremely useful in developing context-based, process-oriented descriptions and explanations of the phenomenon.

Case Study Research

Case study design becoming spreading in social research. The case study approach generally can choose number of possible events, such as people, social movement and organization. The understanding the case studies, it can be divided in to two main types, and each types can be divided in to sub types. The first type is focus on individual behaviours and experience. The second type consider about the operation of organization, group or social movement. Through these types, a researcher can take the role of "either an outside observer or a participant-observer".. The good case study gives better decision for research. The methodology that follows for case study based on four stages: They are: 1. Design the case study. 2. Conduct the case study. 3. Analyse the case study evidence. 4. Develop the conclusions, recommendation and implication. When we develop the case study we have to consider following things.

- All data about the case is gathered. Example: The case title is based on "A program's failure with client", so we need to collect data about the program, its process and the client. We need collect regarding the documentation things, such as application, historical and records. Also we have to collect questionnaire, interviews and observation.
- Data is organized in to an according to the focus of the study.
- A case study narrative developed. Narrative means it must be readable story that summarised and integrate all the information regarding the case. It must be very clear, so it can be understand the outside the audience very easily.
- The narrative might be validated by review from program participants. It must be fully describe with his/ her experience and results.
- Case studies might be cross-compared to isolate any themes or patterns. We have to explain other case studies regarding that topic with main case study. (McNamara)

"A case study is an empirical inquiry that investigates a contemporary phenomenon within its real-life context, especially when the boundaries between phenomenon and context are not clearly evident."

SOCIAL RESEARCH

Social research refers to research conducted by social scientists. Social research methods may be divided into two broad categories:

- Quantitative designs approach social phenomena through quantifiable evidence, and often rely on statistical analysis of many cases (or across intentionally designed treatments in an experiment) to create valid and reliable general claims
- Qualitative designs emphasize understanding of social phenomena through direct observation, communication with participants, or analysis of texts, and may stress contextual and subjective accuracy over generality.

Social scientists employ a range of methods in order to analyse a vast breadth of social phenomena; from census survey data derived from millions of individuals, to the in-depth analysis of a single agents' social experiences; from monitoring what is happening on contemporary streets, to the investigation of ancient historical documents. The methods rooted in classical sociology and statistics have formed the basis for research in other disciplines, such as political science, media studies, and market research.

Methodology

Social scientists are divided into camps of support for particular research techniques. These disputes relate to the historical core of social theory (positivism and antipositivism; structure and agency). While very different in many aspects, both qualitative and quantitative approaches involve a systematic interaction between theory and data. The choice of method often depends largely on what the researcher intends to investigate.

For example, a researcher concerned with drawing a statistical generalization across an entire population may administer a survey questionnaire to a representitive sample population. By contrast, a researcher who seeks full contextual understanding of an individuals' social actions may choose ethnographic participant observation or open-ended interviews. Studies will commonly combine, or 'triangulate', quantitative *and* qualitative methods as part of a 'multi-strategy' design. For instance, a quantitative study may be performed to gain statistical patterns or a target sample, and then combined with a qualitative interview to determine the play of agency. An extreme form of ethnographic participant observation is practiced when a group of social scientists (1) build and occupy an experimental community, (2) observe and record their own behaviours, (3) experimentally test possible solutions to their personal and social problems, (4) deliberately adopt experimentally validated solutions, and (5) publish reports about the evolution of their culture.

Sampling

Typically a population is very large, making a census or a complete enumeration of all the values in that population infeasible. A 'sample' thus forms a manageable subset of a population.

In positivist research, statistics derived from a sample are analysed in order to draw inferences regarding the population as a whole. The process of collecting information from a sample is referred to as 'sampling'. Sampling methods may be either 'random' (random sampling, systematic sampling, stratified sampling, cluster sampling) or non-random/nonprobability (convenience sampling, purposive sampling, snowball sampling). The most common reason for sampling is to obtain information about a population. Sampling is quicker and cheaper than a complete census of a population.

Ethics

The primary assumptions of the ethics in social research are:

- Voluntary participation
- No physical or psychological harm to subjects
- Integrity
- PAC: Privacy, anonymity and confidentiality.

FOUNDATIONS OF SOCIAL RESEARCH

Sociological Positivism

The origin of the survey can be traced back at least early as the Domesday Book in 1086, whilst some scholars pinpoint the origin of demography to 1663 with the publication of John Graunt's *Natural and Political Observations upon the Bills of Mortality*. Social research began most intentionally, however, with the positivist philosophy of science in the early 19th century.

Auguste Comte (1798–1857) first described the epistemological perspective of positivism in *The Course in Positive Philosophy*, a series of texts published between 1830 and 1842. These texts were followed by the 1844 work, *A General View of Positivism*. The first three volumes of the *Course* dealt chiefly with the physical sciences already in existence (mathematics, astronomy, physics, chemistry, biology), whereas the latter two emphasized the inevitable coming of social science. Observing the circular dependence of theory and observation in science, and classifying the sciences in this way, Comte may be regarded as the first philosopher of science in the modern sense of the term. For him, the physical sciences had necessarily to arrive first, before humanity could adequately channel its efforts into the most challenging and complex "Queen science" of human society itself.

Modern social research, and indeed the formal academic discipline of sociology, began with the work of Émile Durkheim (1858–1917). While Durkheim rejected much of the detail of Comte's philosophy, he retained and refined its method, maintaining that the social sciences are a logical continuation of the natural ones into the realm of human activity, and insisting that they may retain the same objectivity, rationalism, and approach to causality. Durkheim set up the first European department of sociology at the University of Bordeaux in 1895, publishing his Rules of the Sociological Method (1895). In this text he argued: "[o]ur main goal is to extend scientific rationalism to human conduct... What has been called our positivism is but a consequence of this rationalism."

Durkheim's seminal monograph, *Suicide* (1897), a case study of suicide rates amongst Catholic and Protestant populations, distinguished sociological analysis from psychology or philosophy.

By carefully examining suicide statistics in different police districts, he attempted to demonstrate that Catholic communities have a lower suicide rate than that of Protestants, something he attributed to social (as opposed to individual or psychological) causes. He developed the notion of objective *suis generis* "social facts" to delineate a unique empirical object for the science of sociology to study. Through such studies he posited that sociology would be able to determine whether any given society is 'healthy' or 'pathological', and seek social reform to negate organic breakdown or "social anomie". For Durkheim, sociology could be described as the "science of institutions, their genesis and their functioning".

Methodological Assumptions

Social research is based on logic and empirical observations. Charles C. Ragin writes in his *Constructing Social Research* book that "Social research involved the interaction between ideas and evidence. Ideas help social researchers make sense of evidence, and researchers use evidence to extend, revise and test ideas". Social research thus attempts to create or validate theories through data collection and data analysis, and its goal is exploration, description and explanation. It should never lead or be mistaken with philosophy or belief. Social research aims to find social patterns of regularity in social life and usually deals with social groups (aggregates of individuals), not individuals themselves (although science of psychology is an exception here). Research can also be divided into pure research and applied research. Pure research has no application on real life, whereas applied research attempts to influence the real world.

There are no laws in social science that parallel the laws in the natural science. A law in social science is a universal generalization about a class of facts. A fact is an observed phenomenon, and observation means it has been seen, heard or otherwise experienced by researcher. A theory is a systematic explanation for the observations that relate to a particular aspect of social life. Concepts are the basic building blocks of theory and are abstract elements representing classes of phenomena. Axioms or postulates are basic assertions assumed to be true. Propositions are conclusions drawn about the relationships among concepts, based on analysis of axioms. Hypotheses are specified expectations about empirical reality which are derived from propositions. Social research involves testing these hypotheses to see if they are true.

Social research involves creating a theory, operationalization (measurement of variables) and observation (actual collection of data to test hypothesized relationship). Social theories are written in the language of variables, in other words, theories describe logical relationships between variables. Variables are logical sets of attributes, with people being the 'carriers' of those variables (for example, gender can be a variable with two attributes: male and female). Variables are also divided into independent variables (data) that influences the dependent variables (which scientists are trying to explain). For example, in a study of how different dosages of a drug are related to the severity of symptoms of a disease, a measure of the severity of the symptoms of the disease is a dependent variable and the administration of the drug in specified doses is the independent variable. Researchers will compare the different values of the dependent variable (severity of the symptoms) and attempt to draw conclusions.

Rules for Social Research

Although there are no laws in social science that parallel laws in the natural sciences, there is consensus about fundamental rules or principles about how to do social research. When social scientists speak of "good research" the focus is on how the research is done – whether the research is methodologically sound – rather than on whether the results of the research are consistent with personal biases or preconceptions. Glenn Firebaugh summarizes the principles for good research in his book *Seven Rules for Social Research.* The first rule is that "There should be the possibility of surprise in social research." As Firebaugh elaborates: "Rule 1 is intended to warn that you don't want to be blinded by preconceived ideas so that you fail to look for contrary evidence, or you fail to recognize contrary evidence when you do encounter it, or you recognize contrary evidence but suppress it and refuse to accept your findings for what they appear to say." In addition, good research will "look for differences that make a difference" (Rule 2) and "build in reality checks" (Rule 3). Rule 4 advises researchers to replicate, that is, "to see if identical analyses yield similar results for different samples of people". The next two rules urge researchers to "compare like with like" (Rule 5) and to "study change" (Rule 6); these two rules are especially important when researchers want to estimate the effect of one variable on another (e.g. how much does college education actually matter for wages?). The final rule, "Let method be the servant, not the master," reminds researchers that methods are the means, not the end, of social research; it is critical from the outset to fit the research design to the research issue, rather than the other way around.

Types of Explanations

Explanations in social theories can be idiographic or nomothetic. An idiographic approach to an explanation is one where the scientists seek to exhaust the idiosyncratic causes of a particular condition or event, i.e. by trying to provide all possible explanations of a particular case. Nomothetic explanations tend to be more general with scientists trying to identify a few causal factors that impact a wide class of conditions or events. For example, when dealing with the problem of how people choose a job, idiographic explanation would be to list all possible reasons why a given person (or group) chooses a given job, while nomothetic explanation would try to find factors that determine why job applicants in general choose a given job.

SURVEY RESEARCH

Survey research is one of the most important areas of measurement in applied social research. The broad area of survey research encompasses any measurement procedures that involve asking questions of respondents. A "survey" can be anything form a short paper-and-pencil feedback form to an intensive one-on-one in-depth interview.

We'll begin by looking at the different types of surveys that are possible. These are roughly divided into two broad areas:

Questionnaires and Interviews. Next, we'll look at how you select the survey method that is best for your situation. Once you've selected the survey method, you have to construct the survey itself. Here, we will be address a number of issues including: the different types of questions; decisions about question content; decisions about question wording; decisions about response format; and, question placement and sequence in your instrument. We turn next to some of the special issues involved in administering a personal interview. Finally, we'll consider some of the advantages and disadvantages of survey methods.

TYPES OF SURVEYS

Surveys can be divided into two broad categories: the questionnaire and the interview. Questionnaires are usually paper-and-pencil instruments that the respondent completes. Interviews are completed by the interviewer based on the respondent says.

Sometimes, it's hard to tell the difference between a questionnaire and an interview. For instance, some people think that questionnaires always ask short closed-ended questions while interviews always ask broad open-ended ones. But you will see questionnaires with open-ended questions (although they do tend to be shorter than in interviews) and there will often be a series of closed-ended questions asked in an interview.

Survey research has changed dramatically in the last ten years. We have automated telephone surveys that use random dialing methods. There are computerized kiosks in public places that allows people to ask for input. A whole new variation of group interview has evolved as focus group methodology. Increasingly, survey research is tightly integrated with the delivery of service.

Your hotel room has a survey on the desk. Your waiter presents a short customer satisfaction survey with your check. You get a call for an interview several days after your last call to a computer company for technical assistance. You're asked to complete a short survey when you visit a web site. Here, I'll describe the major types of questionnaires and interviews, keeping in mind that technology is leading to rapid evolution of methods.

Questionnaires

When most people think of questionnaires, they think of the mail survey. All of us have, at one time or another, received a questionnaire in the mail. There are many advantages to mail surveys. They are relatively inexpensive to administer. You can send the exact same instrument to a wide number of people. They allow the respondent to fill it out at their own convenience. But there are some disadvantages as well. Response rates from mail surveys are often very low. And, mail questionnaires are not the best vehicles for asking for detailed written responses.

A second type is the group administered questionnaire. A sample of respondents is brought together and asked to respond to a structured sequence of questions. Traditionally, questionnaires were administered in group settings for convenience. The researcher could give the questionnaire to those who were present and be fairly sure that there would be a high response rate. If the respondents were unclear about the meaning of a question they could ask for clarification. And, there were often organizational settings where it was relatively easy to assemble the group (in a company or business, for instance).

What's the difference between a group administered questionnaire and a group interview or focus group? In the group administered questionnaire, each respondent is *handed an instrument* and asked to complete it while in the room. Each respondent completes an instrument. In the group interview or focus group, the interviewer facilitates the session. People work as a group, listening to each other's comments and answering the questions. Someone takes notes for the entire group — people don't complete an interview individually.

A less familiar type of questionnaire is the household drop-off survey. In this approach, a researcher goes to the respondent's home or business and hands the respondent the instrument. In some cases, the respondent is asked to mail it back or the interview returns to pick it up. This approach attempts to blend the advantages of the mail survey and the group administered questionnaire. Like the mail survey, the respondent can work on the instrument in private, when it's convenient.

Like the group administered questionnaire, the interviewer makes personal contact with the respondent — they don't just send an impersonal survey instrument. And, the respondent can ask questions about the study and get clarification on what is to be done. Generally, this would be expected to increase the percent of people who are willing to respond.

Interviews

Interviews are a far more personal form of research than questionnaires. In the personal interview, the interviewer works directly with the respondent. Unlike with mail surveys, the interviewer has the opportunity to probe or ask follow-up questions.

And, interviews are generally easier for the respondent, especially if what is sought is opinions or impressions. Interviews can be very time consuming and they are resource intensive. The interviewer is considered a part of the measurement instrument and interviewers have to be well trained in how to respond to any contingency.

Almost everyone is familiar with the telephone interview. Telephone interviews enable a researcher to gather information rapidly. Most of the major public opinion polls that are reported were based on telephone interviews.

Like personal interviews, they allow for some personal contact between the interviewer and the respondent. And, they allow the interviewer to ask follow-up questions. But they also have some major disadvantages. Many people don't have publicly-listed telephone numbers. Some don't have telephones. People often don't like the intrusion of a call to their homes. And, telephone interviews have to be relatively short or people will feel imposed upon.

SELECTING THE SURVEY METHOD

Selecting the type of survey you are going to use is one of the most critical decisions in many social research contexts. You'll see that there are very few simple rules that will make the decision for you — you have to use your judgment to balance the advantages and disadvantages of different survey types.

Population Issues

Can the population be enumerated? For some populations, you have a complete listing of the units that will be sampled. For others, such a list is difficult or impossible to compile. For instance, there are complete listings of registered voters or person with active drivers licenses. But no one keeps a complete list of homeless people. If you are doing a study that requires input from homeless persons, you are very likely going to need to go and find the respondents personally. In such contexts, you can pretty much rule out the idea of mail surveys or telephone interviews.

Is the population literate? Questionnaires require that your respondents can read. While this might seem initially like a reasonable assumption for many adult populations, we know from recent research that the instance of adult illiteracy is alarmingly high. And, even if your respondents can read to some degree, your questionnaire may contain difficult or technical vocabulary. Clearly, there are some populations that you would expect to be illiterate. Young children would not be good targets for questionnaires.

Are there language issues? We live in a multilingual world. Virtually every society has members who speak other than the predominant language. Some countries (like Canada) are officially multilingual. And, our increasingly global economy requires us to do research that spans countries and language groups. Can you produce multiple versions of your questionnaire?

For mail instruments, can you know in advance the language your respondent speaks, or do you send multiple translations of your instrument? Can you be confident that important connotations in your instrument are not culturally specific? Could some of the important nuances get lost in the process of translating your questions?

Will the population cooperate? People who do research on immigration issues have a difficult methodological problem. They often need to speak with undocumented immigrants or people who may be able to identify others who are. Why would we expect those respondents to cooperate? Although the researcher may mean no harm, the respondents are at considerable risk legally if information they divulge should get into the hand of the authorities. The same can be said for any target group that is engaging in illegal or unpopular activities.

What are the geographic restrictions? Is your population of interest dispersed over too broad a geographic range for you to study feasibly with a personal interview? It may be possible for you to send a mail instrument to a nationwide sample. You may be able to conduct phone interviews with them. But it will almost certainly be less feasible to do research that requires interviewers to visit directly with respondents if they are widely dispersed.

Sampling Issues

The sample is the actual group you will have to contact in some way. There are several important sampling issues you need to consider when doing survey research.

What data is available? What information do you have about your sample? Do you know their current addresses? Their current phone numbers? Are your contact lists up to date?

Can respondents be found? Can your respondents be located? Some people are very busy. Some travel a lot. Some work the night shift. Even if you have an accurate phone or address, you may not be able to locate or make contact with your sample.

Who is the respondent? Who is the respondent in your study? Let's say you draw a sample of households in a small city. A household is not a respondent. Do you want to interview a specific individual? Do you want to talk only to the "head of household" (and how is that person defined)? Are you willing to talk to any member of the household? Do you state that you will speak to the first adult member of the household who opens the door?

What if that person is unwilling to be interviewed but someone else in the house is willing? How do you deal with multi-family households? Similar problems arise when you sample groups, agencies, or companies. Can you survey any member of the organization? Or, do you only want to speak to the Director of Human Resources? What if the person you would like to interview is unwilling or unable to participate? Do you use another member of the organization?

Can all members of population be sampled? If you have an incomplete list of the population (i.e., sampling frame) you may not be able to sample every member of the population. Lists of various groups are extremely hard to keep up to date. People move or change their names. Even though they are on your sampling frame listing, you may not be able to get to them. And, it's possible they are not even on the list.

Are response rates likely to be a problem? Even if you are able to solve all of the other population and sampling problems, you still have to deal with the issue of response rates. Some members of your sample will simply refuse to respond. Others have the best of intentions, but can't seem to find the time to send in your questionnaire by the due date. Still others misplace the instrument or forget about the appointment for an interview. Low response rates are among the most difficult of problems in survey research. They can ruin an otherwise well-designed survey effort.

Question Issues

Sometimes the nature of what you want to ask respondents will determine the type of survey you select.

- What types of questions can be asked? Are you going to be asking personal questions? Are you going to need to get lots of detail in the responses? Can you anticipate the most frequent or important types of responses and develop reasonable closed-ended questions?

- How complex will the questions be? Sometimes you are dealing with a complex subject or topic. The questions you want to ask are going to have multiple parts. You may need to branch to sub-questions.
- Will screening questions be needed? A screening question may be needed to determine whether the respondent is qualified to answer your question of interest. For instance, you wouldn't want to ask someone their opinions about a specific computer program without first "screening" them to find out whether they have any experience using the program. Sometimes you have to screen on several variables (e.g., age, gender, experience). The more complicated the screening, the less likely it is that you can rely on paper-and-pencil instruments without confusing the respondent.
- Can question sequence be controlled? Is your survey one where you can construct in advance a reasonable sequence of questions? Or, are you doing an initial exploratory study where you may need to ask lots of follow-up questions that you can't easily anticipate?
- Will lengthy questions be asked? If your subject matter is complicated, you may need to give the respondent some detailed background for a question. Can you reasonably expect your respondent to sit still long enough in a phone interview to ask your question?
- Will long response scales be used? If you are asking people about the different computer equipment they use, you may have to have a lengthy response list (CD-ROM drive, floppy drive, mouse, touch pad, modem, network connection, external speakers, etc.). Clearly, it may be difficult to ask about each of these in a short phone interview.

Content Issues

The content of your study can also pose challenges for the different survey types you might utilize.

- Can the respondents be expected to know about the issue? If the respondent does not keep up with the news (e.g., by reading the newspaper, watching television news, or talking with others), they may not even know about the news issue you want to ask them about. Or, if you want to do a study of family finances and you are talking to the spouse who doesn't pay the bills on a regular basis, they may not have the information to answer your questions.
- Will respondent need to consult records? Even if the respondent understands what you're asking about, you may need to allow them to consult their records in order to get an accurate answer. For instance, if you ask them how much money they spent on food in the past month, they may need to look up their personal check and credit card records. In this case, you don't want to be involved in an interview where they would have to go look things up while they keep you waiting.

Bias Issues

People come to the research endeavour with their own sets of biases and prejudices. Sometimes, these biases will be less of a problem with certain types of survey approaches.

- Can social desirability be avoided? Respondents generally want to "look good" in the eyes of others. None of us likes to look like we don't know an answer. We don't want to say anything that would be embarrassing. If you ask people about information that may put them in this kind of position, they may not tell you the truth, or they may "spin" the response so that it makes them look better. This may be more of a problem in an interview situation where they are face-to face or on the phone with a live interviewer.
- Can interviewer distortion and subversion be controlled? Interviewers may distort an interview as well. They may not ask questions that make them uncomfortable. They may not listen carefully to respondents on topics for which they have strong opinions. They may make

the judgment that they already know what the respondent would say to a question based on their prior responses, even though that may not be true.

- Can false respondents be avoided? With mail surveys it may be difficult to know who actually responded. Did the head of household complete the survey or someone else? Did the CEO actually give the responses or instead pass the task off to a subordinate? Is the person you're speaking with on the phone actually who they say they are? At least with personal interviews, you have a reasonable chance of knowing who you are speaking with. In mail surveys or phone interviews, this may not be the case.

Administrative Issues

Last, but certainly not least, you have to consider the feasibility of the survey method for your study.

- costs : Cost is often the major determining factor in selecting survey type. You might prefer to do personal interviews, but can't justify the high cost of training and paying for the interviewers. You may prefer to send out an extensive mailing but can't afford the postage to do so.
- facilities : Do you have the facilities (or access to them) to process and manage your study? In phone interviews, do you have well-equipped phone surveying facilities? For focus groups, do you have a comfortable and accessible room to host the group? Do you have the equipment needed to record and transcribe responses?
- time : Some types of surveys take longer than others. Do you need responses immediately (as in an overnight public opinion poll)? Have you budgeted enough time for your study to send out mail surveys and follow-up reminders, and to get the responses back by mail? Have you allowed for enough time to get enough personal interviews to justify that approach?
- personnel : Different types of surveys make different demands of personnel. Interviews require interviewers

who are motivated and well-trained. Group administered surveys require people who are trained in group facilitation. Some studies may be in a technical area that requires some degree of expertise in the interviewer.

Clearly, there are lots of issues to consider when you are selecting which type of survey you wish to use in your study. And there is no clear and easy way to make this decision in many contexts. There may not be one approach which is clearly the best. You may have to make tradeoffs of advantages and disadvantages. There is judgment involved. Two expert researchers may, for the very same problem or issue, select entirely different survey methods. But, if you select a method that isn't appropriate or doesn't fit the context, you can doom a study before you even begin designing the instruments or questions themselves.

CONSTRUCTING THE SURVEY

Constructing a survey instrument is an art in itself. There are numerous small decisions that must be made — about content, wording, format, placement — that can have important consequences for your entire study. While there's no one perfect way to accomplish this job, we do have lots of advice to offer that might increase your chances of developing a better final product.

First of all you'll learn about the two major types of surveys that exist, the questionnaire and the interview and the different varieties of each. Then you'll see how to write questions for surveys. There are three areas involved in writing a question:

- determining the question content, scope and purpose
- choosing the response format that you use for collecting information from the respondent
- figuring out how to word the question to get at the issue of interest

Finally, once you have your questions written, there is the issue of how best to place them in your survey.

You'll see that although there are many aspects of survey construction that are just common sense, if you are not careful you can make critical errors that have dramatic effects on your results.

DESIGN OF SOCIOLOGICAL RESEARCH

"Design of Sociological Research" or Research Design is a broad plan of a piece of empirical research specifying the manner in which data are to be collected and analyzed in order to test Research Design derived from theory, or to develop insights into the problem being investigated. It combines relevance of the problem with economy in procedure. The design stage is most crucial phase of the research process. A particular design may specify whether experiment, social survey, participant observation, other methods, or a combination of more than one method will be used.

Nowadays it has became imperative to chart out the research design before starting any work, Modern research in sociology thus specifies the probable method to be used for date collection analysis, etc keeping in view, time money and, of course, the topic of research. Generally, a research design includes the following steps:

a) Universe of Study (whether a tribe, or a village, or an urban areas, or a particular group, etc.)

b) Subject of Study (whether it focuses on the whole society, or any specific institution or a part of it).

c) Tentative relationship between certain variables (Formulating a Research Design but it is not obligatory to start with a Research Design; certain research designs lack Research Design).

d) Sets of selected methods (whether participant observation, Interview, Questionnaire, or some other methods of data collection would be used).

e) Analytical categories (by which the empirical data is subjected to analysis and interpretation).

Although the steps for formulating a research design remain common the designs differ, depending on the research purpose. The latter may be to report an unknown tribe, or to investigate the intricacies of an institution, or to test a specific Research

Design in field situation, or to test a well-designed Research Design in controlled situations.

Depending on the research purpose, one delineates an appropriate research design. However, validity of the steps for forming the design will always have to be there. Every study has its own purpose, but all the research purposes can be conceptualized as falling in one of the following categories. Each category refers to a type of research design. Thus, generally, social scientists identify three types of research design on the basis of different research purposes.

These are:

Explanatory Research Design

When the purpose of the study is to explore a new universe, one that has not been studied earlier, the research design, is called explanatory. The research purpose in this case is to gain familiarity in unknown areas. Often explanatory research design is used to formulate a problem for precise investigation, or aims at formulating Research Design. Thus, often when the universe of study is an unknown community, explanatory design forms the first step of research, after which other types of research designs can be used.

Two very good examples of explanatory designs are:

(i) Malinowski's study of Trobriand society; and

(ii) Whyte's study of the Street Corner Society.

Both these studies for the collection of data have relied on the special method of participant observation. Both researchers had an explanatory objective.

Rather than aiming to test a limited set of specific Research Design, Malinowski and Whyte present in advance only the out line a conceptual model and provide a wide range of detail from which a number of other Research Design can be derived. Instead of concentrating on just unspecific areas and selecting a few aspects for consideration (as may be the case in descriptive research design), researchers gather such a great variety of data that they are able to see the actors in their total life situation.

Explanatory studies are not to be confused with raw empiricism, with fact gathering that is unrelated to sociological theory. The explanatory study always carries with it a set of concepts that guide the researcher to look for the facts.

Descriptive Research Design

Generally, if a researcher is studying a community which is familiar and his research purpose is to depict accurately and in detail the characteristics of a particular institution, group or an event in the community, the appropriate research design is called Descriptive research Design.

Sometimes, descriptive design forms a second step of research, the first step being explanatory design. Thus some times, research Research Design is formulated through explanatory design and to test the Research Design, descriptive design is formulated.

Experimental research Design

The research desig . that is used to test a Research Design of causal relationship under controlled situation is called experimental design. The essence of the experimental design (in sociology) lies in its testing Research Design derived from a theory.

The experimentation in sociology observes the following aspects:

a. In an experimental design, the investigator controls or manipulates an independent variable or stimulus (X),

b. And observes the effects on the dependent variable (Y), and

c. The effect of the independent variable on the dependent variable is observed by minimizing the effects of extraneous variables that might confound the result.

e. These propositions are tested off on the sample, generally called the experimental sample (E).

Experimentation in sociology raises certain important questions, viz. ethical question, difficulties in forming a control sample and retaining it over time; the difficulties encountered in controlling the extraneous environment, etc. Realizing these problems, in some of the 'experiments' carried out by sociologists, the experimental sample is used as the control sample.

It is debatable whether the absence of a control means a non-experimental study. This actually is a modification of the classic experimental design.

The theoretical propositions followed here are the following.

i. Experimental sample is also the control sample.
ii. The experimental sample is measured in the given respect before introducing the independent variable,
iii. After it has been measured, the stimulus for independent variable is introduced.
iv. The experimental sample is measured after stimulus and the change is calculated.

Experimental Methods and Survey

What we've focused on is called Experimental Methods, the true experiment. It involves randomized assignment of subjects, standardized instructions, and at least one IV and one DV. There are several other types of research that are not as rigorous, but that you need to be aware of.

Perhaps the simplest form of research is Naturalistic Observation.

Observing behaviour in their natural environment.

Often involves counting behaviors, such as number of aggressive acts, number of smiles, etc.

Advantages: Behaviour is naturally occurring and is not manipulated by a researcher and it can provide more qualitative data as opposed to merely quantitative information.

Limitations: Even the presence of someone observing can cause those being observed to alter their behaviour. Researcher's beliefs can also alter their observations. And, it is very difficult to coordinate multiple observers since observed behaviors must be operationally defined (e.g. what constitutes an aggressive act)

Survey

Everyone has probably heard of this and many of you have been involved in research involving surveys. They are often used in the news, especially to gather viewer opinions such as during a race for president

Advantages: Can gather large amounts of information in a relatively short time, especially now with many surveys being conducted on the internet.

Limitations: Survey data is based solely on subjects' responses which can be inaccurate due to outright lying, misunderstanding of the question, placebo effect, and even the manner in which the question is asked

Correlational Studies

Correlation means relationship, so the purpose of a correlational study is to determine if a relationship exists, what direction the relationship is, and how strong it is.

Advantages: Can assess the strength of a relationship. Is popular with lay population because it is relatively easy to explain and understand.

Limitations: Can not make any assumptions of cause and effect (explain how third a variable can be involved, or how the variables can influence each other).

2

Survey Methodology

Mailed, self-administered questionnaires are a common data collection method used in family practice research. However, little guidance exists in the medical literature about survey methodology specifically designed for family practitioners. As a result, primary care physicians sometimes struggle with questionnaire design and interpretation. Our goal was to synthesize general survey methodology guidelines (from other disciplines as well as our own) in a manner that would be meaningful to novice family practice researchers.

Research using self-developed questionnaires is a popular study design in family practice and is frequently used for gathering data on knowledge, beliefs, attitudes, and behaviours. A Medline literature search from 1966 to 2000 identified 53,101 articles related to questionnaires, of which 2088 were directly related to family practice. Despite the large number of questionnaire-related articles, however, only 2 in the general medical literature and 1 in the family practice literature were directly related to research methodology.

To obtain guidance on survey research methodology, novice family practice researchers often must go through volumes of information by specialists in other disciplines. For example, a search of a psychology database (PsychInfo) from 1966 to 2000 produced 45 articles about questionnaire methodology. The goal of this chapter is to synthesize pertinent survey research methodology tenets-from other disciplines as well as from family practice-in a manner that is meaningful to novice family practice researchers as well as to research consumers. This chapter is not aimed at answering all questions, but rather is meant to serve as a general guideline for those with little formal research training who seek guidance in developing and administering questionnaires.

Avoiding Common Pitfalls in Survey Research

Although constructing a questionnaire is not exceedingly complex, simple mistakes can be avoided by following some basic rules and guidelines. The Figure is a checklist for conducting a survey research project that combines guidelines and suggestions from published survey research literature, and the cumulative experience of the authors. Two of the authors (M.J.D. and K.C.O.) are experienced survey researchers who have published, in peer-reviewed journals, numerous studies that used questionnaires. One of the authors (MJD) has been teaching research to residents and junior faculty for over a decade, and has been an advisor on scores of resident, student, and faculty research projects. The perspective of the novice researcher is represented by 1 author (C.R.W.).

Getting Started

The "quick and dirty" approach is perhaps the most common pitfall in survey research. Because of the ease of administration and the relatively low cost of survey research, questionnaires can be developed and administered quickly. The researcher, however, should be sure to consider whether or not a survey is the most appropriate method to answer a research question. Adequate time must be given to thoroughly searching the relevant literature, developing and focusing on an appropriate research question, and defining the target population for the study. Large, multisite surveys are more likely to be generalizeable and to be published in peer-reviewed journals.

One way to avoid undertaking a project too rapidly and giving inadequate attention to the survey research process is for novice researchers to avoid independent research. Those with little or no experience must realize that researchers in both family practice and other fields perform research in teams, with the various participants bringing specific skills to the process. Oversights, mistakes, and biases in the design of questionnaires can always occur, whether a researcher is working independently or as a member of a team. It seems reasonable to assume, however, that significant problems are much less likely to occur when a multidisciplinary team approach is involved rather than an individual researcher undertaking a study independently.

Ideally, a research team should include a statistician, a professional with experience in the content areas of the study, and a senior investigator.

The desirable area of expertise, however, is often not readily available to family physicians, especially those in community-based settings. Individuals with some training in research who are interested in being involved can usually be found in colleges and universities, hospitals, and at the local public health department.

Psychologists, sociologists, health services researchers, public health epidemiologists, and nursing educators are all potential resources and possible collaborators. Establishing the necessary relationships to form an ad hoc research team is certainly more time and labour intensive than undertaking research independently, but generally results in the collection of more useful information.

Novices should consult survey methodology books before and during the study. Excellent resources are available that provide a comprehensive overview of survey methods, means for improving response rates, and methods for constructing relatively brief but thorough survey questions. Academic family practice fellowships often provide training in survey methodology. In addition, many family practice researchers respond favorably to requests for information or advice requested by telephone or email contact. The novice author of this chapter reports excellent success in contacting experts in this manner. With the advent of the Internet, a "cyberspace" team comprised of experts in the topic and the methodology is a reasonable and helpful option for the novice.

Survey Content and Structure

Novice researchers often assume that developing a questionnaire is an intuitive process attainable by virtually anyone, regardless of their level of research training. While it is true that questionnaires are relatively simple to construct, developing an instrument that is valid and reliable is not intuitive. An instrument is valid if it actually measures what we think it is measuring, and it is reliable if it measures the phenomenon consistently in repeated applications. By following a few basic guidelines, those with limited research training can develop survey instruments capable of producing valid and reliable information. The 3 primary concerns for developing appropriate questions (items) are: (1) response format; (2) content; and (3) wording and placement.

Format

Questionnaires generally use a closed-ended format rather than an open-ended format. Closed formats spell out response options instead of asking study subjects to respond in their own words. Although there are many reasons for using closed formats, their primary advantages over open formats is that they are more specific and provide the same frame of reference to all respondents, and they allow quantitative analysis. A disadvantage is that they limit the possible range of responses envisioned by the investigators. Questionnaires with closed formats are therefore not as helpful as qualitative methods in the early, exploratory phases of a research project.

Closed-ended items can be formatted into several different categories (classes) of measurement, based on the relationship of the response categories to one another. Nominal measurements are responses that are sorted into unordered categories, such as demographic variables (ie, sex, ethnicity). Ordinal measurements are similar to nominal, except that there is a definite order to the categories. For example, ordinal items may ask respondents to rank their preferences among a list of options from the least desirable to the most desirable.

Survey items that ask for respondents(delete apostrophe) to rank order preferences are often a more useful than items that state, "check all that apply." While checking all relevant responses may be necessary for certain items, such questions often lose valuable information as they can only supply raw percentages without supplying any comparison between responses.

Two additional tools used on questionnaires are continuous variables and scales. Continuous variables can be simple counts (eg, the number of times something occurred) or physical attributes (eg, age or weight). A general rule when collecting information on continuous variables is to avoid obtaining the information in ranges of categories unless absolutely necessary. Response categories that reflect ranges of responses can always be constructed after the information is gathered, but if the information is gathered in ranges from the start, it cannot later be expanded to reflect specific values.

Scales are used by survey researchers to assess the intensity of respondents' attitudes about a specific issue or issues. Likert scales are probably the best known and most widely used for measuring attitudes. These scales typically present respondents with a statement and ask them to indicate whether they "strongly agree," "agree," "neither agree nor disagree," "disagree," or "strongly disagree." The wording of the response categories can be changed to reflect other concepts (eg, approval or disapproval), and the standard 5-response format can be expanded or abbreviated if necessary.

There are no hard and fast rules for determining the number of response categories to use for scaled items, or whether to use a neutral category or one that reflects uncertainty. Research indicates that the reliability of respondents' ratings declines when using more than 9 rating scale points. However, the reliability of a scale increases when the number of rating scale points is increased, with maximum benefit achieved with 5 or 7 scale points. Since the objective of using scales is to gauge respondent's preferences, it is sometimes argued that a middle point or category of uncertainty category should not be used. Odd-numbered rating scales, however, conform better with the underlying tenets of many statistical tests, suggesting the need for including this category. As the number of rating scale points increases, respondents' use of the midpoint category decreases substantially. Thus, based on the available literature, it is generally advisable to use between 5 and 7 response categories and an uncertainty category, unless there is a compelling reason to force respondents to choose between 2 competing perspectives or alternatives.

Content

Items should not be included on questionnaires when the only justification for inclusion is that the investigator feels the information "would be really interesting to know." Rather, for each item, you should ask yourself how it addresses the study's research question and how it will be used in the data analysis stage of the study. Researchers should develop a data analysis plan in advance of administering a questionnaire to determine exactly how each question will be used in the analysis. When the relationship between a particular item and the study's research question is unclear, or it is not known how an item will be used in the analysis, the item should be removed from the questionnaire.

Wording and Placement

The wording of questions should be kept simple, regardless of the education level of the respondents. Questions should be kept as short and direct as possible since shorter surveys tend to have higher response rates. Each question should be scrutinized to ensure it is appropriate for the respondents and does not require or assume an inappropriate level of knowledge about a topic. Since first impressions are important for setting the tone of a questionnaire, never begin with sensitive or threatening questions. Questionnaires should begin with simple, introductory ("warm-up")"questions to help establish trust and an appropriate frame of mind for respondents. Other successful strategies are: (1) when addressing multiple topics, insert an introductory statement immediately preceding each topic (eg, "In the next section we would like to ask you about ..."); (2) request demographic information at the end of the questionnaire; and (3) always provide explicit instructions to avoid any confusion on the part of respondents.

Additional, clear information on survey content and structure is available in 2 books from Sage Publications. By following simple guidelines and common sense, most family practice researchers can construct valid and reliable questionnaires. As a final safeguard, once a final draft of the questionnaire is completed, the researcher should always be the first respondent. By placing yourself in the respondent's role and taking the time to think about and respond to each question, problems with the instrument that were overlooked are sometimes identified.

Analysing Surveys

It is not within the scope of this project to address statistical analysis of survey data. Before attempting data analysis, investigators should receive appropriate training or consult with a qualified professional. There are 3 topics that can and should be understood by novice researchers related to data analysis.

Coding

Before analysing survey data it is necessary to assign numbers (codes) to the responses obtained. Since the computer program that is used for analysing data does not know what the numbers mean, the researcher assigns meaning to the codes so that the results can be interpreted correctly. Coding refers to the process of developing the codes, assigning them to responses, and documenting the decision rules used for assigning specific codes to specific response categories. For example, almost all questionnaires contain missing values when respondents elect to not answer an item. Unique codes need to be assigned to distinguish between an item's missing values, items that may not be applicable to a particular respondent, and responses that have a "none" or "no opinion" category.

Data can be entered into appropriate data files once codes have been assigned to responses and a codebook compiled that defines the codes and their corresponding response categories. It is important to ensure that the data are free of errors (are clean) prior to performing data analysis. Although many methods can be used for data cleaning (ie, data can be entered twice and results compared consistency), at a minimum all of the codes should be checked to ensure only legitimate codes appear.

Frequency distributions are tables produced by statistical software that display the number of respondents in each response category for each item (variable) used in the analysis. By carefully examining frequency tables, the researcher can check for illegitimate codes. Frequency tables also display the relative distribution of responses and allow identification of items that do not conform to expectations given what is known about the study population.

Sample Size

Since it is usually not possible to study all of the members of the group (population) of interest in a study, a subset (sample) of the population is generally selected for study from the sampling frame. Sampling is the process by which study subjects are selected from the target population, while the sample frame is the members of a population who have a chance of being included in the survey. In probability samples, each member of the sampling frame has a known probability of being selected for the study, whereas in nonprobability samples, the probability of selection is unknown. When a high degree of precision in sampling is needed to unambiguously identify the magnitude of a problem in a population or the factors that cause the problem, then probability sampling techniques must be used.

When conducting an analytical study that examines precisely whether statistically significant differences exist between groups in a population, power analysis is used to determine what size sample is needed to detect the differences. Estimates of sample size based on power are inversely related to the expected size of the differences "(effect size)"-that is, detecting smaller differences requires a larger sample. If an analytical study is undertaken to determine the magnitude of the differences between 2 groups, it is necessary to work with a statistician or other methodology expert to perform the appropriate power analysis.

In contrast to analytical studies, exploratory and descriptive studies can frequently be conducted without the need for a power analysis. While some descriptive studies may require the use of probability techniques and precise sample estimates, this often is not the case for studies that establish the existence of a problem or estimating its dimensions. When conducting an exploratory or descriptive study using a survey design and a nonprobability sampling technique, considerations other than effect size or precision are used to determine sample size. For example, the availability of eligible respondents, limitations of time and resources, and the need for pilot study data can all contribute to selecting a nonprobability sample. When these types of sampling techniques are used, however, it is important to remember that the validity and reliability of the findings are not assured, and the findings cannot be used to demonstrate the existence of differences between groups. The findings of these types of studies are only suggestive and have limited application beyond the specific study setting.

Response Rate

The response rate is a measure indicating the percentage of the identified sample that completed and returned the questionnaire. It is calculated by dividing the number of completed questionnaires by the total sample size identified for the study. For example, if a study is mailed to 500 physicians questionnaires and 100 returned a completed questionnaire, the response rate would be 20% (100/500).

The response rate for mailed questionnaires is extremely variable. Charities are generally content with a 1% to 3% response rate, the US Census Bureau expects to achieve a 99% rate, and among the general population, a 10% response rate is not uncommon. Although an 80% response rate is possible from an extremely motivated population, a rate of 70% is generally considered excellent.

The effect of nonresponse on the results of a survey depend on the degree to which those not responding are systematically different from the population from which they are drawn. When the response rate is high (ie, 95%), the results obtained from the sample will likely provide accurate information about the target population (sampling frame) even if the nonrespondents are distinctly different. However, if nonrespondents differ in a systematic way from the target population and the response rate is low, bias in how much the survey results accurately reflect the true characteristics of the target population is likely.

When calculating the response rate, participants who have died or retired can be removed from the denominator as appropriate. Nonrespondents, however, who refuse to participate, do not return the survey, or have moved should be included. This bias tends to be more problematic in "sensitive" areas of research than in studies of common, nonthreatening topics. Imputing values for missing data from nonrespondents is complex and generally should not be undertaken.

Given the importance of response rate, every effort must be made to obtain as many completed questionnaires as possible and strategies to maximize the response rate should be integrated into the study design. Some simple means for improving response rates include constructing a short questionnaire, sending a well-written and personalized cover letter containing your signature, and emphasizing the importance of the study and the confidentiality of responses. It is also advisable to include a self-addressed, stamped envelope for return responses, and sometimes a small incentive is worthwhile. The National Centre for Education Statistics notes that all surveys require some follow-up to achieve desirable response rates. Survey researchers, therefore, should develop procedures for monitoring responses and implement follow-up plans shortly after the survey begins.

Generally, 2 or 3 mailings are used to maximize response rates. Use of post card reminders is an inexpensive, though untested, method to increase response. Several randomized studies have reported an increase in response rate from physicians in private practice with the use of monetary incentives, although the optimum amount is debated. Everett et al compared the use of a $1 incentive vs no monetary incentive and found a significant increase with the incentive group (response rates: 63% in the $1 group; 45% in the no incentive group; P <.0001). Other studies have compared $2, $5, $10, $20, and $25 incentives and found that $2 or $5 incentives are most cost effective. Similar findings have been reported for physician surveys in other countries. In an assessment of incentive for enrollees in a health plan, a $2 incentive was more cost effective than a $5 incentive. A $1 incentive was as effective as $2 in significantly increasing response rate in a low-income population. Quality of responses have not varied by use of incentives and there does not appear to be an incentive-bias.

Use of lottery appears to also increase response rate in both physicians and the lay public, although there are no studies comparing lottery to a monetary incentive enclosed for all participants. Use of either certified or priority return mail appears to increase response rates, and may be more cost effective when used for the second mailing.

Pilot Testing

Though pilot testing is generally included in the development of a survey, it is often inadequately conducted. Frequently, investigators are eager to answer their research question and pilot testing is synonymous with letting a few colleagues take a quick look and make a few comments. One of the questions in the survey asked about how time is allotted for faculty to pursue scholarly activities and research (Format A). Unfortunately, the question mixes 2 types of time in 1 question: extended time away from the institution (sabbatical and mini-sabbatical) and time in the routine schedule. This was confusing to respondents and could have been avoided by separating the content into 2 separate questions (Format B).

Investigators should consider carefully whom to include in the pilot testing. Not only should this include the project team and survey "experts", but it should also include a sample of the target audience. Pilot testing among multiple groups provides feedback about the wording and clarity of questions, appropriateness of the questions for the target population, and the presence of redundant or unnecessary items.

One of the authors (C.R.W.) recently worked on her first questionnaire project. Among the many lessons she learned was the value of a team in providing assistance, the importance of considering if the time spent on a particular activity makes it cost effective, and the need to be flexible depending on circumstances. She found that establishing good communication with the team cuts down on errors and wasted effort. Rewarding the team for all of their hard work improves morale and provides a positive model for future projects.

The mailed self-administered questionnaire is an important tool in primary care research. For family practice to continue its maturation as a research discipline, family practitioners need to be conversant in survey methodology and familiar with its pitfalls. We hope this primer-designed specifically for use in the family practice setting-will provide not only basic guidelines for novices but will also inspire further investigation.

SURVEY QUALITY

In mono-cultural surveys, assessing the quality of survey data requires adequate documentation of the entire survey lifecycle and an understanding of protocols used to assure quality. In such surveys, there may be challenges to overcoming methodological, organizational, and operational barriers to ensuring quality. For example, a country may not have the infrastructure or an organization may not have the means to implement a study entirely according to survey best practices.

In cross-cultural survey research, the challenges increase. Cross-cultural surveys hinge on the comparability or equivalence of data across cultures. Moreover, cross-cultural survey quality assessment procedures and criteria become more complex with additional survey processes, such as adaptation and translation of questions and harmonization of data across multiple surveys.

The survey production lifecycle as represented in these guidelines. The lifecycle begins with establishing study structure (Study, Organizational, and Operational Structure) and ends with data dissemination (Data Dissemination). In some study designs, the lifecycle may be completely or partially repeated. There might also be iteration within a production process. The order in which survey production processes are shown in the lifecycle does not represent a strict order to their actual implementation, and some processes may be simultaneous and interlocked (e.g., sample design and contractual work). Quality and ethical considerations are relevant to all processes throughout the survey production lifecycle. Survey quality can be assessed in terms of fitness for intended use, total survey error, and the monitoring of survey production process quality, which may be affected by survey infrastructure, costs, respondent and interviewer burden, and study design specifications.

QUALITY FRAMEWORK

The framework adopted by these guidelines for assuring and assessing quality is informed by research on survey errors and costs and quality management, and highlights three aspects of quality: total survey error, fitness for intended use, and survey process quality.

Total Survey Error

The total survey error (TSE) paradigm is widely accepted as a conceptual framework for evaluating survey data quality. TSE defines quality as the estimation and reduction of the mean square error (MSE) of statistics of interest, which is the sum of random errors (variance) and squared systematic errors (bias). TSE takes into consideration both measurement (construct validity, measurement error, and processing error)—i.e., how well survey questions measure the constructs of interest—and representation (coverage error, sampling error, nonresponse error, and adjustment error) —i.e., whether one can generalize to the target population using sample survey data. In the TSE perspective, there may be cost-error tradeoffs, that is, there may be tension between reducing these errors and the cost of reducing them.

With advances in computerized interviewing software and sample management systems, data related to quality increasingly can be collected with survey data, and can be used to measure various components of error. These include paradata, data from experiments embedded in a survey, and supplementary data, such as nonresponse followup questions.

Each of these facilitates evaluation of survey data in terms of TSE.

Fitness for Intended Use

Biemer and Lyberg argue that the TSE framework lacks a user perspective, and that it should be supplemented by using a more modern quality paradigm— one that is multidimensional and focuses on criteria for assessing quality in terms of the degree to which survey data meet user requirements (fitness for intended use). By focusing on fitness for intended use, study design strives to meet user requirements in terms of survey data accuracy and other dimensions of quality (such as comparability and timeliness). In this perspective, ensuring quality on one dimension (comparability) may conflict with ensuring quality on another dimension (timeliness); and there may be tension between meeting user requirements and the associated cost of doing so on one or more dimensions. There are a number of multidimensional quality frameworks in use across the world.

The seven dimensions that are often used to assess the quality of national official statistics in terms of both survey error and fitness for use: comparability, relevance, accuracy, timeliness and punctuality, accessibility, interpretability, and coherence. In this framework, TSE may be viewed as being covered by the accuracy dimension.

Cost, burden, professionalism, and design constraints are factors that may also affect fitness for use on these dimensions:

- Cost — are monetary resources optimized?
- Burden — are interviewer and respondent burden minimized?
- Professionalism — are staff provided with clear behavioural guidelines and professional training, are there adequate provisions to ensure compliance with relevant laws, and is there demonstration that analyses and reporting have been impartial?
- Design Constraints — are there context-specific constraints on survey design that may have had an

impact on quality (for example, using a different mode of interview in one culture than in others)?

The aim is to optimize costs, minimize burden and design constraints where appropriate—based on the need to be sensitive to local survey contexts, and to maximize professionalism. The dimensions of quality and factors that affect quality in terms of fitness for use. It also shows the accuracy dimension in terms of TSE.

The dimensions of quality (comparability, coherence, relevance, accuracy, and so on) and factors that may have an impact on quality (cost, burden, professionalism, and design constraints) apply to all surveys. However, in a cross-cultural context, challenges increase:

- The quality dimensions of coherence and comparability are the raison d'être for cross-national and cross-cultural survey research. Fitness for intended use cannot be met without quality on these dimensions.
- Relevance may be harder to achieve in comparative research, in that decisions have to be made about what level of relevance to aim for with a standardized survey across many cultures and countries.
- Accuracy in terms of TSE may be difficult to estimate consistently across cross-cultural surveys.
- Timeliness and punctuality may be a challenge in cross-national research; for example, data collection may occur in vastly different climates or with varying organizational infrastructures.
- Accessibility in the cross-national context can mean more than simply making survey data publicly available, particularly in majority countries, where it also may be necessary to include capacity building or data user training to make the data truly accessible to local users. Country-level data access laws and regulations may also come into play.
- Interpretability of data may be difficult without metadata documentation about the data that would facilitate comparison across cross-cultural surveys.

Survey Process Quality

Fitness for intended use provides a general framework for assessing the quality of cross-cultural surveys, and defines the essential dimensions of quality, one of which is accuracy (TSE). A third approach to quality monitoring and assessment is survey process quality management, and the notion of continuous process improvement. This approach focuses on quality at three levels: the organization, the process, and the product. Quality products cannot be produced without quality processes, and having quality processes requires an organization that manages for quality.

A focus on survey production process quality requires the use of quality standards and collection of standardized study metadata, question metadata, and process paradata. The elements of survey process quality management that allow users to assess the quality of processes throughout the survey lifecycle: quality assurance, quality control, and a quality profile.

Cross-cultural survey organizations may vary in what cost-quality tradeoffs they can make, as well as processes they generally monitor for quality purposes. However, if each organization reaches a minimum standard through adherence to the quality guidelines of the study's coordinating centre, the coordinating centre can assess the quality of each survey based on quality indicators (paradata) from each organization, and create a quality profile that allows users to assess survey data quality and comparability across cultures.

3

General Social Survey

The General Social Survey (GSS) is a sociological survey used to collect data on demographic characteristics and attitudes of residents of the United States. The survey is conducted face-to-face with an in-person interview by the National Opinion Research Centre at the University of Chicago, of a randomly-selected sample of adults (18+) who are not institutionalized. The survey was conducted every year from 1972 to 1994 (except in 1979, 1981, and 1992). Since 1994, it has been conducted every other year. The survey takes about 90 minutes to administer. As of 2008 27 national samples with 53,043 respondents and 5,364 variables had been collected.

The data collected about this survey includes both demographic information and respondent's opinions on matters ranging from government spending to the state of race relations to the existence and nature of God. Because of the wide range of topics covered, and the comprehensive gathering of demographic information, survey results allow social scientists to correlate demographic factors like age, race, gender, and urban/rural upbringing with beliefs, and thereby determine whether, for example, an average middle-aged black male respondent would be more or less likely to move to a different U.S. state for economic reasons than a similarly situated white female respondent; or whether a highly educated person with a rural upbringing is more likely to believe in a transcendent God than a person with an urban upbringing and only a high-school education.

STATISTICAL SURVEY

Statistical survey is a method used to collect in a systematic way information from a sample of individuals. Although most people are familiar with public opinion surveys that are reported in the press, most surveys are not public opinion polls (such as political polling), but are used for scientific purposes. Surveys provide important information for all kinds of research fields, e.g., marketing research, psychology, health professionals and sociology.. A survey may focus on different topics such as preferences (e.g., for a presidential candidate), behaviour (smoking and drinking behaviour), or factual information (e.g., income), depending on its purpose. Since survey research is always based on a sample of the population, the success of the research is dependent on the representativeness of the population of concern.

Modes of Data Collection

There are several ways of administering a survey. The choice between administration modes is influenced by several factors, including 1) costs, 2) coverage of the target population, 3) flexibility of asking questions, 4) respondents' willingness to participate and 5) response accuracy. Het e the most common modes of administration are listed :

Telephone

- use of interviewers encourages sample persons to respond, leading to higher response rates.
- interviewers can increase comprehension of questions by answering respondents' questions.
- fairly cost efficient, depending on local call charge structure
- good for large national (or international) sampling frames
- some potential for interviewer bias (e.g. some people may be more willing to discuss a sensitive issue with a female interviewer than with a male one)
- cannot be used for non-audio information (graphics, demonstrations, taste/smell samples)

- unreliable for consumer surveys in rural areas where telephone density is low
- three types:
    - o traditional telephone interviews
    - o computer assisted telephone dialing
    - o computer assisted telephone interviewing (CATI).

Mail

- the questionnaire may be handed to the respondents or mailed to them, but in all cases they are returned to the researcher via mail.
- An advantage is, is that cost is very low, since bulk postage is cheap in most countries
- long time delays, often several months, before the surveys are returned and statistical analysis can begin
- not suitable for issues that may require clarification
- respondents can answer at their own convenience (allowing them to break up long surveys; also useful if they need to check records to answer a question)
- no interviewer bias introduced
- large amount of information can be obtained: some mail surveys are as long as 50 pages
- response rates can be improved by using mail panels
    - o members of the panel have agreed to participate
    - o panels can be used in longitudinal designs where the same respondents are surveyed several times.

Online Surveys

- can use web or e-mail. Web is preferred over e-mail because interactive HTML forms can be used
- often inexpensive to administer
- very fast results
- easy to modify
- response rates can be improved by using Online panels-members of the panel have agreed to participate

- honesty of responses can be an issue
- if not password-protected, easy to manipulate by completing multiple times to skew results
- data creation, manipulation and reporting can be automated and/or easily exported into a format that can be read by PSPP, DAP or other statistical analysis software
- data sets created in real time
- some are incentive based (such as Survey Vault or YouGov)
- may skew sample towards a younger demographic compared with CATI
- often difficult to determine/control selection probabilities, hindering quantitative analysis of data
- used in large scale industries.

Personal in-home Survey

- respondents are interviewed in person, in their homes (or at the front door)
- very high cost
- suitable when graphic representations, smells, or demonstrations are involved
- often suitable for long surveys (but some respondents object to allowing strangers into their home for extended periods)
- suitable for locations where telephone or mail are not developed
- skilled interviewers can persuade respondents to cooperate, improving response rates
- potential for interviewer bias.

Personal Mall Intercept Survey

- shoppers at malls are intercepted-they are either interviewed on the spot, taken to a room and interviewed, or taken to a room and given a self-administered questionnaire

- socially acceptable-people feel that a mall is a more appropriate place to do research than their home
- potential for interviewer bias
- fast
- easy to manipulate by completing multiple times to skew results.

How to Write Good Survey Questions

Rules for writing good questions are given in classical survey books such as Dillman (1978)..A summary of these rules was made by Ten Brink (1992)..

- Rule 1. Use correct spelling, punctuation and grammar style.
- Rule 2. Use specific questions. For example, "did you read a newspaper yesterday?", instead of "did you read a newspaper?".
- Rule 3. Use a short introduction to question of behaviours. In this way you cannot only refresh the memory of the respondent, but also explain what you mean with the concept you are using. For example, with wines, you may not only mean red or white wine, but liqueurs, cordials, sherries, tables wines and sparkling wines.
- Rule 4. Avoid the use of technical terms and jargon. An exception to this rule are questions that are made for a specific group of respondents, who regularly use jargon, e.g., doctors, lawyers and researchers.
- Rule 5. Avoid questions that do not have a single answer. For example, "do you like to walk and to bike to school?". Somebody who likes to walk, but does not like to cycle, cannot answer this question in the right way.
- Rule 6. Avoid negative phrasing, e.g., "should the school not be improved?". This can lead to confusion and cost more effort to answer the question correctly.
- Rule 7. Avoid words and expressions with multiple-meanings, like any and just.

- Rule 8. Avoid stereotyping, offensive and emotionally loaded language.

Response Formats

Usually, a survey consists of a number of questions that the respondent has to answer in a set format. A distinction is made between open-ended and closed-ended questions. An open-ended question asks the respondent to formulate his own answer, whereas a closed-ended question has the respondent pick an answer from a given number of options. The response options for a closed-ended question should be exhaustive and mutually exclusive. Four types of response scales for closed-ended questions are distinguished:

- Dichotomous, where the respondent has two options
- Nominal-polytomous, where the respondent has more than two unordered options
- Ordinal-polytomous, where the respondent has more than two ordered options
- (bounded)Continuous, where the respondent is presented with a continuous scale.

A respondent's answer to an open-ended question is coded into a response scale afterwards.

ADVANTAGES AND DISADVANTAGES OF SURVEYS

Advantages

- Surveys are an efficient way of collecting information from a large number of respondents. Very large samples are possible. Statistical techniques can be used to determine validity, reliability, and statistical significance.
- Surveys are flexible in the sense that a wide range of information can be collected. They can be used to study attitudes, values, beliefs, and past behaviours.
- Because they are standardized, they are relatively free from several types of errors.
- They are relatively easy to administer.

- There is an economy in data collection due to the focus provided by standardized questions. Only questions of interest to the researcher are asked, recorded, codified, and analyzed. Time and money is not spent on tangential questions.
- Sample surveys are usually cheaper to conduct than a full census.

Disadvantages

- They depend on subjects' motivation, honesty, memory, and ability to respond. Subjects may not be aware of their reasons for any given action. They may have forgotten their reasons. They may not be motivated to give accurate answers; in fact, they may be motivated to give answers that present themselves in a favorable light.
- Structured surveys, particularly those with closed ended questions, may have low validity when researching affective variables.
- Although the individuals chosen to participate in surveys are often randomly sampled, errors due to nonresponse may exist. That is, people who choose to respond on the survey may be different from those who do not respond, thus biasing the estimates. For example, polls or surveys that are conducted by calling a random sample of publicly available telephone numbers will not include the responses of people with unlisted telephone numbers, mobile (cell) phone numbers, people who are unable to answer the phone (e.g., because they normally sleep during the time of day the survey is conducted, because they are at work, etc.), people who do not answer calls from unknown or unfamiliar telephone numbers. Likewise, such a survey will include a disproportionate number of respondents who have traditional, land-line telephone service with listed phone numbers, and people who stay home much of the day and are much more likely to be available to participate in the survey (e.g., people who are unemployed, disabled, elderly, etc.).

- Survey question answer-choices could lead to vague data sets because at times they are relative only to a personal abstract notion concerning "strength of choice". For instance the choice "moderately agree" may mean different things to different subjects, and to anyone interpreting the data for correlation. Even yes or no answers are problematic because subjects may for instance put "no" if the choice "only once" is not available.

Nonresponse Reduction

Dilman (1978) gives detailed recommendations on how to reduce nonresponse in telephone and face-to-face surveys :

- Advance letter. A short letter is send in advance to inform the sampled respondents about the upcoming survey. The style of the letter should be personalized but not overdone. First it announces that a phone call will be made/or an interviewer wants to make an appointment to do the survey face-to-face. Second the research topic will be describe. Last, an expression of the surveyor's appreciation to cooperate and an opening to ask questions on the survey.
- Training. The interviewers are thoroughly trained in how to ask respondents questions, how to work with computers and making schedules for callbacks to respondents who were not reached.
- Short introduction. The interviewer should always start with a short instruction about him or herself. She/he should give her name, the institute she is working for, the length of the interview and goal of the interview. Also it can be useful to make clear that you are not selling anything.
- Respondent-friendly survey questionnaire. The question asked must be clear, non offensive and easy to respond to for the subjects under study.

Other Methods to Increase Response Rates

- brevity-single page if possible
- financial incentives

  - o paid in advance
  - o paid at completion
- non-monetary incentives
  - o commodity giveaways (pens, notepads)
  - o entry into a lottery, draw or contest
  - o discount coupons
  - o promise of contribution to charity
- preliminary notification
- foot-in-the-door techniques-start with a small inconsequential request
- personalization of the request-address specific individuals
- follow-up requests-multiple requests
- emotional appeals
- bids for sympathy
- convince respondent that they can make a difference
- guarantee anonymity
- legal compulsion (certain government-run surveys).

SURVEY METHODS

The survey is a non-experimental, descriptive research method. Surveys can be useful when a researcher wants to collect data on phenomena that cannot be directly observed (such as opinions on library services). Surveys are used extensively in library and information science to assess attitudes and characteristics of a wide range of subjects, from the quality of user-system interfaces to library user reading habits. In a survey, researchers *sample* a *population*. Basha and Harter (1980) state that "a *population* is any set of persons or objects that possesses at least one common characteristic." Examples of populations that might be studied are 1) all 1999 graduates of GSLIS at the University of Texas, or 2) all the users of UT General Libraries. Since populations can be quite large, researchers directly question only a *sample* (i.e. a small proportion) of the population.

TYPES OF SURVEYS

Data are usually collected through the use of questionnaires, although sometimes researchers directly interview subjects. Surveys can use qualitative (e.g. ask open-ended questions) or quantitative (e.g. use forced-choice questions) measures. There are two basic types of surveys: cross-sectional surveys and longitudinal surveys.

Much of the following information was taken from an excellent book on the subject, called *Survey Research Methods*, by Earl R. Babbie.

Cross-Sectional Surveys

Cross-sectional surveys are used to gather information on a population at a single point in time. An example of a cross sectional survey would be a questionaire that collects data on how parents feel about Internet filtering, as of March of 1999. A different cross-sectional survey questionnaire might try to determine the relationship between two factors, like religiousness of parents and views on Internet filtering.

Longitudinal Surveys

Longitudinal surveys gather data over a period of time. The researcher may then analyse changes in the population and attempt to describe and/or explain them. The three main types of longitudinal surveys are trend studies, cohort studies, and panel studies.

Trend Studies

Trend studies focus on a particular population, which is sampled and scrutinized repeatedly. While samples are of the same population, they are typically not composed of the same people. Trend studies, since they may be conducted over a long period of time, do not have to be conducted by just one researcher or research project. A researcher may combine data from several studies of the same population in order to show a trend. An example of a trend study would be a yearly survey of librarians asking about the percentage of reference questions answered using the Internet.

Cohort Studies

Cohort studies also focus on a particular population, sampled and studied more than once. But cohort studies have a different focus. For example, a sample of 1999 graduates of GSLIS at the University of Texas could be questioned regarding their attitudes toward paraprofessionals in libraries. Five years later, the researcher could question another sample of 1999 graduates, and study any changes in attitude. A cohort study would sample the same class, every time. If the researcher studied the class of 2004 five years later, it would be a trend study, not a cohort study.

Panel Studies

Panel studies allow the researcher to find out why changes in the population are occurring, since they use the same sample of people every time. That sample is called a panel. A researcher could, for example, select a sample of UT graduate students, and ask them questions on their library usage. Every year thereafter, the researcher would contact the same people, and ask them similar questions, and ask them the reasons for any changes in their habits. Panel studies, while they can yield extremely specific and useful explanations, can be difficult to conduct. They tend to be expensive, they take a lot of time, and they suffer from high attrition rates. *Attrition* is what occurs when people drop out of the study.

INSTRUMENT DESIGN

One criticism of library surveys is that they are often poorly designed and administered, resulting in data that is that is not very accurate, but that is energetically quoted and used to make important decisions. Surveys should be just as rigourously designed and administered as any other research method. Meyer (1993) has identified five preliminary steps that should be taken when embarking upon any research project: 1) choose a topic, 2) review the literature, 3) determine the research question, 4) develop a hypothesis, and 5) operationalization (i.e., figure out how to accurately measure the factors you wish to measure). For research using surveys, two additional considerations are of prime importance: representative sampling and question design. Much of the following information was taken from the book *Research Methods in Librarianship: Techniques and Interpretation* by Charles H. Busha and Stephen P. Harter.

Representative Sampling

A sample is *representative* when it is an accurate proportional representation of the population under study. If you want to study the attitudes of UT students regarding library services, it would not be enough to interview every 100th person who walked into the library. That technique would only measure the attitudes of UT students who use the library, not those who do not. In addition, it would only measure the attitudes of UT students who happened to use the library during the time you were collecting data. Therefore, the sample would not be very representative of UT students in general. In order to be a truly representative sample, every student at UT would have to have had an equal chance of being chosen to participate in the survey. This is called *randomization*.

If you stood in front of the student union and walked up to students, asking them questions, you still would not have a random sample. You would only be questioning students who happened to come to campus that day, and further, those that happened to walk past the student union. Those students who never walk that way would have had no chance of being questioned. In addition, you might unintentionally be biased as to who you question. You might unconsciously choose not to question students who look preoccupied or busy, or students who don't look like friendly people. This would invalidate your results, since your sample would not be randomly selected.

If you took a list of UT students, uploaded it onto a computer, then instructed the computer to randomly generate a list of 2 percent of all UT students, then your sample still might not be representative. What if, purely by chance, the computer did not include the correct proportion of seniors, or honours students, or graduate students? In order to further ensure that the sample is truly representative of the population, you might want to use a sampling technique called *stratification*. In order to stratify a population, you need to decide what sub-categories of the population might be statistically significant. For instance, graduate students as a group probably have different opinions than undergraduates regarding library usage, so they should be recognized as separate strata of the population. Once you have a list of the different strata, along with their respective percentages, you could instruct the computer to again randomly select students, this time taking care that a certain percentage are graduate students, a certain percentage are honours students, and a certain percentage are seniors. You would then come up with a more truly representative sample.

ETHICAL CONSIDERATIONS IN SURVEYS

These guidelines focus on ethical concerns with regard to cross-cultural surveys as human subject research. The World Health Organization defines human subject research as the "...systematic collection or analysis of data...in which human beings (i) are exposed to manipulation, intervention, observation, or other interaction with investigators either directly or through alteration of their environment, or (ii) become individually identifiable through investigators' collection, preparation, or use of biological material or medical or other records".

There is no lack of source material on ethical guidelines for human subject research. For example, the Declaration of Helsinki, originally adopted by the World Medical Association in 1964 and most recently revised in 2004, defines the ethical responsibilities of physicians to their patients and to the subjects of biomedical research. The principles in the Declaration of Helsinki have been extended to include social science human subject research. Professional organizations, such as the American Association for Public Opinion Research (AAPOR), the World Association for Public Opinion Research (WAPOR), the European Society for Market Research (ESOMAR), and the International Statistical Institute (ISI), have also developed ethical codes and guidelines for their members.

In addition to these self-regulatory measures, many countries have legislation in place that affects human subject research (e.g., data protection legislation and requirements for ethics review boards). Whether working in familiar surroundings or in new contexts, researchers must make sure they are informed about, and comply with, relevant legislation. When working in other countries or locations, researchers may need to comply not only with local requirements, pertaining to the place where they are collecting data, but also with their own country's requirements. A compilation of laws, regulations and guidelines from 96 countries has been prepared by the US Office for Human Research Protections and can be found on the Internet.

As might be expected, there is considerable overlap in the principles contained in the various ethics codes, professional association guidelines, and government regulations. This section attempts to consolidate their common elements, as well as to highlight concerns particular to cross-cultural studies, including cross-national variation in laws and regulations relevant to human subject research and cultural differences that affect the conduct of ethical research across cultures. It is important to recognize that researchers may confront tradeoffs between ethical principles. For example, maintaining sensitivity to cultural differences by having other family members present during the interview may conflict with ethical obligations to protect confidentiality and to minimize error in respondent reporting. For further information on the ethical principles presented here, please see the listing of ethics codes, declarations, guidelines, and other resources for researchers conducting cross-cultural human subject research that is provided in the Further Reading section.

The survey production process lifecycle (survey lifecycle) as represented in these guidelines. The lifecycle begins with establishing study structure (Study, Organizational, and Operational Structure) and ends with data dissemination (Data Dissemination). In some study designs, the lifecycle may be completely or partially repeated. There might also be iteration within a production process. The order in which survey production processes are shown in the lifecycle does not represent a strict order to their actual implementation, and some processes may be simultaneous and interlocked (e.g., sample design and contractual work). Quality and ethical considerations are relevant to all processes throughout the survey production lifecycle. Survey quality can be assessed in terms of fitness for intended use (also known as fitness for purpose), total survey error, and the monitoring of survey production process quality, which may be affected by survey infrastructure, costs, respondent and interviewer burden, and study design specifications.

SURVEY RESEARCH

Survey research a research method involving the use of questionnaires and/or statistical surveys to gather data about people and their thoughts and behaviours.

This method was pioneered in the 1930s and 1940s by sociologist Paul Lazarsfeld. The initial use of the method was to examine the effects of the radio on political opinion formation of the United States. One of its early successes was the development of the theory of two-step flow of communication. The method was foundational for the inception of the Quantitative research tradition in sociology.

4

History and Methodology of Demographic Surveys

Demographic surveys are surveys that wholly or primarily collect information on population characteristics and on the causes and consequences of population change. In addition, demographic surveys can be a name given to surveys that contain mostly demographic information although they also contain information of a non-demographic nature.

HISTORICAL OVERVIEW OF POPULATION SURVEYS

Population censuses attempt to measure characteristics of the total population of a country or territory through the *full* enumeration of all persons and relevant events. Surveys have emerged as alternatives to census taking with the development of statistical sampling techniques that permit interviewing only a part of the population of interest to obtain estimates that are valid for the population as a whole.

Population surveys have a long history, including the 1086 Domesday survey in England. This survey, as well as most other early surveys, was a social survey dealing with living conditions and poverty. Many of these studies were carried out in the eighteenth and nineteenth centuries, but none was based on true probability sampling methods. The first study that employed probabilistic sampling was a 1913 study by A. L. Bowley on the living conditions of the working classes in five English cities. Survey research in the demographic field only came into wide usage in the mid-1900s. Demographic surveys are often taken in conjunction with a census. This was done for the first time in 1940, in the United States. The items covered in the census were significantly increased for 5 percent of the census population, making it possible to collect extensive additional information without increasing the burden on all census respondents and at relatively small additional cost.

One of the first demographic surveys was conducted by Raymond Pearl in 1939, covering 31,000 women in American hospitals. Other early U.S. demographic surveys include the Current Population Survey (CPS) carried out monthly by the Bureau of the Census since 1940; the 1941 Indianapolis study by Pascal Whelpton and Clyde Kiser; the 1960 Growth of American Families Study by Whelpton, Arthur Campbell, and John Patterson; and the 1965 and 1970 National Fertility Surveys carried out by Charles F. Westoff and Norman B. Ryder of Princeton University. The National Centre for Health Statistics (NCHS) carried out six rounds of the National Survey of Family Growth (NSFG) between 1973 and 2002.

The CPS is focused on employment and unemployment and economic activity but additional questions are added from time to time to obtain information on other population characteristics. One of its advantages is its large sample size: 50,000 households. The data from the CPS serve to update information on the U.S. population between the decennial censuses.

Annual demographic data files are available from this source. The other early surveys mentioned above were designed to provide information specifically related to fertility, family planning, and family formation. They sampled women in the fertile age group, with sample sizes below 10,000.

The NCHS undertakes a number of health related survey activities that provide significant demographic information, such as the National Health and Nutrition Examination Survey, which has been carried out eight times since 1960. The round that began in 1999 has been converted into a continuous survey in which 5000 people are surveyed annually in 15 locations in the United States.

Most developed countries have survey activities similar to those in the United States. Periodic labour force surveys are a major source for demographic information. Special demographic surveys have been more rare. The 1946 survey on fertility in Britain by David Glass and Eugene Grebenik was a forerunner for fertility surveys that were carried out in the 1960s in Belgium, Canada, Greece, Hungary, The Netherlands, the United Kingdom, and the Soviet Union. In the 1970s similar surveys were conducted in 15 European countries as an offshoot of the World Fertility Survey (WFS) program, which operated from 1973 to 1984 but was mainly focused on developing countries. A further round of fertility surveys, the Fertility and Family Surveys in Countries of the Economic Commission for Europe Region, was carried out in the 1990s in about twenty countries under the sponsorship of the United Nations Population Fund (UNFPA).

In developing countries, the main sources of demographic information, aside from population censuses, are labour force and economic surveys, and surveys on population and health. Among the latter, the Puerto Rico studies on family planning by Paul K. Hatt in 1947 and Reuben J. Hill, Mayone Stycos, and Kurt W. Back in 1959 were some of the earliest. In India, the 1952 Mysore study was groundbreaking. In the 1960s more than 125 fertility and related surveys were carried out in the developing world, a majority in Africa. Special demographic surveys have most often been achieved through participation in international survey programs like the WFS. The ongoing Demographic and Health Surveys (DHS) program funded by the United States Agency for International Development (USAID) has sponsored over 150 surveys in the period from 1984 to 2001. Among other international programs that have contributed significantly to the availability of demographic survey data in developing countries are the World Bank–sponsored Living Standards Measurement Surveys (LSMS) program, which has carried out over 30 complex surveys since 1985; the UNICEF sponsored Multiple Indicator Cluster Survey (MICS) program, with over 120 surveys since 1995; the Centres for Disease Control and Prevention (CDC) USAID-sponsored surveys, in operation since 1985, with over 40 surveys; the Contraceptive Prevalence Surveys (CPS), also sponsored by USAID, which carried out 39 surveys over 1976–1984; and numerous smaller survey efforts.

LONGITUDINAL SURVEYS

There is a basic distinction between surveys that are planned to provide a snapshot of the population under study at the time of the survey and those planned to provide repeated information on the same sample populations. The former are usually called single-round surveys, the latter are called panel or longitudinal surveys. A longitudinal survey can measure changes in the population with greater precision than could be achieved by drawing on retrospective information collected in single-round surveys (given the likelihood of recall error by respondents) or by comparing the results from two surveys that are based on independent samples. The effect of programmatic interventions in the period between surveys can also be measured more easily.

These advantages of the longitudinal design are balanced by a number of important disadvantages. Longitudinal surveys are generally more costly; the sample population is affected by death and migration; and the respondents may suffer respondent's fatigue if interviewed on too regular a basis. In developing countries an added problem is locating the exact households to be revisited, given the absence of good addresses and the inaccessibility of some sample areas. A particular example of longitudinal surveys are demographic surveillance systems (DSS) These systems reinterview the residents of a small and specific geographic area on a regular schedule. Interviews can happen as often as once every two weeks, as in the Matlab area of Bangladesh. The DSS design is ideal for studying change in a population. The major drawback is that the survey area is typically not representative of the population in the country.

Some of the problems of longitudinal surveys can be overcome in a hybrid design that combines a single round and a longitudinal survey. In this design the sample clusters are the same in each successive survey, but the individual respondents need not be the same. The characteristics of people in a specific sample cluster are more homogeneous than the characteristics of people in different clusters, thus making the samples more similar than if the samples had been totally independent. This provides greater precision in the estimates of change.

Sampling Strategies

Sampling is a difficult task even when the necessary baseline data about the population to be sampled are readily available. In the United States, most research institutions obtain their basic data from the U.S. Bureau of the Census and other government agencies that collect basic statistical information or from commercial firms that sell samples and sampling frames. Most developing countries lack updated census and other information that can serve as secure sampling frames. More often than not, special field operations are necessary to develop an appropriate sample frame by creating up-to-date listings of households or dwellings.

Probability sampling consists of randomly selecting the desired number of subjects from a complete list of all similar subjects in the sample universe. It depends on mechanical random selection and ensures that every element in the population of interest has a known, positive probability of selection. The way samples are actually drawn will depend on what the samples are expected to represent. For instance, if a sample is expected to provide information for a country as a whole and also for each of four of its provinces, each of those provinces needs to be allocated a large enough sample to permit calculation of the required indicators with the desired level of precision.

One factor that helps determine the type of sample to be drawn is whether the sampled individuals will be interviewed through a personal or a phone interview. For personal interview samples, it is typically too costly to interview people who are chosen individually from a list of all individuals in the sample universe. Kish calls this element sampling. For this and other reasons, most personal interview samples are drawn under cluster sampling. Cluster sampling selects groups of elements, with each group or cluster containing contiguous sampling elements (e.g., an urban block). Using cluster sampling implies that all the elements of the population are represented and identifiable in one of the clusters. The size of the clusters and the number of elements to be selected in each selected cluster will be determined by the objectives of the study and the field costs of the survey. The major advantage of cluster sampling is cost savings in the fieldwork; the major drawback is that the homogeneity of elements within each cluster means that the variance *between* elements is greater.

DEVELOPMENTS IN DATA PROCESSING

Some of the main bottlenecks in getting survey data published shortly after data collection have traditionally been the hardware, software, and manpower available for processing the information collected. In the 1960s and early 1970s most surveys were still processed by coding the information on special coding sheets and entering that information on punch cards that were then used in computer analysis of the data. Survey researchers typically had to operate through intermediaries at computer centres to have the data tabulated. With the advent of microcomputers in the late 1970s and the creation of appropriate software, it became possible to do most data processing in-house. Until the mid-1980s, the speed of the available processors and software limitations still made the processing of large surveys a difficult enterprise.

Large data collection efforts such as censuses were most often processed using optical readers. This avoided the onerous task of entering the data by hand and speeded up their availability for analysis. Due to special requirements of page layout and the necessarily limited length of the questionnaires, few comprehensive surveys were processed through the optical reader process.

One of the major problems in survey data processing is how to create a file that is free of structural or consistency errors in the variables. Such a file is created through detailed editing of the data and, where possible, imputation of missing data. This editing eliminates the errors introduced during the interview, in the coding process, and in data entry. The availability of microcomputers for data entry made it possible to build structural, range, and some consistency checks into the data entry program and resulted in fewer errors in initial data files. Further consistency checking can eliminate these types of errors altogether. The development of appropriate software for these stages of processing has been a major factor in the earlier availability of survey data. The Demographic and Health Surveys program developed its Integrated System for Survey Analysis (ISSA), which can handle all data entry, editing, and tabulation. The Netherlands' Institute of Statistics developed a similar program called BLAISE, while the CDC developed the widely used program called EPI-info. Statistical analysis packages such as SPSS and SAS also contributed much to the speedier publication of survey data.

The continued development of personal computers and the availability of laptops and handheld computers are further facilitating survey processing. Frequently, data are entered on a handheld computer or laptop during the interview, thus obviating the need for further data entry. In addition, checks incorporated during the interview can ensure that the resulting files are largely free of error, which minimizes the need for extensive cleaning of the data. There are already instances where survey data are instantly transmitted from the interviewer's computer to a central computer for tabulations.

The proliferation of software and equipment has also had its drawbacks, especially in developing countries. Too many different systems are in use, making it more difficult to build the capacity of organizations to process their own surveys.

TELEPHONE SURVEYS

Telephone surveys are the most common and cheapest way to collect information for marketing and other purposes. For obtaining demographic survey data, they can only be used where all the sample population is reachable by phone. This excludes developing countries. In the United States, the proportion of households with a phone rose above 90 percent in the 1970s, making it possible to sample nearly as well in a telephone survey as through personal interviews. This has generated a fast-growing telephone interviewing industry.

A major advantage of telephone surveys is that the sample design has no impact on the speed of data collection. Distance between sample subjects is not a problem. Another major advantage is quality control, particularly where the telephone interviews are conducted by means of a Computer Assisted Telephone Interviewing (CATI) system. This system can control the sample selection, the flow of the interview, and the quality of data entry. A further advantage is that the use of a CATI system ensures instant availability of the data. Telephone surveys are generally considered to be unsuitable for interviews of longer than 20 minutes, particularly if the subject matter of the interview requires a high degree of cooperation. Due to their cost-effectiveness, telephone surveys are also used in combination with other methods of data collection. Short screening interviews are often done by phone to determine which respondents should receive a more comprehensive personal interview. Sampling for telephone interviews poses its own challenges, however, due to the existence of unlisted phone numbers. A technique called "list assisted random digit dial" is used to decide how many telephone numbers to select from telephone lists with different occurrences of unlisted numbers.

5

Realism and Operationalism in Survey Research

One of the most intractable problems for the social scientist is that of representation. How do we know that of which we speak is the same thing as that which exists in the social world? At a philosophical level the answer to this question will depend on whether one is an empiricist, idealist, or realist (and of course variants of each of these). The empiricist will answer that the question is irrelevant, for all we can speak of is observations. The idealist also would say that the question implies the existence of a social 'reality' and this is to misunderstand the social world.

The idealist maintains that conscious agents construct the social world on the basis of their understandings of it, therefore all we can describe are the meanings that the world holds for agents themselves. The realist, however, wants more and objects to the empiricist response on the grounds that observations can be mistaken and can be accounted for by more than one theory. The realist objects to the idealist on the grounds that there is much more to the social world than agent's understandings of it. Particularly, that real structures in the social world can impose themselves upon agents both in a way they do not understand and without agents' knowledge of their existence.

These positions are well rehearsed in the literature and whilst there have been a number of attempts to transcend them philosophically, they have remained somewhat entrenched at the level of method..

In qualitative research the issue of representation has a long history and was particularly evident in the methodological writings of the Chicago School. Hammersley (1989) shows that the legacy (of Blumer's work in particular) has been an unresolved tension between the desire to move beyond individual description to explanation or to do sociology that is faithful to the natural or actual character of the social world. In the latter case the question inevitably arises as to whether the things we immediately perceive in the social world are in fact representations of its real character, or merely epiphenomena?

Even if this latter point is accepted what can count as evidence of explanation and how can we know if it is correct, or the extent to which it holds in the social world? Although, arguably, there has been no closure on this issue in qualitative research, it has at least been well aired. In survey research this has been much less the case, with its adherents less inclined to methodological soul searching that their colleagues in qualitative research.

THE SOCIAL SURVEY

In the social survey the problem of representation takes on the specific and apparent form of operationalisation. Whilst in qualitative research it could be argued that reality is emergent from the experiences of agents (though of course the experiences recorded by the researcher will be directed by a theory of some kind) in survey research a specific effect must be named beforehand and measurements are made to see if, or to what extent, it is present.

There is then a concern with measuring the presence or extent of what has already been identified as existing. At the level of method (as opposed to methodology) this process in survey research is well described in the literature and an early skill a student of survey research must learn is how to 'operationalise' variables. Most text books on social research and on survey method will contain a section on operationalisation, which will be described as a variant of the idea that theoretical constructs must be translated into tangible observable forms.

The success of this translation process is expressed through the idea of validity, whereby the validity of a measure 'depends on how we have defined the concept it is designed to measure'. de Vaus describes this clearly in terms of three kinds of validity: Criterion; Content and Construct.

The first compares how people answer a new set of questions intended to measure a concept with answers obtained from well accepted measures of a concept. The second evaluates the extent to which indicators measure different aspects of a concept. For example an arithmetic test which measures only an ability to subtract and not to add, multiply or divide would lack content validity. Finally (and perhaps most importantly for our purposes here) construct validity evaluates a measure by how well it conforms with theoretical expectations. De Vaus describes this with the example of alienation and class. Suppose we have developed a new measure of alienation and we want to evaluate it. Our theory may postulate a relationship between class and alienation, whereby the 'lower' the class the higher the amount of alienation. If subsequently the research shows this to be the case then we might say that the new measure has construct validity. But, as de Vaus points out, there are two dangers here:

> Firstly, if using the new measure, the theoretical proposition is not supported, how do we know whether it is our new measure that is invalid: the theory may be wrong or the measure of the other concept (class) may be invalid. Second, we must avoid developing a test so that it supports the theory. If we use a theory to validate our measure and then use the (valid!) measure to test the theory then we have established nothing. de Vaus 1996: 57.

Validity, as a logical concept, refers to relationships within arguments and is not a measure of the truth about the world that the premises or conclusion of the argument claim. Similarly in the social survey, whilst at a technical level we can do much to test, or establish, the validity between criteria, between content and between constructs, our ability to do this with reference to external referents is analogous to that of attempting to establish truths about the world ensuing from logical statements. The logician does not do the latter, but is content to describe valid or invalid relationships, whereas the scientist is interested in achieving validity but wants more. Likewise the survey researcher needs more than validity between variables, but some evidence that those variables are measures of the reality of the population being researched. If this were not the case then there would be little point to survey research.

Broadly speaking, there are two ways this issue can be approached. The first is to begin from what is or can be measured and the second is to theorise what there is and then attempt to measure it. The first of these equates with an operationalist version of empiricism and the second with realism.

Operationalism

Operationalism is not a word much used these days. Indeed in the literature only a few such as Lundberg (1950) and Blalock and Blalock (1971) championed its use in sociology. For the most part it is seen as discredited offshoot of logical positivism (Harré 1972) and like so many other concepts from that era has been quietly forgotten.

Operationalism began life in the natural sciences and is a variant of empiricism. Emphasis is placed onto verification and observation by saying that 'every bona fide scientific concept must be linked to instrumental procedures that determine its values'. Thus what counts as temperature is our measurement of it. Blalock expressed this view very clearly.

Although a concept such as 'mass ' may be conceived theoretically or metaphysically as a property, it is only pious opinion....'mass' as a property is equivalent to 'mass' as inferred from pointer readings.

The operationalist programme in the natural sciences had its origins in the work of Bridgeman, who had been impressed with Einstein's concept of simultaneity. Roughly this concept described signals from events occurring in physical systems which are moving with respect to one another. Judgements by the observer about the signals will depend on the relative motions of the systems and the observer. Thus observer One on system 1 may judge that event *x* on system 1 and event *y* on system 2 are simultaneous, whereas observer Two on system 2 may judge otherwise. From this Einstein concluded that simultaneity is the relationship between two or more events and is not an objective relation between events, thus in Bridgeman's view, it is the operations by which values are assigned that give us the empirical significance of a scientific concept.

In natural science operationalism remained fairly uncontroversial whilst science was dominated by positivism. George Lundberg (1950; 1961), one of operationalism's few champions in sociology, argued that sociologists are wrong in believing measurement can only be carried out after things have been appropriately defined: for example the idea that we must have a workable definition of alienation before we can measure it. For Lundberg the definition comes about through measurement. He maintained that social values can be measured (and therefore defined) by an examination of the extent to which particular things are valued. Do people value X? If so, how much do they value X?

Though Blalock describes the physical concept of mass in the quote above, he was, like Lundberg, firmly of the belief that in social science what counts as a concept is that which is measured (Blalock and Blalock 1971) and for him there is no distinction between operational*ism* and operational*isation* and it is precisely around this issue where the difficulty occurs in survey research.

THE OBJECTIONS TO OPERATIONALISM

There are two main objections to operationalism. The first is generic and is the philosophical problem of the discovery of new phenomena in science. If phenomena can only be known through a given measurement rubric then it must follow that the only new phenomena that can be discovered are those to be found within that rubric. This characteristic was seen as the inevitable outcome of the logical positivist banishment of metaphysical concepts from science. The second objection is specific to the human sciences and has considerable force.

Physical phenomena differ in a crucial respect to social phenomena. Whilst we can describe temperature as that which we define as such, the relationship of the definition to that which is to be measured is a constant. That is, though temperature can vary, what it is we are measuring is the same kind of thing. Furthermore we could substitute Celsius for Kelvin and not only could we find a direct translation, but the phenomena measured remain the same class of thing. In the human sciences such constancy in the relationship is often absent. The lack of constancy occurs in two ways: first in the variability of the meanings of the theories to those who we research, or even the audience to whom the research is addressed and second how do we agree on the operationalisation to begin with?

First consider the question of ethnicity. Ethnicity has both a socio-cultural dimension and a physical one. Our 'standard' measurements often mix the two: thus we commonly use those (in Britain) containing the categories 'White'; Afro-Caribbean; Black British; Asian, sometimes with additional groups, sometimes not (Ahmad 1999). Though these descriptions might become meaningful to their bearers, this was not a consideration when they were derived. Nor was the variability between time and place considered. For example in Plymouth (UK) the principal ethnic minorities include Greek, Maltese, Cornish and Irish. All of these might be subsumed under 'white' and consequently disappear from the sociologist's gaze. Other cities would have quite different ethnic groups. Even if it is argued that the categories need not be meaningful to their bearers, there seems little point in measuring categories that are sociologically meaningless. For example to tell those involved in anti-poverty initiatives that 97% of Plymouth's population is 'white' would remove the consideration of ethnicity as an independent variable in explaining a great deal of disadvantage.

Second (and at the empirical level these issues are not cleanly separated) how do we decide on the operationalisation in the first place? This can be illustrated by a second example, that of the problem of defining homelessness. A number of definitions are available ranging from the 'official' definition (in the UK, effectively the absence or impending absence of shelter) across to subjective ones where people are self defining as homeless. Suppose one uses a variant of the official definition. Quite apart from the same kind of problem as described in the matter of ethnicity (is it meaningful), the definition may change, either as a result of policy change, or because of improved technical competence permitting the measurement of categories of homelessness previously considered not measurable. If for one of these reasons the researcher changes the definition then it is quite likely that the numbers of homeless measured will appear to have increased, or decreased. If on the other hand one tries to ground the definition in the subjective experiences of the homeless, people in identical material circumstances may describe themselves as homeless or not, as the case may be. Unlike the concept of temperature there is no readily available translation language between different measurements of phenomena and between the measurements and the phenomena themselves.

REALISM

Realism is a much more difficult concept to define than operationalism mainly because it comes in so many varieties. Two types of realism: firstly methodological realism which we define as the unreflective stance of the researcher that the objects measured are 'real' and secondly 'critical' realism' a more sophisticated philosophical programme that has yet to bear fruit methodologically. Each of these is an ideal type. Almost certainly no one will admit to being one of the first type, though it can be seen as the outcome in sociology of the quiet accommodation with operationalism (or more generally positivism/empiricism) in the last few decades and is actually something of a non-position. If we reject operationalism and require a firm theoretical foundation for our research then we must embrace a much more sophisticated version of realism that would be at least something like my second ideal type of 'Critical Realism'.

Methodological Realism

Methodological realism can be described as the view that things exist independently of us and in principle are measurable. An example of this is the methodological underpinning of the UK Census (one could presumably include other censuses here, or other government omnibus surveys). The derivation of Census questions is underwritten by the assumption that there is a one to one correspondence between the question and the object it is supposed to measure. Any mismatch between concepts as measured and the measurements themselves is treated as a technical problem (OPCS 1981) and the suggestion that the Census does anything other than measure 'real' things in the world would probably be greeted with incredulity by ONS. Yet one can ask, perhaps, which is the 'real' measure of social class : that used in Censuses up until 1991, or the newly derived Socio-Economic Classification (SEC) ? One would imagine a nice solid concept like a 'room' was about as real as it could get, but the Census must (inevitably) define what a 'room' is and that only about 70% of respondents answer the question accurately or at all, suggests a possible mismatch between the reality of the Census and the reality of the circumstances of those measured. My point is not in favour of an anti-realist interpretation here (or indeed to criticise standards of measurement in the Census), but simply to point out the difficulties entailed in an assumption of a one to one correspondence between object and measure.

The Census is a stark example, because as a research programme it is not linked to explicit theories and hypotheses. Other surveys, whilst beginning from a specific theory nevertheless assume a correspondence between the postulates of the theory and the reality of the agents as measured by variables derived. It is a reality accorded much the same ontological status of near permanence as that of solid objects in the physical world. These kinds of assumptions have long been criticised by 'anti-positivists' for ignoring the meaningful reality of the agents researched. Of course the term 'positivism' is often used by its critics indiscriminately-better the criticism was that of naive methodological realism. The positivism of

Blalock and Lundberg (for example) did not accredit any 'reality' to the objects measured and only a kind of provisional reality to the means of measurement (provisional in that the measurement remained real only whilst it remained a measurement).

The critique of operationalism and that more generally of empiricism hit the mark at a philosophical level, but it was replaced at the empirical level by a naive methodological realism which managed to be 'realist' about the object measured and operationalist in the pragmatic justification for so doing. If the problem, as specified by Blalock, was alternatively resolved it was done so, as Bunge (1996:327) maintains, by just taking the reality of the social world for granted. It is this kind of realism that underpins a great deal of survey research, including the UK censuses.

Yet however misguided positivism or empiricism are considered to be now, it was the case that they advanced a considered epistemological position as a basis for natural and social science. The void left by the demise of positivism (at least as a public position) has been filled with methodological realism. It is an unsatisfactory basis for survey methodology because it is paradoxical, at the same time asserting the necessity of practical definition and the reality of the concepts so defined! It ends up as a non position, or the default state of common sense.

CRITICAL REALISM

Critical Realists mostly trace their intellectual pedigree to the work of Roy Bhaskar (1979; 1989; 1997). Bhaskar's work is wide ranging, sophisticated and often opaque. However there are some core ideas in Bhaskar that seem essential to the success of any realist project in survey research. Bhaskar begins with a philosophical realist ontology.

Things exist and act independently of our descriptions, but we can only know them under particular descriptions. Descriptions belong to the world of society and of men; objects belong to the world of nature... Science, then, is the systematic attempt to express in thought the structures and ways of acting of things that exist and act independently of thought Bhaskar 1997: 250.

However Bhaskar does not assume any kind of direct correspondence between the scientist's theories and reality. Indeed science, he maintains, is a social product that is not independent of its circumstances of production. In other words our observations and therefore the methods that lead to those observations are theory laden. Yet scientists claim to represent the world through there theories. How can this be done without a retreat into empiricism?

Bhaskar talks of the transitive and intransitive objects of science. The former consist of the scientist's theories which are postulated to represent the world. The world itself consists of 'intransitive' objects, that is things exist and act independently of our descriptions and prior to investigation (and indeed possibly after) are not known to science. The aim of investigation is to achieve a correspondence between the two. The way this is done is to uncover the underlying 'generative' mechanisms, which produce 'tendencies'. Tendencies are central to the critical realist version of causation, but unlike the empiricist version it is not simply reliant on the observance of regularities, for these may have occurred through quite different mechanisms. Thus in critical realism there is also a important notion of emergence and complexity. For example Archer holds that a defining characteristic of the reality of the cultural system are its emergent, but real properties.

She writes, As an emergent entity the cultural system has an objective existence and autonomous relations amongst its components (theories, beliefs, values, arguments, or more strictly between the propositional formulation of them) in the sense that they are independent of anyone's claim to know, to believe, to assert or assent to them.

Any investigative programme must presumably get to grips with these components as 'transitive' objects and seek a match with the intransitive objects they are supposed to represent. But the claim that their properties are emergent, that is they take on a character that is different to their components and cannot be deduced from them, is to imply an anti-deterministic ontology of complexity. The complexity leads to the emergence of new phenomena. Tiny perturbations in a system can lead to dramatically different outcomes, a societal version of the 'butterfly effect'. Small changes can produce big effects, but there again they might not. The difficulties in knowing a complex and emergent social world are captured succinctly by Byrne when (in a slightly different context) he says, The real may not become actual because causal mechanisms are complex and contingent and the effects may be blocked. The actual may not become empirical because it is not necessarily observed.

Archer and Byrne are describing different aspects of a complex system and whilst we can produce 'experiments' to show that it is indeed complex, actually doing research on substantive issues is not going to be easy if one is to uphold the theoretical programme of critical realism at an empirical level. In Bhaskar's view (1979: 25-6) discovery is based upon the identification and description of effects, from which hypothetical mechanisms are postulated which, if they existed, would explain the effect. From this, attempts are then made to demonstrate the existence and the mode in which the mechanism operates via experimental activity and the elimination of alternative plausible explanations.

There have been very few attempts to translate this kind of theoretical programme into an empirical one, though an important exception to this is the work of Pawson (1989; 2000). He illustrates how such a programme might work in his discussion of the operationalisation of class. He examines three examples of 'generative models' used to establish class categories (those of Wright, Boudin and Goldthorpe respectively) and concludes that these case studies show remarkable similarities in terms of their explanatory and measurement strategies. None of them relies on common sense categorisation in establishing the measurement properties of key explanatory variables [...] All of them meet the requirement of defining class positions prior to and independently of any operational criterion [...] All of the theories receive support from empirical data and that evidence exonerates not only the substantive theories but also the measurement and classificatory units that go to make up the theories

This approach might be seen as an attempt to bridge the gap between the theoretical prescriptions of Critical Realism and the exigencies of a need to actually name the 'transitive' objects in research. Thus, according to Pawson, it aims to be empirical, without being empiricist (1989: 126).

However do such models adequately capture 'reality' or are they Blalock's 'pious opinion'? Hall (1996) suggests that the similarities resulting from attempts to measure class may be explained by two possibilities. Either there is one fundamental generative and real process, which must be disentangled from externalities and described or there may be manifold mechanisms, processes, events recipes of action, and other phenomena that are tapped by alternative measurements of stratification (1996:194).

In Hall's view what we term 'class' may not be fully described by any one theory, but this does not mean that different theories are mutually exclusive, but may instead describe different social experiences. The three 'models' Pawson examines may not exhaust the possible models. To hope for a theory of 'class' is perhaps analogous to hoping for a theory of movement. Hall ends up as pessimistic of a realist programme such as Pawson's arguing that the complexity of the socio-historical phenomena (of class) undermines a realist agenda for three reasons: the emergent complexity of the 'real' processes would prevent a complete or accurate description; the complexity of the phenomena overwhelms our ability to investigate it; historical change in the phenomena is faster than our technical ability to identify its properties.

Realist Operationalisation?

The problem in trying to recast operationalisation in a realist form is that the rules defining how this must be done are grounded in empiricist concepts and an empiricist vocabulary. The conflation of operationalisation and operationalism in the survey methods literature is therefore unsurprising. A realist alternative to operationalism needs to redefine the rules. An especially pernicious concept in this regard is that of the 'variable'.

Two realists, Carter (2000) and Byrne (2002) have each criticised the idea of a variable as something 'which is real and can be measured'-the default position of naive methodological realism. Carter's critique is specifically concerned with race: that the definitions of race (though the argument could presumably be extended to class, homelessness etc.) fail to capture the complexity of social relations that the term seeks to represent. He argues that the lay use of race 'encompasses a broad variety of propositional and symbolic forms'. That is not to say that the social relations that give rise to the lay and scientific use of the term are not real, simply that race as a social scientific construction cannot stand in for them.

Byrne proposes that we abandon the notion of the variable (as a quantity or force that can vary in value) altogether on much the same grounds, suggesting instead that what we measure are 'traces of the systems that make up reality' (2002: 32). He terms these 'variate traces'. Byrne asks us to think of variate traces as co-ordinates in a multi dimensional system (or 'state space'), which in turn is nested into and contains other systems. A description of the 'system' requires both a taxonomic element and a measurement of those co-ordinates.

Byrne goes on to argue for alternative analysis strategies to those of variable driven ones based on the general linear model and this seems to follow from the 'abandonment' of the variable.

Let us return briefly to the examples of homelessness and class: Just like 'race' homelessness is a social construct that stands in for many heterogeneous states and relationships. The social scientist attempts to describe, measure, predict and explain a concept which is the outcome of a political discourse and not a taxonomic process. In other words it originated as a politicians' not a social scientists' appellation. Like race it is not a single variable that can be operationalised. What is real is that people are staying in hostels, sleeping in doorways, living in squats etc. These are the measurable variate traces and each may be evidence for the same or different underlying mechanisms that have given rise to a local system that gets described as homelessness.

Like race, homelessness is not a valuable analytic concept, there are both good political and methodological grounds for abandoning it, but class may be a somewhat different matter. Let us return to Hall and Pawson. Class, like homelessness, is unlikely to be reducible to one 'fundamental and real process'. It is perhaps the case that we could talk of all class relations and properties as deriving from the relationship of individuals to economic or cultural resources, but because resources would be heterogeneous through time and place, a single process seems unlikely. A simple dictionary definition may therefore be possible, but this does not amount to a definition of a single master mechanism. Moreover it is not a one way relationship between resources and process, but rather that processes that develop through time and place will make a difference to the nature and quantity of those resources. Therefore any specific operationalisation of class must capture process and the processes are complex and emergent. But does this, as Hall suggests, overwhelm our ability to measure it?

Perhaps not. Pawson's point that there are similarities between Wright, Boudin and Goldthorpe's models of class and that they each have empirical confirmation may indicate that they are each accessing some relatively stable features of emergent processes. Thus processes of class may be complex and emergent, but such emergence (as in any complex system) does not preclude some stability amenable to measurement.

Though homelessness and class may have similar logical properties, they are perhaps sociologically different. We can say of both that they are complex and heterogeneous, but they differ in two ways. First, unlike class, the manifestations of homelessness are so localised as to exhibit very little stability. Even between towns 30 miles apart there will be significant differences that would impact upon measurement. Social class, on the other hand, as Pawson is suggesting, can be captured in models which extend beyond the purely local, though of course such models will only work as far as the cultural/economic regularities holds. Wright, Boudin and Goldthorpe's models may work in Europe, North America etc., but would probably not work in China or even Japan. Second, homelessness, in its many manifestations, seems to be an outcome of other processes and is an attribute, whereas class is it itself a process and not an attribute, though it may give rise to attributes which may themselves become variate traces-for example cultural practices associated with particular classes.

Byrne's language of the abandonment, or non existence, of the variable seems radical and perhaps linguistically unnecessary. However what seems to be absolutely right is that for the purposes of operationalisation (and probably analysis) we need to re-think the ontological status of the 'variable'.

REALISM AND MEASUREMENT

The change in the way it is thought of (or in Byrne's view its abandonment), should not be construed as the advocacy of the abandonment of measurement, but it does make a difference to how measurement is approached.

Both operationalism and methodological realism, in their different ways, assume a direct correspondence between that which is named and that which is measured, whereas realists emphasise the importance of theorising both the objects and their relationships. This theorising is the attempt to bridge the gap between the transitive objects of science and the intransitive objects of nature.

It is unlikely to ever be a completed process, especially in the social world where complex feedback mechanisms exist to transform reality as it is uncovered. Such feedback mechanisms have the character of transitive objects. A folk psychological theory of how the social world is transitive in the same way as the social scientists theory is about how the social world is and the latter often will change the former. Social scientific discourse about race and class will impact on folk psychological constructions of race and class. The attempt to close the gap between transitive objects and intransitive objects in the social world therefore has an additional layer.

The implication is that for the survey researcher measurements should be derived from the meanings of the agents whose social world is the object of research. How then do we decide what to measure? Realism depends on theorised (intransitive) objects in two senses. First, that as phenomena they require some kind of theorising to made sensible. A 'room' or an 'ethnic group' is not a given, but a theorised object. Second that the object is theorised as real. This perhaps becomes clearer in a consideration of how ethnicity might be theorised in these two senses. Compare, for example, the derivation of 'Greek' with that of 'White'.

When a person ticks a box labelled 'Greek' the researcher assumes that the person would normally identify with that ethnic group as a result of a range of experiences/attributes, not the same ones for all, but many overlapping between those identifying as Greek. The category Greek is a representation of being Greek. Second, being Greek is a real property, the outcome of causal processes and the bearer of causal powers or liabilities. Conversely 'white', like homelessness, is a politicians' appellation and of limited analytic value. In one sense 'white' is rather like the alchemist's phlogiston, we can describe it and name its properties etc., but it doesn't exist as an ethnic group just as phlogiston did not exist as a substance. Though in another sense it is different to phlogiston in that however much one talks up the former it doesn't exist or have properties, whereas the category 'white' may come to do so as a result of such activity. This caveat aside Greek can be seen to be a social category that it real and meaningful to those who describe themselves as such and therefore the variable Greek is a better representation than 'white'. In Bhaskar's vocabulary there is a closer fit between the instransitive object of Greekness and the scientist's transitive object of Greek as a measurement than there is in the case of 'white'.

A necessary, though not sufficient, condition of a realist approach to operationalisation is that the transitive objects are realistic, that is they are derived from those categories that are real for the agents that the survey researcher will produce predictions and explanations about. Now an objection to this is that why should we prioritise an individual meaning (say of being Greek) over the researcher's (or anybody else's) definition? The answer is not straightforward, but depends on the principle that in the social world whilst all of the features which comprise social reality cannot be known to each agent, they are each known to one or other agent at some time. When enough of these features are held in common by many agents at the same time, then this seems like evidence for 'real' characteristics. Thus being Greek may be a matter of holding meanings/characteristics individual to one agent, but also a range of meanings/attributes in common with other agents who are also Greek. Greek, as a realistic category, can be identified.

CONCLUSION

In survey research operationalisation is unavoidable. However the status we give it and the way it is done need not be operationalist. Though it is right to say that those objects we attempt to measure must be capable of measurement it does not follow from this that there is a straightforward relationship between an object and its measurement, the assumption underlying operationalism and methodological realism. All measured objects in the social world are theorised either actively or passively, as is the broader phenomena they represent. Operationalism and methodological realism by prioritising observables passively theorise their existence and form.

Thus the difference between these and a (critical) realist approach to measurement is that the former begins with observation, the latter with theorisation. Neither is dispensable, but to begin with observation reifies the act of operationalisation. There is nothing methodologically radical about a realist approach to operationalisation, it simply redescribes and combines what are fairly standard theoretical and methodological procedures. In summary:

First, that measurement in survey research is an attempt to represent social reality, but that reality is not directly given. Those things we measure are the traces of that reality, just as a high temperature is not the disease, but may be evidence for the disease.

Second, whilst the objects we measure can be regarded as traces of that reality they additionally have ontological status of their own. In Bhaskar's vocabulary these are the 'transitive' objects. The aim of science being to produce a match between these and the 'intransitive' objects of 'reality'. Social reality can be said to consist of a web of meaning, so a realist operationalisation must aim to measure objects that are meaningful to the agents whose reality the researcher wishes to describe and explain. In practice this means that operationalisation is not just one moment within the survey, but in the operationalisation of variables such as class and ethnicity requires prior exploratory qualitative research.

Third, that social reality is complex and dynamic. It follows from this that variables as operationalised will not always be traces of the same mechanisms and conversely, mechanisms may be known by different kinds of variables over time. Objects as operationalised may not retain the same relationship to reality and consequently operationalisation needs to be dynamic.

6

Qualitative and Quantitative Research Methods

OVERVIEW

If you happen to be an avid reader of FQS, you may have noticed that the title of this volume has changed since it was first announced as "Qualitative and quantitative methods: How the two research traditions see each other". This first title reflects the original orientation behind the volume: to take a look at qualitative researchers' views of quantitative methods and at quantitative researchers' views of qualitative methods. Is there anything that they value about the "other" tradition, and in what way do they believe that their own methodological orientation might profit from integrating such elements?

As it has turned out, this was obviously an overly optimistic idea, presupposing the existence of researchers on both sides of the methodological divide willing to take an unbiased look both at what they themselves do and what the "others" do in their research practice. Presumably it will not be much of a surprise, either, that qualitative researchers were often quite willing to go along with this idea—whereas it proved to be much more difficult (although not completely impossible: cf. ALISCH) to find quantitative researchers willing to consider that there might be a point to doing things the qualitative way at least some of the time. This situation quite accurately reflects the methodological situation in the social sciences. In many disciplines, the quantitative paradigm is still the dominant one (although there is some within-discipline variation from one country's social and behavioural science community to another). As a consequence, qualitative researchers usually cannot get by without some (sometimes even quite substantial) knowledge of quantitative methods and methodological standards, whereas in several disciplines there is no immediate need for quantitative researchers to "bother" much with qualitative methods. Thus the orientation (and with it the title) of the volume have changed, reflecting the concern of qualitative researchers in particular with the combination of qualitative and quantitative methods.

We have grouped the resulting contributions into three sections. The first and in a sense most "abstract" section comprises papers that are concerned with the logic underlying qualitative and quantitative approaches and the consequences for the inter-relation of method ("The logic of relating qualitative and quantitative method").

It is in this section that topics such as the conceptualisation of triangulation, abductive logic, or questions concerning the reconciliation of positivist and constructivist epistemologies are dealt with. In Section two, papers presenting methodological approaches for inter-relating qualitative and quantitative methods have been assembled ("Different approaches for inter-relating qualitative and quantitative method").

In some cases the proposed methodologies extend over the entire research process; other suggestions for method integration concentrate on one phase of the research process in particular, such as the "initial telephone contact" in survey studies. In Section three, the focus is on the application of the most prominent among such integrative methodological approaches—i.e. triangulation—to actual research practice in different disciplines such as economics, media studies, and sociology ("Innovative applications of methodological inter-relation"). In the following, we will first give an overview of the papers (2.) and then go on to outline the major types of the inter-relation of qualitative and quantitative method exemplified by the contributions (3.). This is most notably triangulation which will therefore be dealt with in some detail.

THE CONTRIBUTIONS IN THIS VOLUME

Section one on the logic of relating qualitative and quantitative method begins with a contribution that takes us into the very methodological centre of the volume. Combining qualitative and quantitative methods is almost by definition an issue of across-method triangulation. Since it was introduced into the social sciences by DENZIN (1970), the term triangulation has become something of a catchphrase. "Triangulation" is now ubiquitous in the methodological literature of the social sciences—and as it is often the case with such ubiquitous terms, its precise meaning has become lost over time. In his contribution, Udo KELLE proceeds to identify the various meanings in which "triangulation"—which he regards as a metaphor rather than a precise concept—has come to be used and to determine which of these meanings is most appropriate for conceptualising the combination of qualitative and quantitative methods.

He distinguishes three meanings or models of triangulation: (1) triangulation as the mutual validation of results obtained on the basis of different methods (the validity model), (2) triangulation as a means toward obtaining a larger, more complete picture of the phenomenon under study (the complementarity model), and (3) triangulation in its original trigonometrical sense, indicating that a combination of methods is necessary in order to gain any (not necessarily a fuller) picture of the relevant phenomenon at all (the trigonometry model). These three models are in turn brought to bear upon the potential relationships between the results yielded by qualitative and quantitative methods employed in the same study.

In order to determine the applicability of these models to the combination of qualitative and quantitative methods, KELLE goes on to examine the results of three mixed-method studies from life course research, thus tying his methodological considerations back to the actual research process. Judging the applicability of different understandings of triangulation, however, is something which from KELLE's point of view should involve not only methodological and epistemological considerations, but also include theoretical considerations. KELLE's conclusion that it is the trigonometric model of triangulation which holds the greatest promise for conceptualising the combination of qualitative and quantitative methods is thus a qualified conclusion, holding especially for sociological studies with its distinction between micro-and macrolevel descriptions. KELLE thus clarifies the discourse surrounding triangulation by presenting us with a number of models of triangulation to choose from and he adds to the grounds on which to make such a choice by drawing our attention to the relevance of theoretical issues—implicitly raising, of course, the question of what such a choice would look like in other disciplines.

Philipp MAYRING starts out from the observation that the call for the combination of qualitative and quantitative methods has become almost a commonplace in methodology textbooks in the social sciences. This call, reasonable as it may be, MAYRING argues, is nevertheless a long way from actual research practice and does little to tell the researcher how exactly such a combination is to be achieved. By suggesting five levels at which qualitative and quantitative methods can be related—ranging from data to the entire research process—MAYRING alerts us to the details which lie behind the global call for the combination of the two paradigms.

In closing, MAYRING turns to a premise of the inter-relation of the two paradigms which is more often than not left implicit: what are the advantages of such an inter-relation? It is especially in the context of his outline for an integrative documentation of the (qualitative or quantitative) research process that MAYRING shows what the two paradigms stand to gain by no longer ignoring each other. In the case of the quantitative paradigm, this is in particular the greater proximity to the research subject, while the qualitative paradigm will profit most by making the various stages of the research process more transparent and systematic, thus increasing the generalisability of the results.

The ontological position of constructivist realism which is at the heart of Gerald CUPCHIK's contribution may strike one—at first sight—as something of a paradox. "Realism" with its implications of a world out there which can be apprehended and known by scientists, is a position which has gone out of fashion in our postmodern times. "Constructivism", on the other hand, carries associations of precisely such a postmodern discourse, suggesting that "the world" is real only to the extent that we make it so, that there are as many worlds, as many "realities" as there are minds to construe them.

In his explication of constructivist realism, CUPCHIK cuts across such dichotomies. His starting point is the assumption that in everyday life, we usually have very little doubt about the reality of events that befall us, our actions and our interactions with others. To the extent that it is precisely these personally and socially relevant realities which constitute the subject matter of the social sciences, the social sciences deal with phenomena which are real—hence "constructivist realism". Yet their reality is not a given, but it is constructed by imbuing the phenomenon in question with meaning—hence "constructivist realism". If this meaning is socially shared, the process of meaning construction will hardly be noticeable; the more discrepant the social realities of two persons, however, the less they will be able to agree upon the reality of a phenomenon. In stressing the importance of the social constitution of meaning, CUPCHIK's position is thus akin to that of social constructionism.

If one starts out from this ontological position, CUPCHIK argues, the competition between qualitative and quantitative research is resolved into complementarity. While researchers from the two paradigms tend to stress either the realist (quantitative) or the constructivist (qualitative) end point, they are in the same position: they both deal with real phenomena in the above sense, with social processes, and they both have to ascribe meaning to their data. Rather than sequencing qualitative and quantitative research in some way, CUPCHIK sees both approaches as essentially inter-related, with quantitative research contributing towards the precise identification of relevant processes, and qualitative research providing the basis for their "thick description".

While most contributors to this volume unanimously advocate the inter-relation of qualitative and quantitative methods, Harald WITT cautions us against the indiscriminate combination of methods from the two paradigms. He points out that a major difference between quantitative and qualitative research is to be seen in their research strategies which he describes as linear and circular respectively. Both research strategies, he argues, are cut out for different research goals, they accomodate different kinds of data and different sample types. WITT goes on to show how combining qualitative and quantitative methods does not necessarily result in getting the best from both worlds. Rather, certain types of method inter-relation may be cumbersome at best; at worst, the results achieved by such an “unhappy” combination will fall far short of what could have been achieved by remaining exclusively within one of the two paradigms. This applies in particular to the use of a qualitative method for data collection in the context of a circular research strategy. WITT thus draws attention to what is easily forgotten in the enthusiasm over transcending the boundaries between the qualitative and the quantitative paradigm: Combining qualitative and quantitative methods is not a good thing at all times, but only provided that such a combination is in line with the overall research goals. WITT also shows that the willingness to combine methods is not enough to make such an informed choice of method or method combination. The researcher who wants to combine methods had better know them all, qualitative and quantitative—no mean feat considering the proliferation of methods both in the quantitative and the qualitative area.

For Gary SHANK, qualitative research is the systematic empirical inquiry into meaning. If, at the broadest level, triangulation is about adopting a sceptical attitude that represents “genuine doubt”, and maintaining a receptiveness to any method of inquiry which offers to assuage that doubt, then SHANK is opening up a perspective which prompts researchers to inspect and always keep in mind an awareness of the logical foundations of their inquiries. Logic informs all reasoning, whether it is the hypothetico-deduction we associate with much quantitative inquiry or the inductive efforts often associated with qualitative work. For many researchers, awareness of logic and how it informs the epistemology which supports their empirical work does not get far beyond this distinction. But SHANK alerts us to the several kinds of induction, and to the critical (but widely unremarked) role of abduction in inquiries motivated by an analytic interest in meaning.

SHANK's illustration of the six forms of abduction, or "reasoning to the best explanation", has an affinity with the other, relatively rare, meta-commentaries on the formal properties of qualitative analysis. Its central ground is the logic of inference. When SHANK confronts the relation of quantitative and qualitative methods he first asserts that it is not the method but the question which is important. But, beyond this, he emphasises the effect on the questions we can ask, and answer, if quantitative work were to define research methods. In particular, the valuable fruits of abductive reasoning would be lost.

Drawing on a background in the analysis of political discourse and in the study of Artificial Intelligence, Francisco GUTIERREZ takes our discussion into the issue of how we know what we think we know. Using the case of the famous Turing Test, GUTIERREZ explores the logic by which we establish identity (or any kind of categorical knowledge) more generally. His empirical application is the possibility of discriminating between political actors holding different ideological orientations using only criteria internal to their discourse. Here we are in a central realm of qualitative work, the application and validation of classificatory systems such as typologies. The Artificial Intelligence community, as a result of its efforts to model human reasoning, has developed a close interest in classificatory practices, and the more formal methods of quantitative work can contribute to a better understanding of how people make fundamental distinctions in the course of everyday practical reasoning. Closing his chapter, GUTIERREZ offers an overview of the several points of connection at meta-level between supposedly competing schools of thought, using the notion of paradigm shift to suggest the artificiality of a bipolar contrast between hermeneutic and formal reasoning, "hard" and "soft" methods, and "subjectivity" and "objectivity".

The concluding part of GUTIERREZ's contribution considered inter alia the implications of paradigm shifts in intellectual disciplines, and this serves as the starting point for Dietmar JANETZKO's contribution. He notes that the debate over the status of qualitative and quantitative methods has been subject to its own changes of perspective over time. This fact serves as the basis on which to address a method for analysing conceptual changes (or changes of representation). These changes are amenable to qualitative or quantitative analysis. JANETZKO unfolds an approach to analysing changes of representation on the basis of symbolic, sequential data, which he calls "knowledge tracking", and which allows researchers to investigate both qualitative and quantitative aspects of changes. The approach is embedded in the network representation of cognition and requires the re-casting of the sociologist's or psychologist's theory of the data into the formal terms of a relational structure. JANETZKO argues that, while methods usually are either qualitative or quantitative, knowledge tracking is either or both: used quantitatively, knowledge tracking conducts a data-driven selection between competing theories, while used qualitatively it carries out a data-driven reduction of one theory. In this approach, then, the relationship of quantitative and qualitative can be calibrated to the requirements of the analytic work in hand.

We mentioned that JANETZKO's approach involves a transformation of data and its associated theory into formal terms. In discussing triangulation, the benefits of iterative research designs which develop a programme of research through, for example, a sequence of quantitative inquiry followed by qualitative inquiry followed by further quantitative inquiry have been highlighted. This can be offered as a means of more rigorously and systematically pursuing the object of inquiry. It seems to us that the formalising project represents an alternative to the iterative research design where there is a series of studies alternating quantitative and qualitative approaches. In that the benefit of the latter is a more rigorous understanding of the relationships that have emerged from qualitative and quantitative work separately, JANETZKO's formal manipulation offers the prospect of similar benefit but with an intrinsic gain in efficiency, in that it may reduce the need for further empirical work.

As we outlined above, in our plan for this issue of FQS a central interest was that we should not confine our attention to the established constructions of the relationship between quantitative and qualitative methods, such as the position which sees them as competing and irreconcilable modes of inquiry, or the position which seeks a systematic relationship based on the concept of triangulation. We wanted to stand back a little from these concerns and attend to the contemporary qualitative researcher's perspective on quantitative research, and the contemporary quantitative researcher's perspective on qualitative research. Another point we wanted to pick up was based on the perception that the diffusion of methodological approaches, understandings and practices is never uniform, even within a national community of scholars. When we take a global perspective we see fascinating local developments which feed a distinctive approach into the global social science community (for example, the "participatory research" variant of action research which is strong in Latin America) and we also see backwaters where the penetration of contemporary approaches has been impeded, sometimes reflecting the obstructive influence of political structures or the dominance of approaches associated with perspectives which have in the meantime become outmoded in their culture of origin.

This was one reason for our particular interest in gaining contributions to this issue of FQS from scholars outside the dominant North American/western European social and behavioural science circuit. Jean SALUDADEZ and Primo GARCIA offer us an illuminating glimpse of the perspectives dividing—and relating—the researchers in an applied research institute in the Philippines which speaks directly to our interest in the contemporary relationship of qualitative and quantitative researchers. They profile the quantitative researcher's construction of qualitative research, and the quantitative researcher's understanding of the qualitative researcher's construction of quantitative research. While the study testifies to the continuing reign of quantitative work in such a setting, it also reveals an awareness of the merits and demerits of these modes of inquiry which is a good deal more subtle than a bipolar distinction would permit, thus setting up a framework for viewing the different approaches for interrelating qualitative and quantitative method presented in Section Two.

For these authors, the relationship shows scope to evolve to a more complementary and less conflictual form than has prevailed in the past. Lest it be thought our view of this is as a pretty example of the "maturing" of social science in a post-colonial setting, we might observe that significant developments, such as the withdrawal of a requirement that all doctoral research proposals must be assessed and accepted by a quantitative social scientist or a statistician, are not entirely widespread in the universities of countries such as the United States of America.

Nicole WESTMARLAND addresses the relationship between quantitative and qualitative method from a feminist perspective. She profiles the debate within feminist research over the value of qualitative and quantitative work, where central issues have been the conduct of the research process, the extent to which the two approaches to research adequately capture the reality of women's experiences, and thus the validity of the data upon which quantitative or qualitative researchers base their analyses. This last point means that, of course, the critiques raised by feminists interested in methodology are significant outside the confines of feminist research itself, and are of interest to the wider methodological community. It remains broadly the case that feminist research is drawn largely to qualitative methods, and WESTMARLAND explores the affinities which make this so. However, there is a substantial and important stream in feminist thought on methodology which sees a place for quantitative work in feminist inquiry. WESTMARLAND helps us to see the several ways in which quantitative work is valuable, even necessary, in those approaches to feminist work which prioritise the transformation of the place of women in society. She does so methodologically by contrasting and comparing the role of the survey questionnaire and the semi-structured interview, and empirically by tracing the role of qualitative and quantitative methods in her own researches into the situation of female taxi drivers. For WESTMARLAND, different feminist concerns speak to different research methods, and a dichotomy of qualitative and quantitative based on the claimed superiority of one over the other is a diversion from identifying the best tools for the job.

Annette SCHMITT, Ulrich MEES and Uwe LAUCKEN present and illustrate an approach designed for analysing the structure and the rules underlying everyday social knowledge as it becomes manifest in texts: logographic analysis. Logographic analysis was developed precisely for this purpose; it is informed by the research goal, not by the affinity to either qualitative or quantitative methods (even though the authors are somewhat more at home in the qualitative paradigm), nor was it designed with a view towards combining the two paradigms.

The approach thus constitutes a perfect example of the dictum of the priority of the research question over the method. Considering the research goal and the textual as well as the social character of the data, SCHMITT et al. localise logographic analysis predominantly within the qualitative paradigm. At the same time, however, the analysis also comprises quantitative aspects.

In some cases, these are steps which are interleaved with the qualitative ones, such as hypothesis testing and comparative frequency analyses. In other cases, as in assessing the reliability and validity of the initial coding of the texts, qualitative and quantitative aspects of the procedure are so closely linked that it makes little sense to separate the two. Logographic analysis thus evades description in terms of qualitative and quantitative "parts". It is not a combination of qualitative and quantitative methods, but integrates the two and thus transcends the traditional dichotomy.

Numerically aided phenomenology, the approach presented by Don KUIKEN and David MIALL, constitutes another method which, in integrating qualitative and quantitative aspects, succeeds in going beyond the dichotomy between "qualitative" and "quantitative" research. The criterion by which to evaluate research, KUIKEN and MIALL argue, is above all precision in the sense of distinctiveness, coherence, and richness. Where the description of lived experience is concerned, quantitative research is frequently lacking in precision to the extent that it underestimates the complexity of categories of experience, resulting in the reduction of the phenomenon to a few conventional meanings. Qualitative research, on the other hand, lacks precision in that it fails to distinguish between different extents to which a category of experience may be present.

Numerically aided phenomenology, a method for the description of categories of lived experience, is aimed at increasing the precision of qualitative phenomenological research by instituting a quantitative algorithm at the very centre of qualitative data collection. In this, KUIKEN and MIALL regard categories of experience as "polythetic classes", i.e. as arrays of attributes where some attributes will characterise some instances of the category, but presumably no attribute will characterise all instances. Following the identification of relevant attributes by means of an in-depth analysis of the phenomenon, the specification of categories is achieved by drawing upon HUSSERL's concept of "imaginative variation", a kind of thought experiment in which the presence of individual attributes is varied systematically. Within numerically aided phenomenology, this imaginative variation is achieved by means of the quantitative step of cluster analysis. This is again followed by a qualitative procedure, the close inspection of the data on the basis of those clusters which may in turn result in an expansion and further differentiation of the classes or types. Numerical phenomenology may thus be regarded as an approach toward the construction of a typology which combines qualitative and quantitative procedures (while most approaches existing to date are restricted to either of the two paradigms; cf. the overview in KLUGE 1999).

Most contributors to this volume who are in favour of relating qualitative and quantitative methods suggest ways in which such an inter-relation may be actively realised, as in the above numerologically aided phenomenology, in triangulation, etc. Gerhard KLEINING and Harald WITT take a somewhat different approach. The apparent incompatibility of the qualitative and the quantitative paradigm, they argue, is basically just a byproduct of the almost exclusively interpretive orientation of qualitative research in the social sciences. This orientation, however, is thought to imply a number of drawbacks culminating in a "crisis of qualitative research". KLEINING's and WITT's major concern is thus not with the combination of qualitative and quantitative research as such, but with overcoming the interpretive bias of qualitative research. In order to do this, they suggest the reinstatement of heuristic, exploratory methods which are aimed at discovery rather than interpretation. They present their own approach developed along these lines, the Hamburg qualitative heuristic methodology, which combines classic heuristic elements with systematic rules for their application. This methodological orientation toward discovery, the authors argue, can act as a kind of common roof for both qualitative and quantitative designs, thus overcoming the divide between the two paradigms; they go on to demonstrate this by presenting one qualitative and one quantitative example from their own research.

Obviously, an orientation towards discovery as it is advocated by KLEINING and WITT inevitably carries certain implications of a realist ontology and epistemology—which is very much at odds with the ontological stance found, for instance, even in modified versions of postmodernism. By making their ontological assumptions explicit, these authors thus draw attention to the way in which methodological issues relate to the philosophy of science in general, raising the question of the compatibility between our way of combining qualitative and quantitative methods on the one hand and our ontological premises on the other.

Giampietro GOBO argues in accord with the famous dictum that "the devil is in the detail". It is a commonplace that quantitative and qualitative approaches should be integrated, but the prevailing examples of their integration very often revolve around the macro-level comparison of findings from independently-conducted, discrete applications of each type of method. Instead, GOBO argues that our notion of integration needs to become more specific, and he illustrates this by a discussion of how a qualitative research practice can be applied as an integral part of a quantitative inquiry. Survey non-response is a widely-remarked and increasing problem, as GOBO's useful summary of recent methodological research on the matter indicates. This methodological research shows that an important element in non-response to survey interviews is the tactics and persuasive techniques that are used in the first moments of contact between researcher and potential respondent. In the context of telephone interviewing, GOBO demonstrates how an understanding of the communicative process, drawing on discourse analysis, conversation analysis and narrative analysis, can enable researchers to identify analytically the effects of different interviewer tactics, indicate best practice, and thus improve survey techniques.

Section three on innovative applications of methodological inter-relation begins with an example from economics, a discipline we normally do not associate either with an acknowledgement of subjectivity or with the use of qualitative or fieldwork-based methods. There are illuminating exceptions, but the fact remains that the exceptions are occasional and isolated from the mainstream of the discipline. It follows that triangulation or more broadly, work which integrates quantitative and qualitative method, is a rarity in the economics discipline. At the same time, though, economists are well-aware of the critiques the other social sciences bring to its central convention, the homo economicus or "rational" economic actor, all of whose actions can be modelled, understood and made the basis for prediction precisely because these actors' decisions are wholly and reliably captured by the calculation of costs versus benefits. Since economic models have been known to fail (!), it is plain that there are deficiencies in the cost/benefit heuristic as an exclusive way of understanding those (preponderant) aspects of the social world which relate in one way or another to the allocation of resources (be they material, intellectual or spiritual). This spurs some economists, at least, to pursue additional means of capturing human decision-making. Stefan MANN provides us with an example, drawing on his research on factors influencing the decision whether to invest in a new agri-business development in a rural region of Germany. It is an example of the classic form of triangulation, with the following twist: MANN argues that the qualitative element of the research exposed only the factors that participants were willing to explicitly articulate (while not being obvious to the researcher), whereas the quantitative element enabled the identification of factors that were effective but not consciously articulated during the research process.

There are different postures towards the integration of quantitative and qualitative methods, only one of which is triangulation. But the established literature might be characterised as being dominated either by approaches which argue that triangulation is possible because, if methods are systematically understood and rigorously used, points of connection can be identified such that both types of methods are addressing the same phenomenon, or by approaches that argue that because the types of method are founded on contrasting epistemologies, their differences are irreconcilable and so triangulation is impossible. During its emergent phase, postmodernist schools of thought have overwhelmingly fallen into the latter category. But as postmodernism has begun to establish its own approach to understanding empirical phenomena (rather than being preoccupied with the need to carve out space for its approach by a backwards-looking critique of what has gone before, in similar fashion to other emergent schools of thought, as can be seen in the stages of the relationship between ethnomethodology and sociology), a more interesting and sophisticated position has emerged. This position naturally acknowledges and even valorises relativism, as a sign of the inevitably multi-perspectival nature of knowledge of the social, but also sees no reason to refrain from quantitative work simply because notions of objectivity have been discarded. Such work must be done alongside, and in articulation with, qualitative work, so as to increase awareness of multiple perspectives and the contingency associated with situated knowledge (rather than to draw quantitative and qualitative findings together into a monolithic framework as in conventional triangulation). Natilene BOWKER offers us a significant example of this approach in a report of her programme of research into online behaviour in Internet Chat Rooms, concluding that multiple methods enable researchers to integrate their, and the research participants', situated knowledge.

In Alexander JAKOB's contribution, the concept of triangulation is applied to the sociological reconstruction of employment biographies of officers in the German army who are about to become civilians.

The focus of the study is on the extent to which and the way in which these officers experience uncertainty in facing this substantial change in their life course. JAKOB approaches his topic by means of an across-method triangulation: in a first quantitative phase, a large representative sample is drawn; data are collected by questionnaire and subjected to probabilistic cluster analysis. In a subsequent qualitative phase, a smaller subsample is selected on theoretical grounds and interviewed in depth.

The study thus constitutes an example of realising different research phases where the quantitative is followed by a more detailed qualitative step of data collection and analysis (which corresponds to one of the designs for combining qualitative and quantitative research as suggested by MAYRING). Yet JAKOB's study differs from the standard design of this type in that the two phases do not consist of separate studies, but are in fact interdependent and thus complementary. Quantitative data analysis, for instance, is informed by the results of the qualitative phase and in turn allows to draw conclusions concerning the frequency of each of the types in the population. In describing the characteristics of the types, JAKOB also draws upon his analysis of the interviews, aiming for a "thick description". In applying the concept of triangulation, JAKOB is thus not concerned with a mutual validation of "qualitative" and "quantitative" results, but with their complementarity which he employs towards realising a description of the phenomenon under research which is at once more precise and has greater depth than any description he could have obtained by restricting himself to one method only.

APPROACHES TO METHOD COMBINATION: THE TRIANGULATION PARADIGM

As these applications in Section three demonstrate, triangulation is clearly a core issue in any approach to methodological combination. The contributions in this volume also show, however, that triangulation is not the only way in which qualitative and quantitative methods can be combined. Besides triangulation, two other approaches to method combination can be distinguished: sequencing and what we will term "hybrids".

In the case of sequencing, qualitative and quantitative methods are employed within one and the same study, although in different phases of the research process. The most common example would be a qualitative phase of data collection which is followed by a quantitative phase of data analysis, as in the case of interviews which are coded and for which coding frequencies are determined; alternatively, data analysis might involve the construction of types by means of cluster analysis, the reduction of categories to a smaller number of dimensions by means of multiple correspondance analysis, etc..

Sequencing in this sense can be employed within otherwise "quantitative" studies which aim at hypothesis testing. To the extent that qualitative research wishes to go beyond individual cases and to say something about the sample at large, maybe even the population, sequencing can also be part of a qualitative research strategy, taking place whenever a generalisation of qualitative findings occurs on an aggregate level. Looked at from this perspective, sequencing may even be said to constitute an inherent characteristic of many typically "qualitative" approaches, such as grounded theory, objective hermeneutics, comparative casuistics, and so on.

By "hybrids" we mean approaches which do in themselves constitute a combination of qualitative and quantitative elements. These elements may be so closely "packed" as to be practically indistinguishable—systematic content analysis which combines the (qualitative) coding of texts with the (quantitative) calculation of coefficients of interrater agreement would be a case in point. More often, hybrid approaches comprise a number of phases, some of which are qualitative, others quantitative; all, however, are equally necessary for achieving the objective of the approach. There are some examples in this volume, such as logographic analysis, numerically aided phenomenology, or the qualitative experiment; others, such as the research program subjective theories or KUCKARTZ' approach toward case-oriented quantification are not covered here. To the extent that these latter approaches combine qualitative and quantitative research phases, these "hybrids" are very similar to the strategy involved in sequencing. Hybrids and sequencing differ, however, in the sense that hybrids require precisely one and only one specific combination of qualitative and quantitative phases, whereas in sequencing any kind of combination is possible.

There do, of course, exist other issues concerning the relation between qualitative and quantitative methods which might have been raised by the contributions to the volume—such as strategies for the analysis of qualitative data on an aggregate level or questions concerning the methodological standards for evaluating the results of qualitative research. That this was not the case is probably to some extent due to the original orientation of the volume which did not really invite such strictly methodological papers. Instead, as we said above, it is triangulation which drew the greatest amount of discussion.

The usual emphasis in triangulation is on combining methods, e.g., survey questionnaires with non-standardised interviews, although examples are also common of studies where triangulation is claimed on the basis of using a number of data sources (self, informants, other commentators), a number of accounts of events, or a number of different researchers. The broad idea in the conventional approach to triangulation is that if diverse kinds of data support the same conclusion, confidence in the conclusions is increased. It is implicit here that this is only to the extent that different methods or different kinds of data have different types of error. Further implied is that these sources of error can be anticipated in advance and that their effects and magnitude can be traced when analysis is carried out. It is in this sense that LEVINS' (1966) declaration that "our truth is the intersection of independent lies" is so apt.

The classical approach represented by CAMPBELL's work, and still widely encountered in psychology, is one seeking convergence or confirmation of results across different methods. In effect, this amounts to conducting two studies with the hope of arriving at the same conclusions, thus demonstrating that the conclusions are not artifacts of method and, in particular, associated with sources of invalidity characteristic of a given method. A key example is DENZIN (1970), whose original conceptualization of triangulation is explicitly related to the work of WEBB, CAMPBELL, SCHWARTZ and SECHREST (1966) on "unobtrusive measures". However, the term "triangulation" has acquired so many meanings and usages that it is now safer to use the terms "convergence" or "confirmation" when seeking cross-validation between methods.

In fact this classic goal of seeking convergence across methods has always been relatively rare and is increasingly so as a motive for combining quantitative and qualitative methods. This is so particularly in social science research and even more so in applied social research. One reason for this is the obstacle one encounters when results fail to converge. But the rarity of classical triangulation as a reason for combining methods is also a response to the amount of effort that it takes to pursue the goal of producing convergent findings. As MORGAN (1998) notes, researchers in applied fields often cannot afford to put so much effort into finding the same thing twice. On the other hand, applied problems such as the factors influencing health are so various and complex that applied researchers are readily driven to appreciate the different strengths that different methods offer. This makes for a more flexible approach to methodological combination than is found in classic triangulation, but nevertheless represents an important motivation for combining methods.

It must be apparent from the different constructions of triangulation mentioned above that there are degrees of rigour and/or formality in the operationalisation of the broad idea of triangulation. We might, for example, regard the idea that validity will be enhanced simply by drawing on data collected by different researchers using the same method as a relatively weak form of triangulation, while an approach based on the combination of different methods might be regarded as somewhat more rigorous. Even so, we have already begged a significant question—what is to count as "valid"? As virtually all readers of this journal will be aware, validity (or the idea of a "conclusion" about which we can be "confident") is a highly contested idea.

While epistemological debate continues, with the virtual certainty that it will never conclude, we can nevertheless safely proceed with our concept of triangulation provided in each case where it is claimed the researchers make clear what criteria of adequacy and/or validity they intend to apply. But this is really only an extension of the idea that, for triangulation to be credibly claimed and demonstrated, it is necessary to identify in advance the characteristic weaknesses or types of error associated with given methods so that, when data from the different methods is combined, the possibility can be discounted that the methods might be susceptible to the same kinds of validity-threat. Where they are susceptible to the same weaknesses, combining them will, of course, do no more than multiply error.

Thus, a great deal depends on the logic by which researchers draw on and mesh together data from the different methods.

What is involved in triangulation is not the combination of different kinds of data per se, but rather an attempt to relate different sorts of data in such a way as to counteract various possible threats to the validity of (their) analysis.

While the social science application of triangulation is widely regarded as having originated in psychology, there is an established argument to the effect that qualitative research, and especially ethnography, is particularly well-suited to triangulation. Many have followed DENZIN's (1970) argument that triangulation should not only involve multiple methods ("data triangulation") but multiple investigators ("investigator triangulation") and multiple methodological and theoretical frameworks ("theoretical and methodological triangulation"). Each of the main types has a set of sub-types in DENZIN's formulation. Data triangulation may include time triangulation, exploring temporal influences by longitudinal and cross-sectional designs; space triangulation, taking the form of comparative research; and person triangulation, variously at the individual level, the interactive level among groups, and the collective level. In investigator triangulation, more than one person examines the same situation. In theory triangulation, situations are examined from the perspective of different theories. Methodological triangulation has two variants, "within-method", where the same method is used on different occasions (without which, one might suggest, one could hardly refer to "method" at all), and "between-method", where different methods are applied to the same subject in explicit relation to each other.

Ethnography nearly always involves collecting different kinds of data (fieldnotes, interview transcripts, documents) from different sources (members, the researchers—e.g., through fieldwork diaries, and independent commentators on the setting, e.g., those from another discipline or journalists). BURGESS (1984) adds to this an important elaboration, that the distinctive thing about ethnography in the context of triangulation is that it involves developing "relationships between the researcher and those researched". Such relationships make available a range of techniques for checking interpretations which arise from the more intimate and sustained nature of this form of fieldwork.

It may be thought that all of this is to disregard the powerful critique of social and behavioural science epistemology brought to bear by postmodernism in recent years. However, one need not subscribe to the notion of absolute standards, objectivity and "truth" to see that triangulation has an important place in the research process. As BREWER (2000) puts it, "even in this type of (postmodern) ethnography, practitioners recognise that all methods impose perspectives on reality by the type of data that they collect, and each tends to reveal something slightly different about the same 'symbolic' reality". This means that data triangulation is necessary even in the type of ethnography where the applicable criterion is not the achievement of the objective knowledge of the social world, "not as a form of validity... but as an alternative to validation".

Even for those not in accord with postmodern perspectives, and who are oriented to notions of validity and reliability, triangulation in itself is no guarantee of internal and external validity. For example, let us consider KELLE's third empirical case, where a qualitative enquiry took place into the operation of the job placement scheme in former-socialist East Germany, which had been endorsed as effective by (official) statistical analyses. The qualitative study suggested-to some, revealed-that what was in fact happening was that the job placement system was being manipulated by potential employees, who were merely finding their own work using informal channels, then colluding with employers to report a "vacancy" to the job placement scheme, which was then quickly "filled" by the collusive employee, yielding an apparent success for the job placement system. Let us assume that there is no doubt at all of an internal methodological kind about the rigour with which both the statistical analysis of the job placement system and the qualitative study of employees apparently placed by it were conducted. Does this example represent a successful case of triangulation or does it actually mean that we always need qualitative methods, since the quantitative findings do not seem to have contributed anything?

Our answer would be that it is a case justifying the value of triangulation—because, without the quantitative data providing one version of social reality we would not know how to value or assess those reports from the qualitative study about the workers manipulating the system. In order to identify in our analytic work with the qualitative data that data about the manipulation of the system raised a point worthy of enquiry we had to have the quantitative data suggesting that the official system was operating rather well. Even so, doubt remains. We might, for example, worry that, due to the almost-intrinsically limited scope of qualitative work, our research had simply managed to uncover those few renegade workers who had manipulated the system.

One way we could address that—within the confines of qualitative method—would be to inspect the data for talk in which workers reported satisfaction with the state job placement system. Perhaps this balanced the accounts where manipulation was reported? But another way we could address such doubt (and these procedures have their mirror image in studies where the quantitative data repudiate the qualitative data) would be to extend our programme of research to a third step, where, in light of the findings of the qualitative work, we constitute a further quantitative enquiry, but this time instead of using official employment data, we carry out an independent survey which specifically asks questions about the respondents' experience of the job placement process, for example, precisely how they learned of the vacancy which they then filled (i.e., did they hear about it from a friend or see it posted on a job card in the state job placement bureau). In this approach, initial quantitative data gives an official version of reality, this is called into question by qualitative work, and we seek a resolution of the conflicting versions by highlighting the process suggested by the qualitative work and seeking to establish whether it is more widely applicable.

Thus, we might take the more modest view that the real value of triangulation is not that it guarantees conclusions about which we can be confident but rather that it provokes in researchers a more critical, even sceptical, stance towards their data. All too often in qualitative research (and examples exist in quantitative work, too), researchers are drawn to facile conclusions, of the sort which frequently lead outsiders to complain that the main product of social and behavioural research is the confirmation of what everyone knew by commonsense in the first place. Further, when analyses are challenged, qualitative researchers are prone to claim "ethnographic authority", that is, they defend their interpretation not by adherence to systematic, established, externally-validated analytic procedures but by the (usually unassailable) fact that "they were there". They did the fieldwork, they collected the data, therefore they have the "best sense" of what the data may mean.

Such a criterion for warranting inferences is deeply unsatisfactory. Among its several defects is the way it contrasts with the grounds on which the warrant for inferences from quantitative data can be established. Here use is made of statistical procedures whose steps are standardised, so that adherence to each stage can be checked by critics, and whose criteria for drawing a particular conclusion are not only explicit but precisely define the conditions under which a given conclusion can be assumed to hold or to break down. Triangulation offers a means for qualitative researchers to be more discriminating and discerning about their data, to take on the stance so often characteristic of the quantitative researcher, for whom conclusions are always "on test", hold only under specified conditions, and whose relationship to the data is not uncritical "immersion" but measured detachment.

We are not arguing that qualitative researchers need to transform their approach to resemble that of the statistician, but we do argue that when we look at triangulation its value lies more in its effects on "quality control" than in its guarantee of "validity". A further benefit is that this approach promotes more complex research designs and that these oblige researchers to be more clear about what it is they are setting out to study. There will always be value in the relatively diffusely-focussed exploratory study, but as qualitative research gains legitimacy (and there is little doubt that it has done so in recent years in western Europe and in North America; FIELDING & LEE 2000), it increasingly tackles more precisely-specified topics and becomes more prominent in applied spheres such as policy-related research in fields like health behaviour and crime, where relevant research audiences (including research subjects and researchers themselves) want to feel "confidence" in the "conclusions". Indeed, it seems perverse even in purely exploratory work for researchers to be indifferent to the accuracy of their analyses. One might even argue that it is incumbent on researchers exploring hitherto obscure corners of the social world to employ research designs which accurately depict what has previously been unknown and which has thus far proved resistant to study by more conventional means.

In that triangulation is much about the comparison and integration of data from different methods it is worth reminding ourselves of SIEBER's (1979) seminal argument on what qualitative work can do for quantitative work and what quantitative work can do for qualitative work. Bearing in mind that SIEBER's approach is grounded in a firmly positivist perspective, and beginning with data collection issues, qualitative work can assist quantitative work in providing a theoretical framework, validating survey data, interpreting statistical relationships and deciphering puzzling responses, selecting survey items to construct indices, and offering case study illustrations. In some cases the theoretical structure itself is a product of field experience. For SIEBER, quantitative data can be used to identify individuals for qualitative study and to delineate representative and unrepresentative cases. Turning to data analysis, SIEBER maintains that quantitative data can correct the "holistic fallacy" that all aspects of a situation are congruent, and can demonstrate the generality of single observations. Field methods sometimes suffer "elite bias", an over-concentration on certain respondents due to their articulacy, strategic placing in terms of access, and because researchers like to share their high status. Quantitative data can deal with this fault by indicating the full range that should be sampled. Among the things that SIEBER suggests qualitative data can contribute to quantitative research are depth, an idea of the range of core concepts, and the ability to solve puzzles that the more superficial quantitative data cannot address.

It is worth making explicit that accepting the case for interrelating data from different sources is to accept a relativistic epistemology, one that justifies the value of knowledge from many sources, rather than to elevate one source of knowledge (or more accurately, perhaps, to regard one knowledge source as less imperfect than the rest). Those taking an approach favourable to triangulation in conventional terms are more likely to work from a perception of the continuity of all data-gathering and data-analysing efforts (e.g., as several of our contributors hold, to perceive that all data analysis involves "interpretation"). They are more likely to regard all methods as both privileged and constrained: the qualities that allow one kind of information to be collected and understood close off other kinds of information.

It is important, then, not to be led by an enthusiasm for multiplying sources of information into forgetting to monitor the biases to which each method is susceptible. The conventional logic of triangulation's multiple sources of information is that by using several we can diversify biases in order to transcend them. We use a variety of independent methods with predictable and different characteristic kinds of error so we can look for things which are invariant or identical in the data which have been produced using different knowledge sources. But it is not just the search for points of co-incidence or agreement. In this conventional approach to triangulation, we have further to identify the scope of the processes across which they are invariant, the conditions under which the invariance occurs. We also need to explain failures of invariance, why given limits or conditions apply. It follows that the differences between findings from different knowledge sources can be as analytically illuminating as their points of coherence (as in, for example, the third empirical study in KELLE's contribution to this volume).

Two main sources of bias are apparent in qualitative work: the tendency to select field data to fit a preconception of the phenomenon and how it should be analysed, and a tendency to select field data for analysis which are conspicuous because they are exotic at the expense of less dramatic, but possibly more indicative, data. While the rigidity of positivist methods helps researchers resist these faults, such work is not free of such problems either. But what makes it easier for quantitative researchers to trace such faults is that the character of the data, and the necessity to state hypotheses, make the researcher's assumptions more explicit and available for inspection by third parties.

However, systematic observation can have some of the advantages of the survey, as in HUMPHREYS' (1970) study of impersonal sex in public toilets. He completed "fact-sheet" descriptions for each observation, later augmenting these with conventional fieldnotes, and claimed that this strategy gave "objective validity" to his data. It would be more accurate to say that a quality control mechanism was built into the data by incorporating into the data physical descriptors that could be checked. The point is that the introduction of a systematic element to the field observation facilitated attention to replication and comparison in a similar way to that normally associated with survey work.

The advantages of combining methods should not lead researchers to subordinate their awareness that different approaches are supported by different epistemologies and logical assumptions, which require their handling by different terminologies.

Results from different methods founded on different methods may, then, be combined but for a different purpose than that associated with the established approach to triangulation. Theoretical triangulation does not necessarily reduce bias, nor does methodological triangulation necessarily increase validity. Competing theories are generally the product of different traditions, so when combined they may offer a fuller picture but not a more "objective" one. Likewise, different methods draw on different (and often competing) epistemologies and while combining them can add range and depth it does not necessarily add accuracy. In this approach, when we combine theories and methods we do so to add breadth or depth to our analysis, not to pursue an "objective" truth.

Rejecting absolute versions of truth, and the feasibility of absolute objectivity, is not the same as rejecting the standard of truth or the attempt to be objective. In things social and behavioural, our knowledge is always partial and intrinsically incomplete. We accept the abstraction or conclusion-with-identifiable-and-defined limits as invitational, suggesting implicitly the "constant and unevadable necessity for interpretation and change of aspect". This is, ultimately, the warrant for the triangulation paradigm.

QUALITATIVE RESEARCH

Qualitative research is a method of inquiry appropriated in many different academic disciplines, traditionally in the social sciences, but also in market research and further contexts. Qualitative researchers aim to gather an in-depth understanding of human behaviour and the reasons that govern such behaviour. The qualitative method investigates the *why* and *how* of decision making, not just *what*, *where*, *when*. Hence, smaller but focused samples are more often needed, rather than large samples.

Qualitative methods produce information only on the particular cases studied, and any more general conclusions are only hypotheses (informative guesses). Quantitative methods can be used to verify which of such hypotheses are true.

History

Until the 1970s, the phrase 'qualitative research' was used only to refer to a discipline of anthropology or sociology. During the 1970s and 1980s qualitative research began to be used in other disciplines, and became a significant type of research in the fields of education studies, social work studies, women's studies, disability studies, information studies, management studies, nursing service studies, political science, psychology, communication studies, and many other fields. Qualitative research occurred in the consumer products industry during this period, with researchers investigating new consumer products and product positioning/advertising opportunities. The earliest consumer research pioneers including Gene Reilly of The Gene Reilly Group in Darien, CT, Jerry Schoenfeld of Gerald Schoenfeld & Partners in Tarrytown, NY and Martin Calle of Calle & Company, Greenwich, CT, also Peter Cooper in London, England, and Hugh Mackay in Mission, Australia. There continued to be disagreement about the proper place of qualitative versus quantitative research. In the late 1980s and

1990s after a spate of criticisms from the quantitative side, new methods of qualitative research evolved, to address the perceived problems with reliability and imprecise modes of data analysis. During this same decade, there was a slowdown in traditional media advertising spending, so there was heightened interest in making research related to advertising more effective.

In the last thirty years the acceptance of qualitative research by journal publishers and editors has been growing. Prior to that time many mainstream journals were prone to publish research articles based upon the natural sciences and which featured quantitative analysis.

DISTINCTIONS FROM QUANTITATIVE RESEARCH

First, in qualitative research, cases can be selected purposefully, according to whether or not they typify certain characteristics or contextual locations.

Second, the researcher's role receives greater critical attention. This is because in qualitative research the possibility of the researcher taking a 'neutral' or transcendental position is seen as more problematic in practical and/or philosophical terms. Hence qualitative researchers are often exhorted to reflect on their role in the research process and make this clear in the analysis.

Third, while qualitative data analysis can take a wide variety of forms, it differs from quantitative research in its focus on language, signs and meaning. In addition, qualitative research approaches analysis holistically and contextually, rather than being reductionistic and isolationist. Nevertheless, systematic and transparent approaches to analysis are almost always regarded as essential for rigor. For example, many qualitative methods require researchers to carefully code data and discern and document themes consistently and reliably.

Perhaps the most traditional division between the uses of qualitative and quantitative research in the social sciences is that qualitative methods are used for exploration (i.e., hypothesis-generating) or for explaining puzzling quantitative results. Quantitative methods, by contrast, are used to test hypotheses. This is because establishing content validity — do measures measure what a researcher thinks they measure? — is seen as one of the strengths of qualitative research. Some consider quantitative methods to provide more representative, reliable and precise measures through focused hypotheses, measurement tools and applied mathematics. By contrast, qualitative data is usually difficult to graph or display in mathematical terms.

Qualitative research is often used for policy and program evaluation research since it can answer certain important questions more efficiently and effectively than quantitative approaches. This is particularly the case for understanding how and why certain outcomes were achieved (not just what was achieved) but also for answering important questions about relevance, unintended effects and impact of programs such as: Were expectations reasonable? Did processes operate as expected? Were key players able to carry out their duties? Did the program cause any unintended effects?

Qualitative approaches have the advantage of allowing for more diversity in responses as well as the capacity to adapt to new developments or issues during the research process itself. While qualitative research can be expensive and time-consuming to conduct, many fields of research employ qualitative techniques that have been specifically developed to provide more succinct, cost-efficient and timely results. Rapid Rural Appraisal is one formalized example of these adaptations but there are many others.

Data Collection

Qualitative researchers may use different approaches in collecting data, such as the grounded theory practice, narratology, storytelling, classical ethnography, or shadowing. Qualitative methods are also loosely present in other methodological approaches, such as action research or actor-network theory. Forms of the data collected can include interviews and group discussions, observation and reflection field notes, various texts, pictures, and other materials. Qualitative research often categorizes data into patterns as the primary basis for organizing and reporting results. Qualitative researchers typically rely on the following methods for gathering information: *Participant Observation, Non-participant Observation, Field Notes, Reflexive Journals, Structured Interview, Semi-structured Interview, Unstructured Interview, and Analysis of documents and materials.*

The ways of participating and observing can vary widely from setting to setting. Participant observation is a strategy of reflexive learning, not a single method of observing In participant observation researchers typically become members of a culture, group, or setting, and adopt roles to conform to that setting. In doing so, the aim is for the researcher to gain a closer insight into the culture's practices, motivations and emotions. It is argued that the researchers' ability to understand the experiences of the culture may be inhibited if they observe without participating.

Some distinctive qualitative methods are the use of focus groups and key informant interviews. The focus group technique involves a moderator facilitating a small group discussion between selected individuals on a particular topic. This is a particularly popular method in market research and testing new initiatives with users/workers.

One traditional and specialized form of qualitative research is called cognitive testing or pilot testing which is used in the development of quantitative survey items. Survey items are piloted on study participants to test the reliability and validity of the items.

In the academic social sciences the most frequently used qualitative research approaches include the following:

1. Ethnographic Research, used for investigating cultures by collecting and describing data that is intended to help in the development of a theory. This method is also called "ethnomethodology" or "methodology of the people". An example of applied ethnographic research, is the study of a particular culture and their understanding of the role of a particular disease in their cultural framework.

2. Critical Social Research, used by a researcher to understand how people communicate and develop symbolic meanings.
3. Ethical Inquiry, an intellectual analysis of ethical problems. It includes the study of ethics as related to obligation, rights, duty, right and wrong, choice etc.
4. Foundational Research, examines the foundations for a science, analyses the beliefs and develops ways to specify how a knowledge base should change in light of new information.
5. Historical Research, allows one to discuss past and present events in the context of the present condition, and allows one to reflect and provide possible answers to current issues and problems. Historical research helps us in answering questions such as: Where have we come from, where are we, who are we now and where are we going?
6. Grounded Theory, is an inductive type of research, based or "grounded" in the observations or data from which it was developed; it uses a variety of data sources, including quantitative data, review of records, interviews, observation and surveys.
7. Phenomenology, describes the "subjective reality" of an event, as perceived by the study population; it is the study of a phenomenon.
8. Philosophical Research, is conducted by field experts within the boundaries of a specific field of study or profession, the best qualified individual in any field of study to use an intellectual analyses, in order to clarify definitions, identify ethics, or make a value judgment concerning an issue in their field of study.

DATA ANALYSIS

Interpretive Techniques

The most common analysis of qualitative data is observer impression. That is, expert or bystander observers examine the data, interpret it via forming an impression and report their impression in a structured and sometimes quantitative form.

Coding

Coding is an interpretive technique that both organizes the data and provides a means to introduce the interpretations of it into certain quantitative methods. Most coding requires the analyst to read the data and demarcate segments within it. Each segment is labelled with a "code" – usually a word or short phrase that suggests how the associated data segments inform the research objectives. When coding is complete, the analyst prepares reports via a mix of: summarizing the prevalence of codes, discussing similarities and differences in related codes across distinct original sources/contexts, or comparing the relationship between one or more codes.

Some qualitative data that is highly structured (e.g., open-end responses from surveys or tightly defined interview questions) is typically coded without additional segmenting of the content. In these cases, codes are often applied as a layer on top of the data. Quantitative analysis of these codes is typically the capstone analytical step for this type of qualitative data.

Contemporary qualitative data analyses are sometimes supported by computer programs, termed Computer Assisted Qualitative Data Analysis Software. These programs do not supplant the interpretive nature of coding but rather are aimed at enhancing the analyst's efficiency at data storage/retrieval and at applying the codes to the data. Many programs offer efficiencies in editing and revising coding, which allow for work sharing, peer review, and recursive examination of data.

A frequent criticism of coding method is that it seeks to transform qualitative data into quantitative data, thereby draining the data of its variety, richness, and individual character. Analysts respond to this criticism by thoroughly expositing their definitions of codes and linking those codes soundly to the underlying data, therein bringing back some of the richness that might be absent from a mere list of codes.

Recursive Abstraction

Some qualitative datasets are analyzed without coding. A common method here is recursive abstraction, where datasets are summarized, those summaries are then further summarized, and so on. The end result is a more compact summary that would have been difficult to accurately discern without the preceding steps of distillation.

A frequent criticism of recursive abstraction is that the final conclusions are several times removed from the underlying data. While it is true that poor initial summaries will certainly yield an inaccurate final report, qualitative analysts can respond to this criticism. They do so, like those using coding method, by documenting the reasoning behind each summary step, citing examples from the data where statements were included and where statements were excluded from the intermediate summary.

Mechanical Techniques

Some techniques rely on leveraging computers to scan and sort large sets of qualitative data. At their most basic level, mechanical techniques rely on counting words, phrases, or coincidences of tokens within the data. Often referred to as content analysis, the output from these techniques is amenable to many advanced statistical analyses.

Mechanical techniques are particularly well-suited for a few scenarios. One such scenario is for datasets that are simply too large for a human to effectively analyse, or where analysis of them would be cost prohibitive relative to the value of information they contain. Another scenario is when the chief value of a dataset is the extent to which it contains "red flags" (e.g., searching for reports of certain adverse events within a lengthy journal dataset from patients in a clinical trial) or "green flags" (e.g., searching for mentions of your brand in positive reviews of marketplace products).

A frequent criticism of mechanical techniques is the absence of a human interpreter. And while masters of these methods are able to write sophisticated software to mimic some human decisions, the bulk of the "analysis" is nonhuman. Analysts respond by proving the value of their methods relative to either a) hiring and training a human team to analyse the data or b) letting the data go untouched, leaving any actionable nuggets undiscovered.

PARADIGMATIC DIFFERENCES

Contemporary qualitative research has been conducted from a large number of various paradigms that influence conceptual and metatheoretical concerns of legitimacy, control, data analysis, ontology, and epistemology, among others. Research conducted in the last 10 years has been characterized by a distinct turn toward more interpretive, postmodern, and critical practices. Guba and Lincoln (2005) identify five main paradigms of contemporary qualitative research: positivism, postpositivism, critical theories, constructivism, and participatory/cooperative paradigms. Each of the paradigms listed by Guba and Lincoln are characterized by axiomatic differences in axiology, intended action of research, control of research process/outcomes, relationship to foundations of truth and knowledge, validity, textual representation and voice of the researcher/participants, and commensurability with other paradigms. In particular, commensurability involves the extent to which paradigmatic concerns "can be retrofitted to each other in ways that make the simultaneous practice of both possible". Positivist and postpositivist paradigms share commensurable assumptions but are largely incommensurable with critical, constructivist, and participatory paradigms. Likewise, critical, constructivist, and participatory paradigms are commensurable on certain issues (e.g., intended action and textual representation).

Validation

A central issue in qualitative research is validity (also known as credibility and/or dependability). There are many different ways of establishing validity, including: member check, interviewer corroboration, peer debriefing, prolonged engagement, negative case analysis, auditability, confirmability, bracketing, and balance. Most of these methods were coined, or at least extensively described by Lincoln and Guba (1985)

ACADEMIC RESEARCH

By the end of the 1970s many leading journals began to publish qualitative research articles and several new journals emerged which published only qualitative research studies and articles about qualitative research methods.

In the 1980s and 1990s, the new qualitative research journals became more multidisciplinary in focus moving beyond qualitative research's traditional disciplinary roots of anthropology, sociology, and philosophy.

The new millennium saw a dramatic increase in the number of journals specializing in qualitative research with at least one new qualitative research journal being launched each year.

QUALITATIVE METHODS IN SOCIAL MARKETING RESEARCH

Traditionally, research in the field of health promotion has followed in the footsteps of its "older brother," medicine. However, the reductionistic model of disease causation cannot adequately describe the complex mechanisms that influence health behaviour. Social marketers working to promote health have learned that rigorous quantitative research surveys do not necessarily provide all of the data needed to develop effective communications. Consequently, qualitative methods such as focus groups and in-depth interviews, as well as less precise but useful semi-quantitative approaches, such as intercept surveys, have emerged as part of their research repertoire. In an ideal social marketing program, researchers use both quantitative and qualitative data to provide a more complete picture of the issue being addressed, the target audience and the effectiveness of the program itself. The purpose of this chapter is to look at how these two different research approaches can be integrated to inform the development of an effective social marketing program.

QUALITATIVE AND QUANTITATIVE METHODS: A COMPARISON

An examination of the quantitative and qualitative paradigms will help to identify their strengths and weaknesses and how their divergent approaches can complement each other. In most cases, researchers fall into one of the two camps—either relying exclusively upon "objective" survey questionnaires and statistical analyses and eschewing warm and fuzzy qualitative methods, or using only qualitative methodologies, rejecting the quantitative approach as decontextualizing human behaviour. However, social marketing researchers recognize that each approach has positive attributes, and that combining different methods can result in gaining the best of both research worlds.

Quantitative research uses methods adopted from the physical sciences that are designed to ensure objectivity, generalizability and reliability. These techniques cover the ways research participants are selected randomly from the study population in an unbiased manner, the standardized questionnaire or intervention they receive and the statistical methods used to test predetermined hypotheses regarding the relationships between specific variables. The researcher is considered external to the actual research, and results are expected to be replicable no matter who conducts the research.

The strengths of the quantitative paradigm are that its methods produce quantifiable, reliable data that are usually generalizable to some larger population. Quantitative measures are often most appropriate for conducting needs assessments or for evaluations comparing outcomes with baseline data. This paradigm breaks down when the phenomenon under study is difficult to measure or quantify. The greatest weakness of the quantitative approach is that it decontextualizes human behaviour in a way that removes the event from its real world setting and ignores the effects of variables that have not been included in the model.

Qualitative research methodologies are designed to provide the researcher with the perspective of target audience members through immersion in a culture or situation and direct interaction with the people under study. Qualitative methods used in social marketing include observations, in-depth interviews and focus groups. These methods are designed to help researchers understand the meanings people assign to social phenomena and to elucidate the mental processes underlying behaviours. Hypotheses are generated during data collection and analysis, and measurement tends to be subjective. In the qualitative paradigm, the researcher becomes the instrument of data collection, and results may vary greatly depending upon who conducts the research.

The advantage of using qualitative methods is that they generate rich, detailed data that leave the participants' perspectives intact and provide a context for health behaviour. The focus upon processes and "reasons why" differs from that of quantitative research, which addresses correlations between variables. A disadvantage is that data collection and analysis may be labour intensive and time-consuming. In addition, these methods are not yet totally accepted by the mainstream public health community and qualitative researchers may find their results challenged as invalid by those outside the field of social marketing.

SOCIAL MARKETING RESEARCH

The traditional health promotion professional conducts research at the beginning of a project to develop an intervention, and again at the end to evaluate the effectiveness of the intervention. In contrast, social marketers utilize research throughout the planning, development, implementation and evaluation phases of the program; social marketing is a process of continuous development and testing. Many of the tools used to develop social marketing programs—focus groups, consumer marketing databases, intercept surveys—have their origins in the field of commercial market research, and are based on "what works" for gathering various types of needed data. Social marketing relies upon consumer-focused research to learn as much about the target audience as possible by looking at their lives from many different angles—both quantitatively as part of a larger group and qualitatively to investigate individual attitudes, reactions, behaviours and preferences.

Social marketing programs use research throughout the life of a project. Research in social marketing is conducted specifically to help make better decisions at key points in the process. These decisions may include which target audience, messages and media to choose; whether to make changes in program strategy during implementation; and whether to continue the program. Pinpointing the facts needed to make these decisions will help to identify the best methods for subsequently collecting this data. Some types of information may require quantitative data collection methods, such as detecting any measurable differences in knowledge or behaviours once the program has been implemented. Soliciting audience reactions to a selection of program messages, on the other hand, may be best done through qualitative methods. An effective and responsive program requires a combination of research approaches in order to have the data needed for decision making.

Professionals who come to social marketing from a traditional health promotion background may have a difficult time in reconciling their notion of "what research is" with some of the methods that social marketers have appropriated from the commercial marketing tool kit. Even those who are committed to using a mix of research methods may encounter institutional resistance to deviating from the quantitative paradigm, particularly when the proposed research will occur in a governmental or academic setting. However, as the field of health promotion evolves from a focus on individual lifestyles and risk factors to a broader concept of social and environmental factors influencing morbidity and mortality, researchers must employ a variety of methods to reflect this new perspective.

Toward an Integrative Social Marketing Research Model

As a useful starting point, Steckler et al. (1992) have delineated four possible models of integrating qualitative and quantitative methods in health education research. In the first approach, qualitative methods contribute to the development of quantitative instruments, such as the use of focus groups in questionnaire construction. The second model consists of a primarily quantitative study that uses qualitative results to help interpret or explain the quantitative findings. In the third approach, quantitative results help interpret predominantly qualitative findings, as when focus group participants are asked to fill out survey questionnaires at the session. In the fourth model, the two methodologies are used equally and in parallel to cross-validate and build upon each other's results. Social marketers may operate under one or more of these models; the approaches are not mutually exclusive.

A social marketing model for integrating methods must include quantitative and qualitative methods at each stage of the process for formative research, process evaluation and outcome evaluation. While each program is unique, the model proposed here can be adapted based on available resources.

INTEGRATING FORMATIVE RESEARCH

During the formative research stage, in which the goal is to learn as much as possible about how the target audience thinks and behaves in relation to the issue being addressed, a host of research methods provides many different data "viewpoints" for seeing the big picture. Exploratory research conducted at the beginning of the project reviews previous research involving both quantitative and qualitative data and can include interviews with those who have previously attempted to address the issue. This research will help in the initial development of the project strategy to delineate the parameters of the project, steer the selection of the target audience, specify the potential behaviours to be promoted and identify lessons learned and potential pitfalls. Focus groups conducted for exploration also yield valuable qualitative data regarding the target audience, providing insights into their language, issues and obstacles they identify, and meanings attributed to beliefs and behaviours.

Information learned from the initial focus groups can then be used to inform questionnaire construction for a population survey to collect hard numbers for baseline data. The survey will also help to segment the target audience based upon its distribution across the stages of behaviour change, as described by the Transtheoretical Model of Behaviour Change, or other characteristics. In addition, commercial marketing databases, while quantitative in nature, provide highly detailed profiles of target audience segments for message development and channel selection.

The messages and materials developed based upon the exploratory research should be pretested using both qualitative and quantitative methods so that the results provide depth of understanding as well as generalizability. Focus groups provide a valuable means to pretest messages and materials, for audience members can provide spontaneous reactions and explain their responses. This method, however, can only indicate trends and cannot yield hard quantitative data needed for definitive decision making. If enough focus groups are conducted and participants are considered representative of the target audience, a survey questionnaire may be administered either before or after the focus group to collect numerical data as well.

A central-site intercept survey, in which potential audience members are approached in a public area and asked to respond to a quick questionnaire, provides another method of pretesting materials. The fast turnaround nature of this method and high volume of responses makes it ideal for testing draft executions of materials such as print or television ads prior to production and implementation. This method is considered semi-quantitative because respondents are not selected from a random sample, but questions are usually closed-ended and tabulated statistically. Final decisions, such as choosing from among several possible ads, can be made based on the numbers this method yields.

INTEGRATING PROCESS EVALUATION

Upon implementation of the program, process evaluation helps to keep the project on track and signals when changes are needed in the program strategy. The most common data collection activity in this phase involves counting—materials distributed, number of people attending activities, broadcasts of the television or radio ads, media coverage of events, phone calls to the organization—to ensure that the project proceeds as intended. Other quantitative tracking mechanisms, such as consumer surveys, identify whether the program's message is reaching the target audience and is getting its attention and motivating action. In an ongoing multi-year project, this may be a repetition of the population survey conducted at the beginning; for a shorter-term project, a survey may target a very specific audience segment.

Qualitative process evaluation methods can include periodic interviews or focus groups with target audience members to assess their progress toward behaviour change. Through these activities, participants may inform program administrators of unforeseen barriers or opportunities to adopting the behaviour that need to be addressed to increase chances of success. Observations of audience members may also provide clues to needed changes in program strategy or messages in case they are using the product in an unsafe manner or performing the target behaviour incorrectly. The quantitative and qualitative process research can be conducted simultaneously to collect and react to data.

Integrating Outcome Evaluation

Both types of research are instructive in identifying the program outcomes. A repeat of the quantitative population survey will provide an indication of whether the program realized its objectives in raising awareness, changing attitudes and initiating behaviour change. Related decreases in morbidity and mortality or other major indices will be more difficult to claim without also conducting a matched community intervention study, with the only difference between the communities being the presence of the social marketing program.

In the end, the quantitative data emerging from the survey are generally used as the final arbiters of success. However, qualitative research can point out successes that may have occurred on a more human scale through anecdotes about how the social marketing program made a difference in someone's life. Focus groups, interviews and other methods of collecting individual people's stories and responses to the campaign are valuable in learning which components of the program were successful and how the next project can be improved. Both types of research are necessary to assess the full extent of the program's impact upon the target audience. Integrating quantitative and qualitative research methods lends depth and clarity to social marketing programs. This combination of approaches is necessary because of the wide range of data needed to develop effective communications. However, the potential for problems exists when attempting to combine such divergent research paradigms; one may end up not doing either type of research well. This integrative approach therefore requires a research team with expertise in both types of methods. Using multiple approaches can also be time-consuming, labour-intensive and expensive. Another obstacle, which will likely change as social marketing gains in usage, is that combining multiple methods is still not widely accepted as a viable research strategy—at least in mainstream public health circles. As social marketers demonstrate that such research is necessary to fully understand and address many health-related issues, the research norms and scientific dogma regarding appropriate methods may shift to a new, more integrative paradigm.

QUANTITATIVE APPROACHES INTO THE RESEARCH PROCESS

The Case for Separation and the Case for Convergence

The case for separate paradigms is that qualitative and quantitative researchers hold different epistemological assumptions, belong to different research cultures and have different researcher biographies that work against convergence. Indeed qualitative researchers are embracing even greater reflexivity, for example taking account of the influence of the researcher in the research encounter, finding new ways of relating the voices of marginal groups to academic knowledge and researcher interpretation.

On the quantitative front researchers are constantly urged by bodies such as the UK's Economic and Social Research Council to develop their skills base in order to keep up with developments elsewhere (notably the US); this may serve to maintain the barricades between qualitative and quantitative research through ever greater sophistication and complexity of statistical techniques.

While researchers rationalize their interpretive frameworks in terms of fundamental distinctions of ontology, epistemology and theory, they develop over time habits and dispositions as well as particular expertise and preferences for particular approaches and may lack the time and inclination to extend skills and interests in other directions and across the qualitative/quantitative divide. Research practice is also shaped by the research environment—by the funds available for a research project and by the shortterm contracts of many researchers in the UK.

While research practices diverge, there is considerable pressure for convergence at this present time. Externally, there is increased demand for research to inform policy and for practical rather than scientific research, again a trend that may work against specialization in either qualitative or quantitative research.

The importance placed upon particular types of research evidence is subject to changes in political climates and persuasions. As Janet Finch argued in the 1980s, British government has long preferred quantitative evidence in contrast to more pluralistic methodological preferences of US governments in the same period.

Currently, there are external pressures, from national and EU funders, for researchers to inform policy and therefore to disseminate in lay language. There is a whole industry in Britain and the US, and increasingly Europe, devoted to evaluation of policy that utilizes qualitative as well as quantitative methods. In the US, the demand for qualitative research has been caught up in the wider politics of interest groups who have argued that the benefits of government programmes to the poor did not show up in much quantitative work. Many of these trends suggest greater rather than less convergence between approaches.

Both externally and internally, the pressures of research markets and the marketization of universities in the 1990s and twenty-first century are leading to the institutionalization of research training. The arrival of a skills-based economy in which training has superseded notions of apprenticeship is as influential in research as elsewhere in the labour market. In Britain, in the past ten to fifteen years, we have seen a steady expansion in masters' degrees courses in research methods and in other courses dedicated to research training. Today's students on masters courses are typically introduced to both qualitative and quantitative methods, whereas in the past they were not exposed to such a wide range of methods.

Pressure from users and the enhanced diversity of skills influence the type of research that is done as well as the questions posed, and how they are addressed. They also affect how research is written up for different audiences or 'user' groups.

Researchers today are required to communicate in 'double speak': in the specialized languages that define their 'fields' (as opposed to disciplines) and in a generic, popular language that addresses 'research users'. Such emphasis upon dissemination may have the effect of increasing the importance of research which takes an action perspective, that is draws upon actors' perspectives both in the interpretation and in the presentation of the data. This is not to suggest, however, that quantitative research is being displaced.

However, responding to pressures from funders and the demand to disseminate and to do so in particular kinds of ways can result in epistemological issues vanishing from view in the way data analysis is discussed, while methodological issues may be reduced to skills training. Lack of space in the article format also can mean that methodological issues are relegated to footnotes, while in books they appear in appendices or end notes. These pressures have on the other hand helped to generate an increase in journals and books devoted to methodological issues.

Context of Justification

Our methods and their assumptions are revisited in a second context—what is known as the context of justification where the data are analysed and interpreted. As some would argue, in the context of justification the resulting data sets cannot be linked together unproblematically. For it is at this phase that ontological, epistemological and theoretical issues raise their heads in the encounter with data.

In the cold light of data analysis we are forced to reflect on different kinds of 'truth' or 'validity' and to take account of the fact that our different types of data are constituted by the assumptions and methods that elicit them.

Thus we cannot unproblematically assume that data from different methods will corroborate one another as is implied in the strategy of triangulation—that is where the choice of methods is intended to investigate a *single* social phenomenon from different vantage points. Data collected from different methods cannot be simply added together to produce a unitary or rounded reality. When we combine methods, there are a number of possible outcomes; corroboration of results is only one of at least four possibilities:

Corroboration: The 'same results' are derived from both qualitative and quantitative methods.

Elaboration: The qualitative data analysis exemplifies how the quantitative findings apply in particular cases.

Complementarity: The qualitative and quantitative results differ but *together* they generate insights.

Contradiction: Where qualitative data and quantitative findings conflict.

In other words, when researchers work with different types of data within the same research project, the way they use these data will vary according to the *phase* of the research in which the researcher brings the different data sets into play.

Bryman distinguishes between the ways in which qualitative and quantitative research are combined in terms of: (a) the *importance* given to qualitative and quantitative approaches in the research investigation and (b) the *time ordering* or sequencing of the approaches. However, as he suggests, such distinctions are not always possible in practice because they rely on being able to identify the dominance of one approach.

WORKING QUALITATIVELY AND QUANTITATIVELY IN PRACTICE

The Research Design Phase

The study concerned children's concepts of care and their contribution to family life, which was carried out in two London boroughs. The first phase was a self-completion questionnaire survey of school-based populations—of around 1,000 children aged 11–12. The second phase involved a sub-sample drawn from the survey of groups of children and their parents living in different types of household (63 households). This second phase employed a semi-structured interview schedule.

Each phase had a particular aim and addressed different research questions and concerns. Moreover it was also the case that the second (qualitative) phase depended upon the first (quantitative) phase: The interview cases were embedded within schoolbased surveys located in particular social milieux which we also sought to describe. The surveys therefore provided *contextual* information about the populations of children who had been selected. Where a study is being conducted with a two-stage design, the contextualization provided in the first stage can be very helpful.

The survey provided a sampling frame for the interview studies conducted with children and their parents in different types of family structure. Gaining access to children via schools was essential to reaching particular family sub-groups for the interview study. (The questionnaires were not anonymized but contained codes linked to children's names; this enabled us later to identify and contact the groups we wished to select for the interviews.) Access required careful negotiation with schools but also some reciprocity on the researchers' part. By providing schools with quantitative data drawn from the questionnaire survey phase relating to each school, we hoped to gain access to the qualitative sample. The questionnaire surveys were therefore designed with this additional purpose in mind.

The case to be made for attaching qualitative sub-samples to statistically derived samples such as national cohort studies is a further variant of mixed method designs. Such designs may benefit quantitative researchers through achieving a better handle upon the meanings of underlying statistical associations, while it gives qualitative researchers the chance to select particular cases, to draw upon contextual information from the wider study and to test hypotheses on large, statistically representative samples.

The Fieldwork Phase

Different research methods may be incorporated during the fieldwork phase rather than in the design phase, with one method encompassing more than one type of approach. The exemplar study of the latter concerns a longitudinal study of women's return to employment following maternity leave carried out during the 1980s. The study was initially conceptualized in quantitative terms to examine the 'effects' of maternal employment upon women and children. The impetus for the methodological changes we made was both theoretical and political. The study stretched over a six-year period allowing considerable scope in time and material resource terms for the development of concepts and methodologies that were not articulated in the original research proposal. It was carried out in the 1980s, a period when funders were more generous in terms of project length. The study was moreover funded by the UK's Department of Health, which provided considerable support to researchers for methodological development.

In this study, an important conceptual shift took place, away from a focus upon outcomes and to a focus upon meaning and upon the household: how mothers made sense of their situations and responsibilities and the ways in which they and their households (the children's fathers) actively organized and construed employment and parenthood. This change in conceptual perspective translated into a change in the study's method of interviewing, with a new set of aims that underpinned the collection of qualitative as well as quantitative data. The result was an interview schedule that combined structured questions (the responses to which were categorized according to predefined codes) with open-ended questions giving scope for probing (responses were transcribed and analysed qualitatively).

We remained committed to collecting the structured data originally promised but required the interviewers to collect such data while seeming to adopt a flexible, in-depth mode of interviewing. Indeed this combined interviewing approach was so successful that, in one of the later waves of the longitudinal study when, for resource reasons, we decided to collect only quantitative data, we found the interviewees reluctant to comply; they continued to respond in the way they had done in the earlier semi-structured interviews.

These changes were well made in that they represented the experiences of the mothers in all their complexity and ambiguity. The return to full-time employment in children's early years was unusual in Britain in the early 1980s, with the dominant ideology still favouring full-time motherhood. Many mothers therefore experienced ambivalent feelings about returning to work in that context as well as being subject to the conflicting practical demands of home and work. The development of a methodology that allowed for the expression of contradictory views and feelings was therefore an important development in this study: The responses women gave to single closed questions differed from narratives embedded in their experiences. These different types of data illuminated moreover broader theoretical concerns and served to confront the contradictions in, and to highlight, the fragmented and multifaceted nature of human consciousness. We wrote about 'the inter-penetration of ideology and practice ... the mechanisms by which women reproduce and integrate contradictory elements of their beliefs, actions and the situations in which they find themselves ... beliefs and practices ... [which are] part and parcel of larger ideological debates concerning gender roles and the practice of everyday life'.

Attending to how particular findings are generated by different methods is therefore a fruitful strategy in making sense of data. Another example from this study concerns the sharing of childcare in the household. We noted how women often retracted negative comments about their partners or balanced them with commendations in response to direct questions. We wrote: 'Examination of the qualitative analysis of women's comments suggested a more complex conclusion. In many cases a good deal of criticism or ambivalence (about husbands) was expressed, especially when women recounted particular incidents. Critical comments, however, were often retracted or qualified in response to direct global questions concerning satisfaction with husbands' participation ... the strategy [we] adopted was to examine the contexts in which women's responses were located, together with a content analysis of responses. In this way the contradictions were confronted, and the processes identified by which dissatisfaction was played down or explained away'.

In writing up the study data, we commented upon different ways of combining qualitative and quantitative data. In general we rarely sought to corroborate qualitative results through reference to the quantitative data. Rather we analysed the data sets in relation to the particular research questions underpinning each, while also being attentive to the context of informants' responses, namely the questions the interviewers posed to them. Typically we found that the two types of data analysis were broadly complementary, providing different kinds of insights into the different aspects of the social phenomena which constituted our field of interest.

Such a developmental approach had consequences for a research project's resources. An organic interviewing approach was employed, requiring increased commitment and the development of new skills; the interviews took longer, requiring extensive probing and greater flexibility, concentration and listening skills than originally envisaged in the research proposal.

It had data processing consequences and more time and involvement from the senior members of the team. There were other tensions too in the analysis phase namely between carrying out an analysis across a large number of cases and carrying out a qualitative, in-depth analysis of a smaller number of selected cases.

In Britain's increasingly marketized research world, such an evolutionary approach to research would be unlikely.

However, in so far as research funders aim to encourage capacity building among researchers, allowing for a developmental approach within a project's timetable could be one way whereby researchers build up a broad spectrum of methodological expertise.

Interpretation and Contextualization

The third phase of the research process in which another type of data may be introduced is the phase of interpretation and contextualization of the findings. Drawing upon data across the qualitative/quantitative spectrum can take place at all phases of the research process: shaping the concepts and ideas at the start of the enquiry and influencing the process of analysis, as well as occurring at the later stage when the researcher draws conclusions.

Contextualization is particularly important in cross-national research. My example here is from a study of young people's views of their future work–family lives, funded by the European Union and carried out in five countries. In the empirical phase of the study, focus groups and individual interviews were carried out with different groups of young people aged 18–30, selected according to life course phase relating to education, employment status and occupational level.

It is axiomatic in cross-national studies to be attentive to the social science concepts which the different country research teams draw upon and how these play out methodologically—in terms of how informants make sense of concepts and how researchers translate and interpret them in practice. For such processes of 'translation' in crossnational research are likely unwittingly to reflect rather than reveal the characteristics of the contexts researchers seek to study. There is in short a danger of 'insider bias'.

Thus in this study, the ways in which the focus group moderators framed the questions on the fieldwork guide and the way respondents interpreted them reflected dominant normative and cultural assumptions, in this case concerning the history of maternal employment and childcare in the different countries. Differences later emerged in the ways in which the questions had been put by moderators to young people about combining work and family in the future. In order to make sense of these differences and the assumptions they revealed we (the UK team) were reliant to some considerable extent upon the contextual knowledge gained from our own understandings and in respect of other countries on those of our colleagues.

We were also reliant upon national official statistics while qualitative studies conducted in particular countries were rarely available to us in translation.

Some variation in the way moderators ask questions is allowed in the focus group method. Moreover in some cases we did not do all the moderation ourselves. In analysing some of the focus group material across the five countries, we were struck by how the questions about parents' employment were posed differently depending on the context.

For example, in the UK focus groups, the question was typically posed thus: 'Can you see yourself giving up work when you had a child? Would you carry on working when your children were young?'

Posing the question thus allowed young people to respond in terms of their 'personal choices', which has been the leitmotiv of much British public policy in recent years. It suggested to young people that there may be alternatives, reflecting current UK public policy changes and practices concerning the escalating employment of mothers over the 1990s, especially the employment of mothers with young children.

This framing contrasted with that of the moderator in Ireland who made strongly *gendered* assumptions about full-time motherhood (the norm in Ireland at the time, albeit change was beginning to happen): 'Some people would say that a pre-school child would suffer if his/her mother [our emphasis] was employed and others would say it made no difference?' Here the Irish moderator introduced the possibility of negative effects upon children— signified in the words 'child would suffer'.

The sociologists in the team were particularly mindful of the tendency in much current qualitative enquiry to place undue emphasis upon discourse and the subjectivity of respondents. This danger was to some extent minimized by the study's research design: Young people were selected on the basis of age, educational level and occupational status.

However, during the course of the focus groups we found little reference by young people to the structural context and the constraints upon their lives. For example, young Norwegians university students displayed what we termed a 'confident planning mentality' about their future lives as parents and workers but failed to suggest how such feelings of mastery and independence were premised upon the support of a strong welfare state in Norway.

It was therefore important to reveal the link between the individual's sense of agency within the structural context and to inject this into the interpretation of the focus group data in the analysis and writing up.

Conclusion

A multi-method strategy may enter into one or more phases of the research process: the research design; data collection; and interpretation and contextualization of data. The practice and value of working qualitatively and quantitatively it is necessary to distinguish between the context in which researchers design research for particular purposes and frame particular questions, from the context in which they make sense of their data and recontextualize them in relation to ontological, epistemological and theoretical assumptions.

The paper has given some examples of research in which different methods were chosen to address different aspects of the research design and different research questions. It has also indicated how research designs require us to find particular groups and how a quantitative sample may lead to the identification of relevant groups for in-depth study. Reference was made to linking a qualitative sample to statistically representative samples and the advantages for different parties. Disadvantages may also accrue as when a nationally representative sample does not generate the groups that qualitative researchers wish to access.

The paper has also suggested that a fieldwork method may include a quantitative approach so that data on particular items are collected systematically; some questions on the interview schedule discussed were treated quantitatively while others had a qualitative character.

An interviewing approach which allows interviewers to probe and the interviewees to give narratives of incidents and experiences is likely to result in a more holistic picture of people's understandings than a conventional survey analysis would provide and elucidate the meanings that research participants attribute to their practices and actions.

The paper has also discussed contextualization and interpretation as a separate phase of the research process and as a phase that informs other phases.

Contextualization is a critical part of a multi-method strategy in creating and making sense of data. In methodological texts there is surprisingly little attention given to the issue. Indeed it is only when the issue of working cross-nationally is addressed that contextualization deserves separate attention and is addressed explicitly: in terms of the development of research instruments and question wording and in the interpretation of people's responses in a given national context.

It may well be that it is ignored because of its compartmentalization as reviews of official statistics and the literature. Until the arrival of systematic reviews, literature reviews did not routinely require methodological discussion. The paper has moreover noted that qualitative analysis in its emphasis upon the textual may be rather weak in contextualization, that is in making sense of data in relation to structural contexts and particular historical moments. At worst, quotes from informants are sometimes presented in the written outputs of studies without reference to context, so that meaning is often narrowly interpreted to refer to actors' own interpretations. Thus agency may be attributed to actors without reference to the resources that are available to them. In this way there is a risk that we may fail to make the classic sociological link between the individual and society.

To conclude, the aim of methodology is to help us to *understand*, in the broadest possible terms, not only the products of scientific enquiry but the process itself (Kaplan, 1964). A multi-method strategy should be adopted to serve particular theoretical, methodological and practical purposes. Such a strategy is not a tool kit or a technical fix. Nor should it be seen as a belt and braces approach.

Multi-method research is not necessarily better research. Rather it is an approach employed to address the variety of questions posed in a research investigation that, with further framing, may lead to the use of a range of methods. However, the resulting data need to be analysed and interpreted in relation to those methods and according to the assumptions by which they are generated.

7

Participatory Action Research as a Methodology

In a recent critical assessment regarding the conventional approach to development studies Edwards shows that in most cases research in this field has "become part of the problems of underdevelopment rather than being part of the solutions to these problems".

This is related to the fact that advising developing countries had become a "major industry, employing 80.000 expatriates in Africa south of the Sahara. As an alternative to the conventional academic survey and policy (top-down) research Edwards pleads for the introduction or extension of participatory or action research. This kind of research appears the only type that can seriously take into account the knowledge about their own environment and problems that exists among the common people for whom all the studies are allegedly to serve.

Fortunately, at the margins of the mainstream academic and policy-studies participation-and action-research and-even better-participatory action-research has been carried out over the last few decades in several countries.

This was mostly related to such fields as community-and peasant organization, adult education, and similar grassroots oriented development efforts, designed to lead to "empowerment of the poor". A brief overview of the emergence of action research and participatory action research as its offshoot should be given.

Action research has emerged just before and during the Second World War in social psychology as a form of social research in which the researcher learns about certain group processes or change processes by actively participating in or manipulating certain aspects of these group-or change processes. It is a kind of learning by doing. The inventor of the term action research, Kurt Lewin, once said: "If you want to know how things really are, just try to change them". His work intended to benefit minority groups in the USA, such as Jews and Blacks, but it could well be applied to rural areas in Third World countries. Lewin himself was a Jewish refugee from Nazi Germany with a background in the Frankfurter Schule. He created within social psychology a current or school dealing with democratic and authoritarian leadership patterns in groups and conducted a great deal of group dynamics experimentation among various kinds of people. Later his approach was applied also in group formation and community organization work in Southern Italy and Latin America.

During the 1960's and early 1970's an increasing number of social scientists particularly in Latin America recognized that most current forms of sociological or anthropological research were not able to deal adequately with the political implications of people's participation in development particularly where this manifested itself in acute local contradictions or conflicts. As controversial aspects were too often ignored, it was difficult for such research to contribute to any solution. In fact unintentionally such research often served the most powerful and vested interests in such cases. As an alternative form of social research which proved more apt to play a role in conflict situations and contribute effectively in finding solutions certain types of action research became increasingly practised.

Different forms of action research have been distinguished. One form is manipulative action research: the knowledge acquired through action research can be utilized to manipulate people e.g. workers in industry. This happened in certain fields of industrial "human relations" programmes in USA and Europe where this form of social psychology following Lewin's initiative has been widely used. In grassroots work in Third World countries a form of action research has emerged which tried to utilize the research itself as well as knowledge acquired through it, to enhance the grip of the local people, the participants on their own communities.

From research objects they became research subjects. This was called participatory action research. In this participatory form of action research, several important contributing elements can be distinguished for the activist-researcher:

1. Required is an awareness of one's own limitations, a sense of insecurity and one's relative ignorance (compared with the local people involved). In addition to this one needs consciousness of oneself as working with certain values, which may differ considerably from those of the local people.
2. Accepting one's relative ignorance, one tries to learn from the people concerned through empathy and friendship what their problems and needs and feelings are. Knowledge of the history and the overall political-economic situation in the village or area concerned is essential background information. This can be obtained through data-gathering from official statistics or through local informants and group interviews, where people check one another's information.
3. After acquiring sufficient knowledge and understanding of local problems further dialogue with the local people, particularly through discussions in small groups, searching together for possible solutions is undertaken. This will be done prudently, since most problems are due to conflicts of interest existing in the village or area concerned. Although risky, it is important to not ignore but rather to discover such conflicts and underlying social structural contradictions. It is needed to bring them into the open and initiate step by step, to support or help the people concerned, to undertake activities or create organizations to remedy and correct the situation and to overcome the existing contradictions.

Participatory action research mostly had as a purpose to find solutions to concrete problems and conflicts. The results of such research, however, if carried out systematically and consistently, at the same time contributed to a greater knowledge of conflict-solving methods as such, which apply to a variety of concrete situations. This is important for the replication elsewhere of general theoretical knowledge in this field, from which grassroots groups in a variety of circumstances can benefit. The methodology of participatory action research has gained impact and recognition from the established social science circles in Latin America where special symposia on this method have been organized or sponsored by Unesco, Int. Sociological Association and other bodies, in Cartagend, Colombia (1977), Ayacucho, Peru (1979), Lubljana, Yugoslavia (1980) and Patzcuaro, Mexico (1982), and most recently in Managua (1989).

Also in other parts of the Third World the importance of including participatory strategies into social science methodology has been applied for some time. In the case of African countries where in the rural areas polarization between rich and poor and concentration of land property in few hands has not (yet) taken the alarming forms visible in Latin America and large parts of Asia, the need to practice participatory methods of research to mobilize peasants for effective rural development efforts has also been recognized. Such research was related to study planning and implementation of concrete small self-sufficiency projects such as grain storage or local problem-solving for broader self-reliance as the Jipemoyo-project in Tanzania.

There are several ways in which action research, if properly implemented, can directly serve the population in peasant villages. Properly implemented means here that research should be undertaken in close dialogue with the people concerned. As regards the, often problematic, internal situation of villages it is important to discover the existing stratification and the kinds of contradictions between social strata if they exist. The nature of such contradictions can be discussed with the people concerned, particularly with the lowest categories which generally form the majority. Discussion of these contradictions can be used creatively in a process of conflict-resolution.

Thus dynamic mobilization of the people for their own benefit became an integral part of such action-research as happened in cases in Latin America or India. In cases where such contradictions have not developed too strongly, they can be checked or corrected before they become acute and violent. An important aspect of the uncovering of contradictions and polarization between rich and poor is to study the historical process through which these emerged in the near of far-away past, particularly in respect to land tenure.

As regards the external relations of peasant villages or rural areas study was made of the dependency patterns which existed between the local economy and the broader society, regionally, nationally and internationally (e.g. the world market).

Such studies, also undertaken in close dialogue with the local people tried to design strategies in which relationships of dependence could be managed in such a way that the local villagers achieve a maximum of bargaining power to assure a measure of independence or even self-reliance. Also this research had to include a look into the history of the emergence of such dependency relationships with the broader economic and political structures and what the effects of these relationships were for the local population. In this context the recovering of oral history often was a strongly motivating force.

These forms of action research have contributed to awakening or heightening poor people's awareness about the conflicts and contradictions existing in their situation and ways to overcome these. Researchers supplied the people they worked with, with useful background information which helped those people to interpret more accurately their own situation. Such action research could direct itself simultaneously towards the development of theories and to the solution of concrete social problems. Some forms of action research are undertaken to facilitate the solution of concrete problems while other forms are directed towards a (more theoretical) search for general problem-solving methods which could apply to a variety of concrete situations. Thus in addition to helping conflict-resolution such action research could lead to valid scientific insights supplementing the type of research generally practised with orthodox methodologies which do not always capture sufficiently the realities of rapid social change.

In the course of years of experimenting it was learned that the processes of rapid change in which most communities and societies are involved at present, anywhere, can probably most fruitfully be studied and understood by participating in those change processes, from within, through active but careful participation in ongoing processes. In addition to this, such action research also had to be undertaken from below, which implied that the realities were being seen critically, through the eyes of those who were suffering the effects of changes, and watched these effects with suspicion, distrust and doubt. This view from below implied a kind of structural and historical consciousness about the causes of subordination, which can help poor peasants and women to maintain their self-esteem to some extent in spite of their down-trodden situation.

However, practising this view from within and from below is often difficult as a consequence of the ways in which the social sciences are generally being taught and implemented. At present social scientists are amply trained in tabulating, drafting questionnaires, observation and interviewing, but there is hardly any systematic training to become sensitive to the needs and values of fellow human beings, individually or in groups. Even less attention is given to oneself, as a researcher and as a human being, grown up with all the biases one's society imposes.

Similarly neglected is development of the capacities to bring 'experiences', impressions and biases through introspection and discussion in small groups into the 'objective' sphere, something that can be learnt like good interviewing as is amply demonstrated by many feminist consciousness-raising groups. Such 'sensitivity-training' is probably a good way to overcome the alienating, dehumanizing effects of most of the current social research methodology which is basically manipulative and not emancipatory. Introducing such a sensitive methodology, in addition to possibly helping the people being researched, may well have a liberating effect on the social scientists concerned themselves.

There exists a certain variety in forms of participatory action research in which research and action (understood as processes of social transformation) are related. The most important distinctions are: Participatory Research-for-action and Participatory Research-through-action.

Participatory Research-for-action mostly consists of the regular forms of survey research though questionnaires or interviews, with a view of quantifying data on the situation of villagers. It is self-evident that before starting such investigation in a concrete village or area, statistical and other overall material on the village which is available at competent government offices or statistical bureaus, should be collected and studied. Relevant topics are population, land tenure, economic activities, on-going or past project activities, if available also historical data.

In relation with certain action projects-e.g. various types of people's participation projects-it is necessary to involve participants according to criteria of relative poverty. At the start of a project the activists or promoters visit local families. By making an inventory of the inhabitants of a village and their (lack of) wealth, income, land tenure, measure of indebtedness, number of cattle, they can in dialogue with the people determine who qualifies for participation in the project and who not. It is a principle of people's participation projects to exclude the better-off, to ascertain that they will not become the main beneficiaries of the project or dominate it as happened too often in all kinds of current development schemes as promoted by the World Bank and similar agencies.

The participatory action aspect of this simple quantifying survey research is that the results of inventarization are being fed back into the community in group meetings to verify in open discussions that the data are largely correct (most people in villages know the economic situation of other villagers and a mutual check, particularly if announced beforehand, can be a guarantee for correctness of data supplied). Of course such research should be explained in public meetings in advance, before it actually starts. Such public discussions can enhance awareness and the possible solution of certain contradictions or injustices existing within the village or in its relation with outsiders (merchants, transporters, moneylenders, landlords).

As will be shown below people's participation projects are launched by some governments or nongovernmental organizations in order to specifically help the poor sectors of the rural areas (often the majority) which have not benefited from or were even marginalized by the current Green Revolution and other rural development efforts such as the introduction of large capitalist farms.

There are a number of other forms of participatory research-for-action in addition to such an inventory of existing social conditions which form the starting point of action projects. In many cases in addition to knowing the actual social structure of a community it is important to (re)discover the history of social relationships. Listening to the (oral) histories as told by aged men and women about themselves and their community in the past and discussing the findings in community or group meetings has proved to be a useful way to discover and enhance the aspirations living in a community.

Such research can include economic and political history of struggles and developments but also concern the religious and spiritual life, which in the past has often been more evident and important than to-day, though it still may be slumbering and thus influencing present decisionmaking in covert ways.

Participatory Research-through-action takes as a point of departure that most activities in the field of emancipatory social transformation can be seen as experiments proving (or disproving) that people can use certain group strategies to change their situation for the better and how to do this most effectively through group formation and common action on their own behalf. It implies therefore a careful recording, qualitative and quantitative, of the process of relevant activities undertaken.

This had to be done by the activist or promoter but in part also by the secretaries of the action-groups (e.g. minutes of meetings held). The promoter has to do the summarizing of all the collected records and to assess in dialogue with the participants cases of success and failure, problems or bottlenecks which occurred (e.g. regarding democratic or authoritarian style of group leadership and its effectiveness). The summarized experiences are presented for discussion in the groups concerned and in common meetings or workshops of representatives of various groups, so that feedback can take place and an overall and mutual learning-by-doing process emerges. Thus certain successful activities can be analysed and the factors leading to success be recognized and their occurrence enhanced in future activities. At the same time factors leading to failures can be detected and in the future possibly be avoided.

Participatory research-for-action and research-through-action generally complement each other as components of participatory action research. They can be implemented at various levels. These are mostly undertaken at the village or community level and have in such situations proved to be a useful approach to enhance the empowerment of disadvantaged people (peasants, women) through group formation and common action. The group members and-leaders as well as the activists or promoters learn a great deal from these exchanges. Promoters as well as participants can enhance their learning by keeping in addition to official records and logbooks about occurrences and activities a personal diary with reflections and observations particularly on difficult or controversial aspects of the processes involved. Personal development and group empowerment often go hand in hand and can be explicitly linked by conscious reflective effort. Thus objectivity in participatory action research can be enhanced by the distance, through self-reflection, which researchers can take from themselves and from their own personal and cultural biases and the political-economic context to which they structurally belong.

In the course of the last few years considerable experience has been accrued in some official or many non-governmental agency sponsored projects with various forms of participatory action research. One of the few official and UN sponsored programmes using this methodology is FAO's People's Participation Programme (PPP), working through pilot projects in about 10 different countries. In most of these projects some measure of systematic application of participatory action research has been an essential component.

RESEARCH APPROACH AND METHOD

Social Mapping

Social mapping is a research method which involves asking people to plot out where they see the boundaries of their 'space'. This will be used to develop and refine our understanding of community and place. This involves walking with and talking to people as they move through defined spaces, and seeing how their understandings and shaping of community is informed via their interactions and movements.

Such social mapping in the first instance will be geared towards the central life-world themes of the project (for example, where people work, meet, eat, and play). These are then mapped against the social themes of the project (for example, what a given life-world theme such as work has meant in the past and now), and then interpreted in terms of a series of layers of social analysis that form the theoretical level of our methodology (for example, broader implications about social formations at work in how people define a given thematic).

In summary, the initial stage is to build up profiles of the different communities and places that will be involved in the project. This will be done by drawing on a range of sources through a variety of strategies. This is then mapped against increasingly abstract modes of analysis. Our intention is to move from the empirical to the abstract and back again in a constant journey of return, testing each level against the others.

Gathering the Evidence

Because of the diversity of the communities that will take part in the project, a flexible toolbox of methods is required for gathering research material. Our toolbox ranges across the following techniques:

- writing background social histories for each of the research locales
- writing thematic essays that provide general background to local communities or background to pressing social issues
- conducting interviews and strategic conversations
- collecting stories and life-histories
- eliciting photographic narratives or artistic representations of the locale
- conducting a survey questionnaire
- gathering quantitative data from official and unofficial sources
- collecting policy documents relevant and contextualizing official discourses.

Writing Social Histories

To complement these social maps, social histories will be written to develop a sense of the larger composition of the community. This includes finding out when and how the community came to be, as well as understanding the impact of different formative events on the community. One point of reference here will be, for example, conflict and violence, including the way in which both frontier wars and/or involvement in overseas conflicts have affected and shaped the community.

Writing Thematic Essays

Thematic essays involve the writer exploring some focussed aspect of social history or contemporary social life. It is a way of providing context for understanding contemporary social issues. For instance, in a city such as Sarajevo a thematic essay could take into account all kinds of celebrations and rituals from medieval times to the present associated with the social theme of 'identity-difference'. In relation to a town such as Broadmeadows a thematic essay might take contemporary questions of 'sport and leisure' as its focus. In short, in focussing upon a locale (or locales) a thematic essay should directly address at least one of our social themes or life-world themes listed below. This might range, for example, from the social theme of 'belonging-mobility'—perhaps discussed in relation to pressing social issue of refugees—to the life-world theme of 'arts and symbolism', perhaps discussed in relation to births and marriages. A thematic essay might stretch beyond any one locale to explore issues related to a life-world theme such as 'place and environment' or open up a discussion into dialectical issues contained in the social theme of 'authority-participation'. Thematic essays can present the outcomes of thematic research and/or they can include elements of creative or lyrical writing on a theme.

Conducting Interviews and Strategic Conversations

We will use two particular kinds of semi-structured interviews to explore specific topics and themes with relevant community members; sometimes to capture deeper and more nuanced information about topics that are included in our survey questionnaires and sometimes to get a deep understanding of particular developments or projects within the community concerned.

In the first kind of interview—strategic conversations—considerable thought needs to go into the choice of people to be interviewed in relation to the nature of the topic. The taped interviews thus need to be preceded by background research and preliminary discussions with the interviewees. In such cases the interviewer plays a proactive and strategic role in the discussion of the researched topic. The term 'strategic conversation' indicates that an active dialogue has taken place in which the interviewer and interviewee have pushed each other, based on some prior understanding of each other's views on the subject. A strategic conversation in this sense goes beyond the usual research interview where an interviewer faces an unknown respondent and asks them to answer a series of set questions on the designated topic.

Strategic conversations are supplemented by a second kind interview— response interviews. These are shorter discussions conducted with other people involved in the projects or developments that are relevant to the strategic interviews. These response interviews allow us to cross-reference the experiences of a range of people beyond those involved in the key strategic conversations.

Collecting Life-Histories and Stories

Collecting Stories and Life Histories All kinds of stories already circulate in local communities and some untold stories deserve to go into broader public circulation. These can range from local histories and myths to oral histories to recent experiences and events. We are interested in eliciting local stories that are well-crafted and communicated as concisely as possible without losing their narrative richness. Such stories can be collected by community members, by 'outside' researchers, or by a combination of both. They can be collected in the form of written accounts or as 'digital stories' that combine images and audio. In many cases they will touch on more than one of the life-world or social themes listed below. Life histories are organized around individual life narratives that provide background and context to contemporary community life. They involve background research, lengthy interviews and collaboration with the subject to ensure that the story is told accurately and with a degree of depth and reflection relating to the life-world or social themes. They provide an opportunity to explore the 'lived experience' of changes over time and to capture dynamically-contextualized stories of local community life.

Eliciting Photographic Narratives

Another way of drawing community participants further into the project is to use photography as tool. The approach that will be used is known is reflexive photography. In this approach, community participant observers are given a disposable camera and invited to take photographs of people, places and things in their communities around the life-world themes outlined below. Reflexive photography assumes that community members possess a great deal of 'inside knowledge' about the communities to which they belong. Community participant observers will also be invited to supplement their photos with meaningful photographs from their own collections as well as other personal artefacts that they believe expresses something about their community. They will also be given a mini-photo album and will be asked to arrange their photos and to think about the connections between them. The purpose of this is to encouraging the community researchers to begin to construct reflexively meaningful narratives about the places and events depicted in the photos. Reflexive photography supplements one of the other research tools—interviews.

Collecting Community Life-Profiles

Community life-profiles are developed as a very concise version of a life history and/or a snapshot of local community life as it is experienced by individuals. They begin as interviews of ten to fifteen minutes that follow a schedule of questions relating to the subject's direct experiences of the complexities and dynamics of local community life (relevant to the life-world or social themes listed below). The interviewer turns this into a concise narrative that is returned to the subject for amendment and approval. Because this process is not very time-consuming it is possible to collect a large number of such community life-profiles over time and they can be used as background data for a wide range of research interests.

Conducting a Survey Questionnaire

We have developed a questionnaire that is used as a quantitative indicator drawing upon some of the life-world themes and social themes of the project. The questionnaire allows for comparative analysis across the different places of research. Here we provide a printable copy of the questionnaire that you can either open or download in English, Spanish (Español) and Bosnian.

The questionnaire uses a combination of 10-point Likert scales, multiple-choice questions and open-ended questions, and is designed to gather data from a large number of respondents. It can be used both as a mail-out self-administered questionnaire and as a structured interview schedule. The questionnaire will be analyzed by applying a commonly-used statistical analysis program.

Gathering Quantitative Data

To provide context for other methods of data collection, a number of quantitative strategies are being used. We are developing systematic social profiles of each of the communities across the globe using community statistics or small-area data. These include demographic data at local government level, including population, age, culture, education, employment and income. This will be supplemented with data relating to mortality, morbidity rates and population health.

Collecting Relevant Policy Documents and Contextualizing Official Discourses

This refers to the ways in which communities are constituted via official documents and reports, including those put out by civic and professional organizations and representative bodies. These might include tourist brochures and pamphlets, information regarding cultural activities and events in the communities, business planning documents, health reports and information and the like. Official discourse might also include official mappings of community against which our social mappings can be compared.

Life-World Themes

We have chosen a range of 'life-world' themes, social facts and activities in everyday life. They are treated as broad categories around which to base all our qualitative and quantitative research. These are the primary categories that will be used directly in working with community participants. They are as follows:

- arts and symbolism
- celebration and ritual
- food and drink
- sport and leisure
- learning and education
- health-care and medicine
- work and money

- governance and law
- place and environment
- technology and resources
- conflict and violence.

Social Themes

We have, in turn, chosen a range of 'social' themes, overarching issues that inform daily life over time and space. These will also inform the direct work with community participants, but at a secondary level of reflection on the research outcomes based on the life-world themes. They are as follows:

- identity-difference
- past-present
- wellbeing-wretchedness
- local knowledges-expert systems
- authority-participation
- belonging-mobility
- mediation-disconnectedness
- freedom-obligation
- equality-wealth distribution
- security-risk.

Social Analysis

At the tertiary level, we move to a much more theoretical level of academic reflection, based on a particular theorizsation of 'modes of practice' (James 1996)—that is established sociological, anthropological and political categories of analysis or ways of framing the 'things in the world'.

At the level of conjunctural analysis, categories of production, exchange, organization, communication and inquiry will be used in order to organize and give shape to the information developed in the community profiles. We are interested here in finding out how communities are structured and constituted through these different 'modes of practice'. By such an exploration this project will examine how communities embedded within specific locales are linked into large flows of people, resources and information that are prominent characteristics of the contemporary globalization.

Further, we will determine how the sustainability of such communities is affected—either adversely or positively—by such flows. The analysis will be drawn into forms of social integration that are at work in the community. The notion of integration here refers to the different ways in which individuals are bound into community, ranging from the most concrete, face-to-face forms of social integration to more highly abstracted modes, via information technologies, for example.

While different modes of integration may co-exist with one another—for example, the face-to-face co-exists with email communication—they do not necessarily do so in equal measure. One mode of integration can tend to dominate other forms of integration, framing those other modes in the process. Our hypothesis is that different forms of integration affect the sustainability of communities through time, with communities that are structured primarily through face-to-face social integration facing particular challenges to sustainability in the contemporary conditions of globalization.

ELABORATING THE METHODOLOGY

In the following documents we provide a further explanation of the methodology as outlined thus far. The first document, by Christopher Scanlon, further elaborates on both the ways in which the various research tools will be employed and also begins to integrate an explanation of the levels of theoretical analysis involved which are named below. The second document is an excerpt from Paul James's *Globalism, Nationalism, Tribalism: Bringing Theory Back In* which is the basis for the analytical approach taken here and which gives a precise theoretical categorization of the levels of analysis.

LEVELS OF ANALYSIS

Empirical Analysis

The first level of analytical abstraction is an ordering of 'things in the world', before any kind of further analysis is applied to those 'things'. This is the level at which the research materials are gathered, as outlined above. One of the strengths of this method is that its insistence on reflexive analysis forces us to separate out the first, second and any further levels.

Conjunctural Analysis

The second level of analytical abstraction involves identifying and more importantly examining the intersection of various 'modes of practice' (established sociological, anthropological and political categories of analysis), or ways of framing the 'things in the world' defined in the first level. The continuities or contiguities between these modes are not generally well addressed and to do so allows for a more complex and finely-nuanced reading of historical, political and social events, and social facts.

- production
- exchange
- communication
- enquiry
- organization.

Integrational Analysis

The third level of analytic abstraction involves categorizing ways in which people relate to, or differentiate themselves from, others. These forms of integration and differentiation vary with the kinds of societies that people live in, and are deeply related to the nature of lived social being. These categories or modes are explained in much greater detail in the two downloadable files and in James (1996, 2005).

- face-to-face relations
- object-extended relations
- agency-extended relations
- disembodied relations.

Categorical Analysis

From examining how people relate to each other, the fourth level of analytical abstraction moves to analysing the nature of the categories of social being itself. We concentrate on the four categories below. By mapping the dominant forms of these ways of being in the world we can distinguish a number of fundamentally different social formations—tribalism, traditionalism, modernism and postmodernism. These social formations have historical precedents but are not restricted to a particular time or place: they can and do exist side-by-side, and/or in tension in the same social space.

- time
- space
- embodiment
- knowing.

METHODOLOGICAL ISSUES IN CROSS-CULTURAL RESEARCH

Over the last decades researchers have shown an increasing interest in cross-cultural studies. Despite this interest, research in the field of cross-cultural management seems to lag considerably behind other fields of management science. In this respect, it has been argued that cross-cultural research suffers from many drawbacks creating impediments for further advances. We believe that difficulties encountered in cross-cultural research are various in nature and they may go beyond methodological and practical limitations. While some of these problems can be identified solely as methodological issues, others may be considered as problems related to epistemological positions.

EPISTEMOLOGICAL ISSUES

Epistemology or theory of knowledge is concerned with the nature sources and limitations of knowledge. Epistemological orientations shape and determine our particular view of the world and of reality. They also provide us as researchers with the guiding principles upon which we may base our methodologies. Therefore, the epistemological positions are in close relations with methodological approaches and they, affect research process in that they permit us to develop questions, design the study and adopt appropriate research strategies.

Most of cross-cultural research is based on a realistic perspective both at ontological and epistemological levels. Ontological realism implies that there is an external reality which does not depend upon cognitive structures of human investigators. On the other hand, epistemological realism assumes that the external reality is cognitively accessible to researcher.

The realism ontology views cultures as existing, stable and real systems of beliefs and practices. Therefore, it is argued that culture as an independent and objective phenomenon can be accurately measured, observed and investigated. This view of culture leads to an analytical/positivistic research strategy. In this way, the researcher perceives reality as tangible, concrete, stable, hard and real with deterministic relations among its constituent parts. The goal of analytical/positivistic research is to explain (erklaren) objective reality as fully as possible, and most of the time it is assumed that there is only one possible answer to a research question. Influenced by triumph of natural sciences, the proponents of the positivistic approach insist on methodological unity of all sciences and deny fundamental differences between natural and social sciences.

The researchers who make a distinction between the methods of the classical natural sciences and those of the social sciences are often called hermeneutics. The hermeneutics maintain that natural science methods are essentially unsuitable in social science domains. They underline a decisive difference between two domains. The difference of these two perspectives is, however, more than divergence in methods being used to create knowledge. The very essential difference between the two paradigms can be considered in terms of their objectives in creating knowledge. While the positivists attempt at explaining the phenomena (erklaren), the hermeneutics aim to understand them (verstehen). The explanation (erklaren) and understanding (verstehen) may have some blurred boundaries, but they have substantive differences. To explain (erklaren) is to present general relations among characteristics, behaviours or both. By, contrast, understanding (verstehen) is interpretative understanding of the meaning of actions through some form of contact with actors. In other words, explanation (erklaren) is to provide a deterministic account of external causal variables which shed light on an observed behaviour. The explanations should contain operational definitions as far as possible. Otherwise, these results (explanations) might be based on concepts that are not related to objective reality, something that may lead to misunderstanding and confusion.

A review of the literature shows that most of the cultural/ organizational research is based on a realist perspective and adopts a positivistic approach. However, the extent to which positivistic approach can be used to examine a complex concept such as culture has been questioned by many researchers. It is argued that man and his culture are historical concepts that should be understood in social context and they cannot be studied in vacuum.

Some critiques assert that positivistic approach has rendered cultural phenomena ahistorical, linguistically naive and psychologically unaware. Other scholars assert that the positivistic research can be employed to produce meaningful quantitative measures, but the nature of culture renders its understanding through these research techniques very difficult. The positivistic approach emphasizes the importance of generalizations and universal laws, however, cross-cultural research based on this approach has established quite a few generalizations. Most importantly, these generalizations are neither very general nor exact as those in natural sciences. So, how can we rely on them as knowledge? How can they be applied by other researchers el practitioners? Among so many cross-cultural researches, we know few that can provide us with clear, exact and reliable results. Moreover, the findings of such studies should be viewed as highly embedded in social context. Once removed from their original context, these results are hardly replicable to other cases.

Since culture is a very complicated and fuzzy concept, the researchers adopting a positivistic/analytical approach try to choose for parsimonious models utilizing as few variables its possible, with the variables being of an objective kind. On the other hand, by operationalization, they try to reduce the complex concepts such its culture to concrete indicators. Of course, these parsimonious and highly operationalized models may facilitate the research design, but at the same time they may distort the concepts and reliability of results. Some researchers hope to find cause-and-effect relations by incorporating only a few operationalized variables. However, by trying to increase the internal validity of the research (whether or not what has been identified as the cause produces the effect), they may sacrifice the external validity (the extent to which the research findings can be extrapolated to other cases). Since much of this research is looking for a supposed narrow causal relationship, it focuses only on very limited aspects of phenomena under investigation and fails to provide an in-depth understanding of cultural phenomena. In that way, the impetus of researchers is to make a priori predictions and test hypotheses rather than understanding and explaining the nature of cultural phenomena.

Despite all the criticism, it should be acknowledged that positivistic studies are characterized by rigor, internal/external validity and intelligible results. Since the results are to a great extent context-free and independent of researchers, they may he replicated to similar cases and this enhances the predictability of such studies. According to pragmatist/ instrumentalist perspective that dominates the knowledge creation of modern world, the value of knowledge equals to its practical use.

That is, the more the knowledge is practical, the more it is valuable. Therefore, culture is seen as an instrument to be studied and exploited for better performance and more efficiency. On the other hand, the predictability and practicality may bring more support to further positivistic research. Since these studies try to create practical, hard and relatively context-free knowledge, they are more likely to receive attention and financial support from both scholars and practitioners. For instance, the studies adopting a positivistic/quantitative approach have more chances to be published in top-ranked management journals, especially in USA. The proponents of positivist approach maintain that many of the criticisms directed to this approach are due to poor research methods, and therefore more advanced statistical techniques should be developed. They argue that the problems encountered in positivistic research are due to underdeveloped methods and as more complicated methods are introduced, the quality of research will improve.

SOCIAL CONSTRUCTIVIST PERSPECTIVE

Social constructivist perspective views reality as a social construction which cannot be independent of us as its observers. Accordingly, the objectivity is created by people and can therefore be changed by them. Furthermore, the objective (or objectified) reality and its meanings influence in turn the people who contribute to create them. That is, there are reciprocal and dialectical relations between the realities and people who create them. Based on constructivist perspective the human beings (the generating actors) and the reality (what is generated) stand both in mutual dialectical relation to each other. Therefore, the researcher attempts to understand and describe the dialectical relations that are continuously reinterpreted.

With respect to culture, social constructivist perspective focuses on the actors" interpretations or constructions of cultures. This means how the actors define their characteristics and those of others. Accordingly, culture is an ongoing interpretation process rather than a stable structure of values and norms. Social constructivism may have many forms. At its radical form, constructivist view claims that cultures and cultural differences only exist when people become aware of them in social interaction. Although researchers adopting a social constructivist perspective are few in number, they have provided interesting and insightful discoveries highlighting the importance of the actors' own interpretations of cultural differences. It seems that this paradigm is still in its infancy and more advances are needed to distinguish different processes and mechanisms when studying actors' interpretations and constructions of cultural conceptions.

The Constructivist perspective can have important implications for managing cultural differences. The fact that culture should be considered as a construction of actors underlines the importance of managerial issues and perceptions in dealing with cultural differences. This perspective permits us to view culture and cultural differences as mental constructions that can be managed and exploited.

Vaara (2000) argued that rather than contradictory orientations, the realist and constructivist perspectives correspond to two different epistemological commitments and both of them can contribute to a better understanding of the impacts of culture in organizational research. This means that a better knowledge of cultures should take into account both the real manifestations of cultures and the reflexive processes where the actors make sense of their cultures. In other words, one should view culture both as real systems of beliefs and values and actors' interpretations.

METHODOLOGICAL ISSUES

The term methodology has been used in different and even contradictory ways. Despite the differences, it is possible to view method as a demarcation criterion between scientific approaches to the creation of knowledge and non-scientific modes of exploration. In line with this view, Arbnor and Bjerke (1997) define methods as guiding principles for the creation of knowledge. These principles, on one hand, should be in accord with underlying epistemological assumptions and they should fit the problems under investigation on the other. Thus, by relying upon epistemological positions, the methods provide the link between theory and data, but they remain distinct from theory and independent of the data to be gathered and analyzed. As mentioned earlier, most of the cultural (and even social) research is based on a positivistic (explanationist) tradition. By adopting this approach, the methods look for models, theories and generalizable law-like principles with a considerable degree of external validity. Accordingly, it is possible to consider typical methodology of cross-cultural research as the study of techniques which are characterized by issues such as conceptualization, operationalization, designing research, formulating hypotheses, building instruments, collecting/analysing data and building theories. Based on this view of methodology, the following part of this paper is devoted to reviewing recurrent methodological problems encountered in different stages of cross-cultural research.

Conceptualization and Operationalization of Culture

Culture is a fuzzy and abstract notion and the First challenge for researcher is to define it. If culture has important implications for management practices, how can we define it? The problem is not lack of definition but difficulties in operationalization. Kluckhohn and Kroeber (1961) listed more than 164 different definitions for culture. According to these scholars, the proposed definitions call be divided into descriptive, historical, normative, psychological, structural, genetic and incomplete categories. Despite this abundance, every group of definition insists on very limited aspects and neglects other facets of this complex notion.

In the area of organizational science, review of literature reveals that many researchers view culture as a very vague variable representing a wide range of social and economic factors which may be invoked to explain the results of their studies. This issue can be attributed to a lack of agreement on general scientific paradigms in the field of cross-cultural management. According to Kuhn (1970), scientific paradigms can be considered as "'universally recognized scientific achievements that for a time provide model problems and solutions to a community of practitioners". This community of practitioners is a community of scientists, who create this paradigm through which they can find solutions to the problems defined by the paradigm. Those whose research is based on shared paradigms are committed to the same rules and standards for scientific practice. Therefore, an agreement on general paradigms may serve the definition and operationalization of the concept of culture. Due to this lack of general paradigms, the meanings associated to the concept of culture are very diverse and contradictory.

The problem of definition in cross-cultural research stems from two different but interrelated issues: its complexity as a concept and lack of general agreement on scientific paradigms among researchers. In other words, culture resists operational definition, not only because it is a fuzzy and complex concept, but also because there is no commonly accepted language to describe it.

The need for a general agreement on the definition of culture has two important implications; first it serves as a common language among researchers to advance the creation of knowledge and second it serves conceptual equivalence across borders/cultures. Conceptual equivalence implies that the meaning of research concepts, and materials should be equivalent across population under investigation. If culture is not universally defined, it cannot be studied across borders. Disappointed by the complexity of culture and lack of agreement on its definitions, some researchers suggested that it is better simply to abandon the concept of culture. In this respect, some scholars estimate that cross-cultural management research is still in its infancy and more advances are needed to achieve a general agreement about the meaning of culture. By contrast, others are more cynical and maintain that cross-cultural research has passed its infancy and these shortcomings cannot be justified.

For overcoming the difficulties concerning definition and operationalization of culture, it has been suggested that researchers must be precise in their definition of culture a priori rather than post hoc. Another suggestion is to use more tangible and refined constructs. In this respect. Bhagat and McQuaid (1982) proposed that researchers should replace the term culture with more meaningful constructs. To define and operationalize culture, an approach that might be useful is to identify several of its aspects/dimensions along which cultural differences could be compared. The cross-cultural literature provides us with different frameworks based on some aspects or dimensions of culture. For instance, Kluckhohn and Strodibeck (1961) identified six dimensions along which a society can be categorized; relationship to nature, beliefs about human nature, relationships among people, nature of human activity, conception of space, and orientation to time. Hofstede (1980) has described national cultures in five dimensions; power distance, individualism, masculinity, uncertainty avoidance and long-term versus short-term orientation. In the same way, Herskovits (1989) listed five dimensions of culture: material culture, social institutions, men and universe, aesthetics, and language. Trompenaars (1993) proposed a model that consists of seven dimensions: universalism versus particularism; individualism versus collectivism; neutral versus emotional; specific versus diffuse; achievement versus ascription: attitudes to time; attitudes to the environment. Schwartz el al. (1994, 1992) have proposed a framework by identifying three basic societal issues: relations between individual and group; assuring responsible social behaviour; and the role of humankind in the natural and social world. The cultural adaptations to resolve each of these three issues constitute his framework, which consists of three bipolar dimensions, defining seven cultural domains.

Many cross-cultural researchers focus on a few dimensions and especially those of Hofstede's model to describe and compare cultures. However, dimensionalization of culture has been subject to extensive criticism. Tayeb (2001) asserts that dimensionalization is a convenient approach to study culture across borders, but it simplifies a complex concept and diminishes the accuracy of investigation. By relying on a few dimensions, many cross-cultural studies neglect the contexts of the cultures within which their studies have been conducted, and they view a few dimensions as the only determinants of cultural differences. Moreover, since cultural dimensions rely on the typical members of cultural groups, cross-cultural studies built on dimensionalisation focus overlook the effects of intra-cultural variations. Intra-cultural variation (ICV) refers to the population distribution of a characteristic within a culture. Au (1999) suggests that intra-cultural variation explains as much if not more than inter-cultural variation.

Emic and Etic Approaches

Two mater possibilities for studying cultures are emic and etic approaches. Etic and emic are neologisms coined by,

Kenneth Pike from Phonetic and Phonemic. The emic approach attempts to describe a particular culture by investigating specific aspects of concepts or behaviours. In other words, the emic approach focuses on studying a construct from within a specific culture, and tries to understand that construct as the people from within that culture understand it.

The etic approach, on the other hand, involves developing an understanding of a construct by comparing it across cultures using predetermined characteristics. The use of emic or etic approaches depends upon the nature of study. It should be mentioned that there are important differences between the notions of culture and cultural differences and the ways they are studied. Culture can be studied in every defined society, but cultural differences can be studied only if there are at least two cultures.

This has implications for the research approaches since every culture should be identified by taking in account of the other culture. While the effects of culture are testable from one culture alone, the effects of cultural differences are measurable only when individuals from different cultures are compared. Since the etic approach uses variables which are generalizable across cultures it is more suitable for broader analyses, usually involving two or more cultures. The main assumption in etic research is that there is a shared frame of reference across culturally diverse samples, and that construct measurement can be applied to all of the samples in the same way, ultimately allowing for more generalizability.

While the eric approach permits a better comparison across cultures allowing generalizability by assuming that there are some shared frames among cultures, it may sacrifice conceptual equivalency and precision of the research. On the other hand, if an emic approach ix used, a more precise and thorough description of the construct within one culture is obtained, but the ability to make cross-cultural comparisons diminishes because the constructs are developed within a specific culture and they may not be extrapolated to other cultures. From a measurement standpoint, criteria in an etic approach are considered universal, with less attention being given to the internal characteristics of a particular culture. Furthermore, the use of an etic approach may be more practical for organizational researchers in terms of financial limitations and time pressures.

However, if etic constructs are used to make cross-cultural comparisons, researchers risk not capturing all of the culture-specific (emic) aspects of the construct relative to a particular culture in the study. When researchers choose an etic approach and assume that the concepts being tested exist across all cultures, they are imposing some predetermined constructs developed within other cultures. These imposed constructs may not have the same meanings in target cultures. For instance, some problems may happen when variables designed for one culture (e.g. leadership) are applied to a second culture without modifications. This is the case for comparative studies that try to replicate theories developed in United States to other countries. Some constructs (e.g. performance, leadership) based on western concepts may have different meanings in other cultures.

A suggestion for dealing with this problem is to use a combined emic-etic approach, rather than simply applying emic dimensions of one culture to other cultures. A combined emic-etic approach requires researchers to first attain emic knowledge about all of the cultures in the study. This allows them to put aside their culture biases, and to become familiar with the relevant cultural differences in each setting.

RESEARCH DESIGN

The main interests of cross-cultural researchers are related to cultural influences on organizations and management methods. That is, researchers often try to compare organizations in various cultures to identify similar and different aspects of organizational behaviour in these cultures. Generally, every study attempting to investigate the effects of culture is based on the implicit assumption that culture is a principal variable and that it has some impact on organizations. As Adler (1983) pointed out, comparative cross-cultural research is based on the assumption that culture plays a measurable role in the development of events, beliefs and attitudes. Therefore, the researchers looking to anticipate the effects of cultural phenomena should treat culture as the main variable. Following this perspective, some researchers define cross-cultural research as the study that has culture as its main dependent or independent variable but not as an extraneous and/or residual variable. While this perspective dominates cross-cultural management, some researchers give less importance to culture and treat it as a residual factor. For instance, Ajiferuke and Boddewyn (1970) maintain that much of the importance attributed to cultural factors rests more on speculation than facts. Viewing culture as a residual variable implies that researchers take it not as the principal factor affecting organizational behaviour but as a factor among others.

By taking culture as the main independent variable many researchers tried to find or establish causal relations between culture and organizational aspects such as performance, stability or some aspects of human resource management. While culture can be considered as an important variable affecting some aspects of organizational behaviour, in many cases it is questionable to incorporate it as the only independent variable for research. It is suggested that the goat of research should be to provide large variations of independent and dependent variables. Therefore, considering culture as the principal independent variable can be justified only if there are substantial variations of both independent and dependent variables.

Unit of Cultural Analysis

Hofstede (1997) described culture as "the collective programming of the mind which distinguishes the members of one group or category of people from another". Hofstede (1980) distinguishes culture from human nature on one side, and from individual's personality on the other. According to this view, culture has a collective nature and can be applied to various groups of society such as nation, industry, corporation, department, function, etc. Therefore, cultural groups can be defined and studied tit different levels, which are not necessarily exclusive. For instance, Benedict and Steenkamp (2001) distinguished three major levels: meta-culture, national culture, and micro-culture. Meta cultures are clusters of countries that may exhibit a number of common cultural characteristics. National cultures are delineated by national boundaries and micro cultures are subcultures within a country. Whereas meta-culture is even more comprehensive than national culture, micro or subculture is more specific. A micro-culture preserves is related to not only important patterns of the national culture but also its own unique patterns of behaviour. Such micro-cultures may be defined on various overlapping criteria, including language, ethnicity, religion, age, urbanization, and social class.

8

Participatory Rural Appraisal as Qualitative Research

Judging by the frequency of references to participatory IF methods in the development and anthropological literatures, the methods appear to have been embraced unreservedly. However, given their recent emergence-as action research, cooperative inquiry, participatory action research, and techniques based on the work of Freire (1968)-and their proliferation geographically and across disciplines, it seems wise to pause and take stock of the approach. At this stage in the development and use of participatory methods, it is somewhat premature to attempt to review the applications of such methods in part because the majority of development research that utilizes participatory methods remains unpublished.

One set of participatory methods, participatory rural appraisal (PRA), and with ascertaining the basis of two claims made by its proponents that are directly relevant to anthropological and development research, namely: 1) that PRA, and participatory methods generally, represent a distinct paradigm in social research; and 2) that such methods produce knowledge about the world that is valid and reliable. Such claims are based upon a particular way of knowing the social world, which presumes that a fundamental distinction can be drawn between natural and social science, and between the research methods typically associated with a specific research "paradigm." The task of examining such claims is controversial, in part because they derive from a debate about the superiority of qualitative or quantitative research and from arguments by postmodern theorists that distinctive research paradigms possess their own validity and credibility criteria (e.g., Lather 1986).

However, the latter claim constitutes an antifoundational position in social science and has serious implications for the kind of claims that social science is able to make.

One of the strengths of anthropology has been its inherent skepticism of all types of claims regardless of source and its attempt to achieve a holistic understanding of social and cultural life through the development of research techniques that must be combined with detailed social analysis. However, PRA is typically used as a standalone set of techniques and is not combined with other forms of qualitative research such as participant observation.

A SHORT HISTORY OF PARTICIPATORY RURAL APPRAISAL

Participatory rural appraisal owes it existence to the convergence of a number of research programs, including participatory action research, agroecosystem analysis, applied anthropology, and field research on farming systems. In particular, the current form and use of participatory techniques arose in the 1970s at a time when the expanding aid industry required quick access to socioeconomic data.

These processes culminated in rapid rural appraisal, or RRA, a response to the need of policy makers for access to relevant, timely, accurate, and useable information at a period when development research faced growing constraints. Initially, RRA was a strategy that sought to arrive at a "rough approximation of the value of many variables within a complex system in order to be able to decide what to focus on in more detail through more specialized studies". The initial principle that guided this strategy was "optimal ignorance," the importance of knowing what is not worth knowing (i.e., the level of ignorance that can be afforded).

Optimal ignorance together with lessons from anthropological research, survey work, and short appraisal visits resulted in recognition of the problems of interlocking biases and professional shortcomings that arise in shortterm research or appraisal visits. The biases arise because of the limited time available for field research, which results in random meetings with individuals who happen to be available or accessible at the time (i.e., near the road, in the project office, or at their houses rather than out in the fields).

RRA practitioners were said to have shared a common rationale, principles, and rigor that was embodied in five principles.

1. Optimizing tradeoffs between the cost, quantity, relevance, truth, and benefit of possessing information;
2. Offsetting biases from development "tourism" and hurried visits;
3. Triangulating by using more than one method or source to obtain and cross-check information;
4. Learning directly from with rural people whose knowledge and capacities are generally underrated but required for sustainable development; and
5. Learning rapidly and progressively through flexible, iterative, interactive processes aimed at the consciuos exploration of local peoples' lives.

In recent years efforts have been made to differentiate rapid rural appraisal (RRA) from participatory rural appraisal (PRA). RRA is now seen as extractive and nonparticipatory. PRA is supposed to use participatory techniques to facilitate local peoples' analytic abilities and empower them to plan and undertake sustainable action. RRA supposedly resulted in a situation in which outsiders' "reality blanketed out that of local people"; outsiders, it is now argued, did not know or care to share and extend their knowledge with local people. Chambers and others have argued that this fundamental break between RRA and PRA constitutes an epistemological shift that stems from the altered relation between outsiders (who should be facilitators) and local people (who take responsibility for analysing, planning, and implementing the activity). Consequently, proponents argue that PRA represents a paradigm shift that combines empiricism, the examination of diversity, improvization, and personal responsibility in a manner that embraces and affirms multiple realities and local diversity. Chambers (1994b:1258) has also argued that there is "no reason for anything less than critical rigor in assessing the validity and reliability of RRA and PRA approaches and methods."

THE ORIGIN OF "PARTICIPATORY" TECHNIQUES IN QUALITATIVE RESEARCH

The development and use of PRA has changed considerably over the past 30 years. As Chambers (1994a:959) has noted, "in the early days, RRA seemed to be largely organized common sense" on the part of field researchers. In particular, RRA emphasized the use of secondary sources, semistructured interviews, and observation. At the time researchers understood that RRA was a strategy intended to make the best use of limited time for fieldwork that offered little scope for the rural poor to set the research agenda. However, this appreciation appears to have been at odds with the work of others who sought to devise and promote a field methodology capable of maximizing local participation in development such that proposed projects would better fit the needs of local people and vice versa.

The techniques have been modified and adapted by researchers and development practitioners in a variety of novel ways, with the result that PRA techniques are widely seen as substitutable. Indeed, there now exists a variety of combinations of techniques that have their own name— participatory and learning methods (PALM); participatory learning and action (PLA); rapid assessment procedures (RAP)-and which are used for quite different purposes, including: 1) health research; 2) natural resource planning; 3) pest control; 4) what might be called experiential learning and communication; 5) development planning; and 6) project or program evaluation.

The popularization of PRA, the constant modifying of techniques, the variability in PRA training, and the apparent variation in how they are used, highlight why the academic community should be concerned with PRA and arguments that techniques are similar or substitutable, and indeed about the value of sequencing techniques.

The use of interviewing methods has primarily focused on semistructured interviews (SSIs) as developed in anthropological fieldwork. However, there is a tension between the focus of PRA training that redefines the technique as a team activity-and hinges upon the development and use of an interview guide. Though manuals point out the importance of context and of sensitive listening for the effective use of SSIs, little attention is given to who should be selected to be interviewed or to the need and means to corroborate or cross-check interview data with other information. Furthermore, the short period spent in the field— typically less than one week per site-and the emphasis on facilitating local learning in effect deemphasizes the role of SSI, of observation, and of obtaining data from secondary sources to better understand complex social relationships.

Many PRA techniques are modelled on or borrowed directly from qualitative social research, though practitioners pay little attention to the published literature discussing the limitations of the techniques. In particular, the prominent role of group interviews (i.e., structured interviewing or focus groups) is especially problematic because of the need to carefully select participants and to manage the group interview. As textbooks on qualitative method attest, structured interviewing is intended to "expose every informant in a sample to the same stimuli.... The idea is to control the input that triggers each informant's responses so that the output can be reliably compared". The techniques that rely on this approach include questionnaires, the construction of free lists, sentence frame techniques, triad tests, pile sorts, rankings, paired comparisons, and ratings. With the exception of questionnaires, the techniques were developed to explore what people think, how they think it, and how they organize the material. In short, such techniques attempt to explore specific cultural domains in terms of things that can be listed.

The task of producing data that are valid and reliable requires in part that all participants in a group interview are competent or knowledgeable in the specific domain to be investigated. This is difficult to achieve.

As Frey and Fontana (1991:185) observe, "group responses can be effected by the size of the group, by the group members view of the purpose of the interview, and by the differences in the background of the members." Failure to carefully select participants who are socially homogeneous (and who are strangers) is fraught with problems that include participants who feel under pressure to conform to peers or dominant individuals (the group effect), a stifling of discussion, interpersonal conflict, the production of irrelevant information, and posturing.

A related issue arises from the role of moderators in group interviews because their performance critically affects the data. At issue here is the extent to which group interviewing is more or less directed by the moderator and whether interviewing is more or less structured by the question format, the purpose of the discussion, and skill of the moderator. However, PRA practitioners are primarily concerned with issues of group management (with team building, creating consensus) and give limited attention to the selection of group members, the composition of groups, or the role of the moderator. When other PRA techniques are combined with the group interview, additional problems arise.

Furthermore, there is a tendency to use the information generated by a group interview as if the account speaks for itself. There are two interrelated issues involved: an accurate record of the group's account and the need to analyse the account. Many PRA practitioners appear unaware that a detailed record of group discussions is an important source of data. The record of a focus group is the basis for an analysis of individual statements, group interaction, and the role of the moderator. In PRA, note taking has an undefined role in daily review sessions during fieldwork and in writing up the final report. In this approach, note taking is intended to record process issues-how interviews were conducted, identification of problems-and is not seen as providing data for the research report.

As Maynard (1998) makes clear regarding her use of focus groups to study widowhood, the accounts of the women required analysis because they are historical constructions. Maynard grounded her account in terms of "a gendered analysis of marriage, family/household, domestic career and ideas about aging." Thus, the accounts produced in a group interview require theoretical analysis. Only in this way is it possible to make sense of the perspective of individuals and groups, and only with this type of analysis is it possible to move beyond a focus on discourse to an understanding of the constraints facing individuals and their society.

Visualization techniques are used in group interviews and are intended to enable local people to "conduct their own analysis, and often to plan and take action" through a shift from verbally to visually oriented methods that are not dependent on literacy, which could exclude many people. Thus, Pictures can be a means of focusing on problems and memories that are too painful or too complicated to be expressed in words. They can help individuals come to an accommodation with their past experiences. Pictures can be shown by the individual, the community or the state to project an image or an idea which would be difficult to explain in any other way. They can bridge languages and cultures, they can educate the world and inform a friend.

PRA uses visual techniques in group interviews to explore aspects of the social world that are amenable to diagramming or mapping. Experience is said to be the best guide to the use of these techniques, and facilitators have little more to go on than general guidelines and a list of do's and don'ts. Once again, and despite injunctions-to be nondirective, to facilitate, to listen closely, probe, and question-there appears to be limited awareness about the roles facilitators assume in group interviews or of the importance of carefully selecting participants. Instead, emphasis is placed on comprehending cognitive processes and identifying "simple, schematic devices which present information in a readily understandable visual form" such that, the act of constructing the diagrams is in itself an analytical procedure and helps the constructors to think through the dynamics they are trying...[to represent in visual form, JC). Second the diagrams become a means of creating communication and discussion between different people.

In this way, and supposedly without direction from outsiders, a group: 1) maps a locality; 2) constructs a seasonal calendar, locating itself and agricultural and social practices within it; 3) devises a profile of its use of time; 4) devises a longitudinal time line that indicates key dates, occurrences, and events; and 5) uses VENN diagrams to identify and analyse relationships between key areas and institutions.

PRA practitioners seem unaware of the kind of skills needed by local people to take part in visualization exercises. Drawing on Streets' (1993) research on literacy, Robinson— Pant (1996) has argued that many PRA visualization techniques appear to impose Western cultural practices and require local people to learn new cultural skills. In particular, a distinction must be made between visual literacy and numeracy.

The required literacy may not exist locally. While some degree of visual literacy can be picked up in PRA exercises-reflected in the fun or playfulness experienced by participants in the exercises-there is every reason to believe that each individual (including facilitators and researchers) interprets a map or matrix differently. The only way to address the issue would be to: 1) select individuals for inclusion in a group interview who are likely to share a similar worldview because of gender, age, religion, or caste, but this requires prior knowledge of the community; and 2) undertake research on local literacy and social cognition (Block 1998). PRA must adapt its techniques to accommodate the unevenly distributed skills and competencies that exist in a population.

Ranking and scoring techniques are problematic for the same reasons, namely their use cross-culturally and with groups. The techniques include exercises that solicit information, usually of a very particular type, that is listed, discussed, and ranked. The major types of ranking techniques are: well-being or wealth ranking; scoring or ranking of different options or opportunities; pair-wise ranking; and preference or problem ranking.

One of the defining features of PRA is that during the group interview facilitators should query members about the product of the visual ranking exercise (i.e., the map, the matrix). "Interviewing the diagram" is the principal mechanism used to incorporate the full range of social perspectives. However, the concept is understood in two contradictory ways: that there should be no ambiguity or "blank spaces" and that all perspectives should be accurately represented and incorporated into a group "product." The key concern with maps or matrices is expressed in the observation that "informants tell you something by drawing the diagram, and what they draw, and omit, tells you something about the informants". Interrogating maps and diagrams involves asking what has changed, exploring blank or empty spaces, clarifying the symbols used, and discussing ambiguous or unclear issues. Maps and diagrams are not supposed to be an end in themselves; rather, it is the process of focused discussion that is important. Even so, the number of times a map or diagram has become the objective of PRA must be enormous since it is often seen as a summation of the exercise.

An additional way to clarify and explore this issue would be to repeat the same exercise with other groups. Repetition is important for two reasons. First, the decision to use PRA techniques is presumably because very little is known about a particular problem and its amenability to study by PRA. Second, the decision of who to recruit into groups is related directly to the nature of the problem being investigated. Because development will differentially effect a population, each issue needs to be assessed separately with different sections of the community. Also, it is not possible to generalize findings from a small number of group interviews that are likely to be unrepresentative of the wider community. However, there is little evidence in the literature that repetition is utilized to crosscheck results.

While the emphasis is to build into the map or matrix the full range of local knowledge, the limitations of the technique and the limited knowledge of participants are unlikely to emerge until the document is used and clarified in a second exercise or is put to practical use. Thus, while it is possible to interrogate a map or matrix as it is being constructed, ideally facilitators need to link it to a second technique, to repeat the exercise with a different group, or to make use of other qualitative techniques.

PRA in Practice

Careful attention to method can help define a basis for transparent accounts of the research process and a more informed discussion of the validity and credibility of RRA and PRA.

There is a need to distinguish between the process of participatory research, and claims regarding the nature of local people participating in it, and a range of distinct and logically separate outcomes of research.

The role or contribution of participation in social research is a matter of considerable debate. Participation has been defined to include passive participation, participation in information giving, participation in consultation, participation for material incentives, functional participation, interactive participation, and self-mobilization. Pretty, Thompson, and Kiara (1994) argue that the first four types are superficial and have no lasting impact on people's lives. In any event, claims that participation plays a central role in research require a transparent account of the research process that distinguishes between: 1) the act of bringing people together for research that may or may not involve locals learning from or discussing their situation; and 2) the outcome of the research. Research outcomes may or may not include: 1) increasing and codifying local knowledge in maps or documents; 2) agreeing upon local development priorities; 3) planning and undertaking joint action; and 4) production of a research report. PRA may or may not involve data extraction, and it may or may not facilitate community action or empowerment.' To the extent that PRA produces research data, such information may serve important functions at different levels-facilitate local action, inform policy— and in different ways, including establishing dialogue between communities and government. Each output needs to be documented and assessed separately in research reports before the issue of participation can be fruitfully pursued.

There is a need to provide better documentation on the use and type of group interview utilized, including details on the techniques) it was combined with, its objective, and the information it produced.

Group interviews may serve a variety of purposes other than generating data (e.g., therapy, decision making, education), and they may follow organizational procedures that influence discussion. Most importantly, the role of the facilitator, the research instruments, and the methods used provide differing degrees of structure to the discussions. In PRA, insufficient information is provided about how individuals are recruited into groups and about what actually occurs in them. While general rules of thumb exist to avoid obvious biases, too little attention is given to such issues.

From the perspective of the researcher, a well-designed group interview attempts to elicit local respondents' "hierarchy of importance" in the form of emic understandings expressed in the local language. This task is facilitated by recording and transcribing the discussion for subsequent analysis. A further concern is that visualization, ranking, and scoring techniques have been added to the group-interview technique without a clear appreciation of their limitations. It seems clear that basic research on these techniques-used separately or in combination-is required.

There is a need to distinguish the data produced in a group interview from the knowledge and social competencies of local people.

PRA is premised on the assumption that its techniques effectively access local knowledge, but due to their proliferation it seems certain they are not consistently used. Additionally, there is the presumption that all members of a society are competent in the domain of inquiry that is the focus of research. In such circumstances, it seems reasonable to conclude that the techniques and the data they generate need to be more carefully assessed and that these issues should be addressed in research reports.

A related concern arises from the public nature of PRA exercises that allows a dominant group to construct a normative, unitary narrative that emphasizes consensus. Furthermore, the knowledge produced by PRA "is a construct of the planning context, behind which is concealed a complex micro-politics of knowledge production and use". Local knowledge production has four aspects: 1) the shaping of knowledge by local relations of power; 2) the expression of outsider agendas as local knowledge; 3) local participation in the production of a consensus; and 4) the direct manipulation of peoples' planning by development agents and projects. The complex nature of local knowledge production is unlikely to be adequately grasped by short field visits, assuming that researchers do pursue ambiguous findings and seek to explore minority views.

Finally, "backsliding" in the application of PRA creates problems. The pressure to produce results may lead researchers to skip key preparatory work, resulting in insufficient time spent building rapport with local people and poor or inconsistent training of facilitators, which tends to produce poor and unreliable data. This is particularly the case where divergent local interests are insufficiently explored, a situation that arises in the context of gender and ethnic inequality when insufficient attention is given to strategies of organizational and cultural change as opposed to merely including women or minorities as participants.

There is a need to identify the strengths and limitations of an individual PRA technique prior to integrating or combining it with another PRA technique or with quantitative and qualitative techniques.

While the principles of PRA emphasise iterative learning, the extent to which this occurs is unclear since many reports fail to clarify their techniques or procedures. At the same time, the extent and manner in which a technique is used to cross-check as opposed to obtaining discrete types of information is also unclear. In reality, little or no crosschecking may occur.

Equally problematic is the unexamined assumption that different techniques, and the information they produce, dovetail-as opposed to pointing in different, possibly contradictory directions-to form a coherent analysis or a harmonious and conflict-free society.

Are PRA techniques compatible with qualitative and quantitative techniques? How should the data produced by combining PRA with other techniques be assessed? These issues have yet to be examined, but their resolution would seem to involve: 1) an assessment of a PRA technique— individually and in combination with a second technique— in obtaining specific types of data; and 2) awareness of the possibility that different methodological orientations may render certain techniques and the data they produce incompatible.

Of the techniques used by PRA, only two have been the subject of work that examines the strategy used to collect, analyse, and present data. Focus groups (group interviews) provide the framework in which many PRA techniques are utilized, yet little research exists on the value and problems of combining it with other techniques. Morgan (1996) identifies four ways focus groups have been used in combination with individual interviews or surveys. All the applications are recent, and nearly all raise significant and unanswered questions about sampling and the analysis of data derived from different "paradigms."

Ward, Bertrand, and Brown (1991) compared focus groups to surveys on the extent to which data from these techniques converged or diverged. They found that:

Overall, for 28 percent of variables the results were similar; for 42 percent the results were similar but focus groups provided additional detail; for 17 percent the results were similar, but the survey provided more detail. And in only 12 percent of the variables were the results dissimilar.

The key finding was that to the extent that a focus group was appropriate to the problem being investigated, and was properly utilized, it functioned effectively in combination with surveys, individual interviews, or as a stand-alone technique.

Note, however, that PRA utilizes focus groups in combination with visual and verbal techniques that have not been examined to ascertain their limitations, and that the use of group interviews in PRA diverges sharply from their use by trained focus group facilitators.

The only PRA technique that has been the focus of basic research regarding its strategy of collecting data is wealth ranking, which was compared to data derived from household surveys to determine whether it provided a valid measure of socioeconomic stratification. Wealth ranking can focus either on locally defined household assets, or it can solicit local terms and understandings about household wellbeing or wealth. The solicited terms are then used as the basis for an exercise that ranks all households in a community or setting where the individuals undertaking the ranking know one another. The technique is used in the group interview format; therefore, the caveats identified earlier apply.

Scoones (1995) undertook research in southern Zimbabwe to compare the value of a wealth-ranking exercise that began by eliciting local wealth criteria that were used in group interviews with local households. This is a carefully designed piece of research in which various definitions of household were teased out so that the economic and social relationships between households could be explored: historical and ecological changes were addressed, gender issues were considered, and a differentiated set of indicators about assets, consumption, and perceptions were applied. The study's attention to context, culture, and method is excellent and it successfully demonstrates that when properly conducted, wealth ranking "is a cost-effective research tool for examining issues of wealth and poverty in a rural context".

A second study has examined wealth ranking as a means of analysing social stratification. Adams et al. (1997) attempted the more limited task of comparing findings from a wealth-ranking exercise to data obtained simultaneously from a survey of a small number of households. Unlike Scoones, this research relied upon methodological shortcuts. In particular, local interviewers were trained to use one wealth— ranking technique, and they made use of criteria derived from a previous study of a different area than the one to be ranked. In addition, the ranking exercise was performed by a small number of key informants in each administrative subdivision who were asked as a group to assign a household to one of three predefined wealth groups. Fifty-five villages were ranked; then a random sample of 30 households was selected for in-depth interviews to obtain a household census and collect information against which the results of the ranking exercise were compared.

The authors examined whether wealth ranking provided an adequate empirical measure of stratification; however, there are important caveats in their use of the technique :

1. The study fails to examine the nature of the social unit (households) being ranked;
2. The ranking criteria were derived from a study that may not adequately reflect local social variability;
3. It relied upon an unrepresentative number of key informants to do the ranking; and finally,
4. Ranking was undertaken as a group exercise. Had it been undertaken by individuals, an independent check on the bias of the exercise would have been possible.

It may be, as Adams et al. (1997:1170) argue, that measured differences across households "are consistent with our hypotheses and support the construct validity of the wealth—ranking technique." It may also be that their use of the technique does not measure what it purports to measure. Given the absence of comparable studies, the validity of the method as demonstrated by these authors must remain in doubt.

Finally, the extent to which different methodological orientations may be incompatible is suggested by Jodha's (1988) study of rural poverty in Rajasthan over a 20-year period. Jodha was unable to reconcile quantitative data on household income which showed that for 38 percent of households in two villages per capita income had substantially declined, with qualitative indicators suggested by villagers that indicated dramatic improvements in well-being, including reduced reliance on patrons, reduced dependence on low-pay options, improved mobility and household liquidity, improvements in consumption, and improved acquisition of consumer durables. Jodha (1988:2421) explains this paradox as one that arises from factors underlying rural poverty that "are too detailed and at times too complex to be captured by standard and simplistic methods".

Jodha's study illustrates a major disagreement between those who advocate a consumption-based approach to measuring income and expenditure (IDS 1996) and those who argue that local people's perceptions are fundamental to identifying what poverty is and how it is experienced. However, epistemological differences need not prevent research from exploring both positions by, for instance, focusing on issues of agreement and overlap or by integrating PRA with quantitative and qualitative techniques. The integration of different techniques and measures of poverty in a carefully designed study should increase the scope for a more nuanced analysis and appreciation of policy issues than is possible through studies that are confined to one methodology or set of techniques. Such a study would also have greater validity.

SEQUENCING AND TRIANGULATION

A major concern for PRA is with sequencing techniques. We have found that practitioners use or adapt established qualitative techniques in novel ways and that current practice may produce partial, invalid, and unreliable information. Though its proponents argue that validity is secured by sequencing techniques, there is little consensus about how to do it. The single exception refers to the "power" that derives from the experience of using the techniques that involves participants in a mix of enjoyment, enlightenment, and insight. Regardless, the PRA literature is vague on the subject of sequencing and refers generally to the wider social science literature on triangulation and to postpositivist "trustworthiness" criteria.

The social science literature identifies four types of triangulation and requires that research be designed to enable a researcher to cross-check a technique and the data a technique generates. The idea behind triangulation is that the limitations of any one technique can supplement or validate findings from a second, thus improving the accuracy of findings by incorporating more than one point of view. However, as Jick (1979:604) has pointed out, in the writing on triangulation one basic assumption is buried. The effectiveness of triangulation rests on the premise that the weaknesses in each single method will be compensated by the counterbalancing strengths of another..it is assumed that multiple and independent measures do not share the same weakness or potential for bias (emphasis added).

With respect to methodological triangulation, the absence of basic research means that the limitation of PRA techniques is unknown. In short, when they are combined with another technique, whether PRA, qualitative, or quantitative, unforeseen problems may arise with the validity of the data generated and which call into question the reliability of the technique. In addition, the lack of methodological rigor and the short time spent in the field means that data triangulation (which uses as many different sources of data as possible to analyse an event) and investigator triangulation (in which multiple investigators are used to provide greater reliability of observation) are also problematic. This leaves the possibility of theory triangulation. However, this technique involves formulating a research program to explicitly test rival theories and forms of explanation, an approach that has not been pursued by PRA.

Far from rejecting efforts to validate data, Bloor argues that such efforts are essential because they require the researcher to reconsider initial findings from "a novel standpoint." The point here is that the reliance of PRA on sequencing to achieve triangulation and provide a degree of validity is as problematic as its reliance on the unexamined nature of its techniques. Such a position is not an argument for paradigm— dependent validity criteria (with all due respect to Lather 1986 and Lincoln and Guba 1985). On the contrary, all researchers need to demonstrate how they have arrived at their conclusions by carefully documenting the research process so the research community can be confident of the reported conclusions. Thus, the issue is not adherence to technique, but rather the need to demonstrate that sufficient attention has been given to the practice of social inquiry and to a reflexive awareness of the process and the limitations of research findings.

Participatory Rural Appraisal-A Valid and Credible Knowledge?

What lessons can we draw from this discussion? Does PRA constitute a coherent research methodology? Does it produce knowledge of the world that is valid and reliable? First, let us be clear that regardless of claims that distinguish RRA from PRA, both approaches encounter the same methodological problems. Recall that RRA arose as a response to rising demands for information and from a shortened time frame to collect data-RRA and PRA were not intended to substitute for in-depth qualitative and quantitative research.

Even so, many of those who use PRA do so without employing other qualitative methods, and the few published accounts available do not provide very transparent accounts about how research was conducted. Though RRA and PRA were intended to provide roughly accurate information, the tendency has been to use them as a stand-alone set of techniques to undertake research. However, a balance is needed between exploratory research, the development of new research techniques, and an appreciation of what is required to produce "objective" social science. In this regard, the conventions of qualitative research require that sufficient evidence and information about research methods and procedures be provided to allow research conclusions to be assessed for bias and fallibility by the wider research community. Indeed, this chapter has attempted to set out the kind of information PRA reports should include. Only by producing transparent research accounts will it become possible to disentangle methodological questions from issues of participation and empowerment. Despite the proliferation of participatory techniques and their use in an expanding range of applications, the core techniques have emerged from qualitative research, and it would seem reasonable to suggest that participatory researchers should engage with the issues of validity and reliability as defined in the qualitative research tradition. Failure to engage with these issues will result not merely in eclectic and unfocused work, but it is also likely to produce work that is of limited practical, theoretical, and policy value.

The proliferation of PRA and its adoption by governments and development agencies provides a strong rationale for a funded program of basic research into PRA and other participatory techniques. However, given the impatience of the research community and the time it will take before benefits will be realized from basic research, researchers and practitioners are advised:

1. That in addition to providing transparent research reports, there is a need to strike a balance between the innovative use of PRA and the development of better-designed research and evaluation that explicitly create opportunities to triangulate methods in a conscious attempt to ensure reflexive practice.
2. To insist on funding for sufficient time to undertake fieldwork to ensure that research questions are adequately addressed through the integration of PRA with qualitative and quantitative methods to produce greater insight and more in-depth understanding than is possible from casual observation or from forms of inquiry that depend upon highly structured ways of interacting with respondents.
3. To publish research that attempts to advance our understanding of how PRA can be used as a research methodology, as opposed to its value in exploratory research or in facilitating social interaction and discussion.
4. To distinguish between the use of PRA and other forms of qualitative research to undertake academic versus applied or practitioner research. The different purpose and function of these two types of research suggest that different considerations may apply in assessing the reliability and validity of their respective accounts.

METHODS FOR QUALITATIVE MANAGEMENT RESEARCH

In this special issue the term "social systems" is derived chiefly from the theoretical starting point propounded by Niklas LUHMANN (1995). The issue is intended to raise the profile of his work in the wider English speaking research community. His work on organizations as autopoietic social systems has only recently and partly been made available in English. Although used by a broad but relatively exclusive German speaking scientific community, the theory is only gradually being acknowledged developed, applied and critiqued in the English speaking research community.

This special edition draws from a range of theoretical standpoints such as, complexity science as applied in the management domain, social constructionism and the (re-)construction of organizations as distributed self-regulating knowledge systems. Other related streams reflecting a systemic understanding of organizations/institutions include GIDDENS' structuration theory (1984), BOJE's (2001) work on metaphors, narratives, and storytelling, LATOUR's (1987) and WOOLGAR's (1996) use of "actor-network theory" as well as MACKENZIE and WAJCMAN's (1999) focus on the social construction of technology.

A key underlying assumption for this special issue is our belief that the reluctance of the scientific community to apply LUHMANN's social system theory in management research boils down to first the relative difficulty readers face when trying to follow his writing and the complexity of the theoretical approach, and, second and more significantly, a missing methodological basis for conducting research grounded in LUHMANN's social system theory and related theoretical approaches. In particular this special issue comprises

- theoretical articles reviewing the broad landscape of existing qualitative research methods and developing an adequate methodological canon for research grounded in LUHMANN's social system theory and related theoretical approaches;

- empirical articles describing the application of specific qualitative research methods used in research projects grounded in LUHMANN's social system theory.

All articles present a discussion of the issues, questions and challenges related to the application of systemic research designs using qualitative methods in management studies, both in reference to theoretical approaches, as well as to the research practice. Authors demonstrate how management science can benefit from viewing organizations through a "systemic lens." Furthermore, attention is drawn to the limitations and constraints of using systems theory for the study of phenomena in organizations as social systems.

OBSERVATION, RESEARCH DESIGNS AND IMPLICATIONS

With one exception, the papers in this special issue focus upon the study of organizations through the lens of LUHMANN's social system theory (1995). The exception explicitly expands on this theoretical perspective by complementing it with a social constructionist approach. Whilst conceding that the constructionist approach already shapes most of LUHMANN's thoughts (particularly in his later work), Jens MEISSNER and Martin SPRENGER (2010) consider it appropriate to deconstruct these thoughts down to their constructionist base. In so doing they attempt to demonstrate how one is given clues on how to do empirical research, and on how to organize observations while acting oneself as an observer, and thus get insights into how observing in research contexts both enables and limits what a study can provide.

While reviewing papers of this special issue, we recognized three thematic threads that seem to be of particular importance to qualitative management research from the stance of systems theory. The first of these themes relates to observation in management research, the second to methods and the design of studies for application in empirical research using systems theory, and the third to the implications of those studies on what was studied, i.e. management in organizations. The themes are reflected and discussed by all authors, although with different intensity.

Observation

Applying a systems theory perspective to management and organizational studies implies that the focus of the analysis should be on systemic communication processes rather than on the single actions of individual actors. Gian-Claudio GENTILE (2010), in arguing the case for LUHMANN's systems theory as operative constructionism, contends that meaning no longer resides in individuals' descriptions of "what happened" (first order observation) but into understanding how reality is constructed and maintained, i.e. how sense making patterns are processed between two or more actors in a way that systemic structures emerge and sustain. The LUHMANNian management research approach, therefore, compares distinctions applied by members of the organizations studied. These distinctions serve to guide the perceptions of the researcher.

Contributors to this special issue are unified in acknowledging that the perspective of a systemic researcher is situated and self-constructed, thus impacting upon what researchers can observe and recognize about the phenomenon they study. Tina KEIDING (2010) even argues that observations may say more about the observer than about the situation itself and her paper reflects about how to minimize this impact. She states: "Observation is always participation" (paragraph 76). She draws our attention to LUHMANN's mandate for construction of the "other" when participating in and observing communication.

In constructing the "other," the scholar is required to be present in interactions and, therefore, to participate in the interactions. In distinguishing between persons and human individuals LUHMANN insists that scholars observe others in a way which does not take first impressions for granted by seeking other descriptions and interpretations. VON GRODDECK (2010) describes observation practices as a three-folded form with a marked and an unmarked space (i.e. what is in the focus and what is not in the focus of the empirical investigation) and the distinction itself. Morten KNUDSEN (2010) suggests that researchers should analyse and reflect upon the distinctions that guide their observations so that research "can surprise itself."

Against this background, regarding the role of researchers as observers and the situatedness and constructedness of their perspectives on organizational phenomena, the discussion shifts to focus upon the reciprocity between the findings researchers bring about and the phenomena they are investigating. For instance, Harald TUCKERMANN and Johannes RÜEGG-STUERM (2010) suggest that management research is a communicative social practice where organizational practices become recursively interwoven with research practices, to include the involved actors in their contexts.

They analyse how a "research system" emerges from relationships between the system of the researchers (for example a research project) and the system of the researched (for example an organization) as a "third system." This research system reproduces itself through relational episodes. Similarly, Patricia WOLF (2010) describes the dynamic interactions between these three systems which can have a strong impact on the research question and the research design. Harald TUCKERMANN and Johannes RÜEGG-STUERM (2010) conclude that LUHMANN's social system theory (1995) provides a useful grounding for studying these recursive dynamics.

Authors also acknowledge the importance of conducting a careful analysis and reflection of their own position when applying this theoretical understanding. In all empirical studies, author-researchers position themselves explicitly as NOT belonging to the system(s) which they observe.

The most interesting case in that sense is the article by Patricia WOLF (2010) who was employed as doctoral student by the organization she studied. As a member of the organization, she constructed her organizational role as an "autonomous observer" and portrayed herself as such to other organizational members. Armed with this self-awareness she herself felt obliged to write a project diary to help maintain a reflective distance, between her and the "normal" members of the system.

System Theoretic Research Designs and Methods

LUHMANN's approach to methodological correctness is revealed in the article by Christina BESIO and Andrea PRONZINI (2010) as being deeply rooted in human-conscious systems and their evanescent nature—as existing only in the present as thoughts or perceptions. He further emphasizes the contingent nature of systems, of management and of decisions—each of which could be formed or done in a different way.

The research designs reported reflect the dynamic interactions between the systems under scrutiny. Often, research designs are adapted or amended during the research process to the extent that change is evolutionary in its nature. Gathering data from multiple (sub system) perspectives provides an approach for accommodating the comparative nature of systems theory into the design of a study. The papers reflect a requirement for gathering data which represents the perspectives of actors from a variety of sub systems, such as organizational members from different departments and with different roles, from different institutions belonging to the educational system.

As social systems theory also implies, much data gathering is conducted through observing communication and decision chains. Cristina BESIO and Andrea PRONZINI (2010) summarize extant studies outlining observations at different system levels. Other authors provide insights into research methods which offer different "sorts" of data: Gian-Claudio GENTILE (2010) studied real-time communication relating to construction of collective meanings about corporate volunteering during group discussions. Patricia WOLF's (2010) research diary contained actors' statements recorded shortly after the statements were made, having been selected according to subjective relevance structures. This rapid recording of data alleviates the possible problems arising from having to analyse material that has been reconstructed from memory. Other approaches to data gathering employ very open, i.e. narrative or problem centred, qualitative interviews on topics such as innovation management, unsuccessful management strategies, strategy implementation, transformation processes in education management the (re)construction of management identity as a function.

A number of authors compare different methods for processing information within the social system they study. Several authors highlight the potential of functional analysis in allowing researchers to capture and visualize the distinctions which operate at the system level for classifying (management) problems and solutions. Gian-Claudio GENTILE (2010) describes a documentary method of analysing discussions in detail as content (what is said), structural (how collective sense making structures are processed) and inter-case level (what distinguishes sense making patterns between one case study and another). In addition authors report on how processes used for validating data complement and support the research data. Examples include feedback workshops with, or presentations to, former interviewees and the structural analysis conducted by former interviewees of the relationship of terms which they themselves had used. All authors of empirical papers confirm that triangulation methods for validating data were applied.

Implications of System Theoretic Research on Organizations

The implications arising from theoretical findings are rarely discussed here, with authors preferring to focus on the performance of the investigation of communication and decision patterns rather than any requirement to transform these patterns. This non-interventionist stance is legitimated by recognizing that science is itself a sub system of society. Consequently, authors tend to formulate their findings and contributions at an abstract level, such as those insights provided by Thorsten PEETZ, Karin LOHR and Romy HILBRICH (2010) into the increasing commoditization of education; by Katharina MAYR and Jasmin SIRI (2010) into the functional role of management in organizations, by Gian-Claudio GENTILE (2010) into collective patterns of sense making that impact the implementation of a corporate volunteering concept, by Patricia WOLF (2010) into the impact of the implementation of a knowledge management concept on organizational decision structures and by Jens MEISSNER and Martin SPRENGER (2010) into the design of an innovation process and dynamics of organizational renewal.

Although research findings from these studies were made available for organizational members to scrutinize, the aim of these feedback loops into the system was to validate findings and rather than to intervene. Consequently, authors acknowledge that findings of research projects might have a potential for irritation, for stimulating reflection and for providing orientation in a complex transformation process Cristina BESIO and Andrea PRONZINI (2010) for example highlight that the second order observation would enable the researcher to question the functions of "taken for granted" systemic structures. System theoretic researchers however leave it to the organization to make use of their findings.

Conclusions

A key question arising out of this special edition of FQS is, how does Niklas LUHMANN's theory impact upon methodology? We attempt to answer this question by dwelling on the subject-object dialectic as a characteristic of scholarly practice. LUHMANN also considers this dialectic to be of great significance, in his quest to discover the nature of the systems under examination. In so doing LUHMANN differentiates between adjoining systems by applying specific methodological rules appropriate to the system in question. For many scholars, having chosen to adopt Niklas LUHMANN's methodology, the task may appear daunting. An easier route is to avoid his "trivia" and, instead, make an "opportunistic study of everything". For the scholar then, personal implications arise from the methodological choices he or she makes and will, in turn, affect the methodological process itself.

According to the authors of this special issue, one of the methodological key challenges for empirical scholars applying a system theoretic point of view in their management studies is that LUHMANN's theory and perspective of systems forces them to engage with a fundamental, almost existential, dilemma:

is what we think we observe really observable? Existential phenomenology, as we know, is a thoroughly constructionist social phenomena by which, "meanings are constructed by human beings as they engage with the world they are interpreting". LUHMANN urges the scholar to look beyond meanings and interpretation in seeking further levels of granularity in the data. As Katharina MAYR and Jasmin SIRI (2010) outline, LUHMANN's notion of management as a symbolizing construction plays with the falsity of considering management as an objective entity or as a sequence of actions. Instead management "exists" as an enabler for generating meaning among employees. As the articles in this special issue discuss, decision making is perhaps the central task of management, this action connecting and creating meanings both within the organization and between it and the outside world. Thus in a sense management is semantically constructed.

This constructionist notion has considerable implications for research. The mandate by system theory to study communication instead of actions or actors raises several challenges related to the researcher's position in relation to the studied organization as well as his or her research interest which determines what distinctions are made in observing. This constitutes a blind spot in which researchers operate. The system theoretic perspective demands that observing communications results in a sociological observation which sets aside ontological prerequisites about the social or about human beings. Such prerequisites are usually applied in quantitative studies. The articles in this special issue discuss how scholars can deal with this challenge through applying qualitative methods in their research designs. In general, qualitative methods appear as appropriate for system theoretic research because they enable researchers to observe the distinctions that are operative in social systems. One important insight is that triangulation of methods plays a crucial role because it supports the observation of communication processes from multiple perspectives.

As far as the explanatory power is concerned, we see that the findings of system theoretical studies have the potential to support practitioners/managers in translating their own observations into distinctions relevant for their organization. Second order observation by researchers provides practitioners with an input that can potentially stimulate reflection as it visualizes how sense making patterns in organizations are created and constrained. For the organization and its members, this usually constitutes a blind spot. The strength of systems theory lies in the possibility to not only observe social practices but also to reconstruct the different systemic logics that determine the particular situation. As KLEIN (1994) explains, organizations display recursive symmetries between scale levels which tend to repeat a basic structure at several levels. Within organizations humans make decisions based upon patterns, seeing the world both visually and conceptually as a series of spot observations filling in the gaps from previous experience. Humans will rationalize decisions in whatever way is acceptable to the society or system to which they belong.

This rationalizing tendency holds equally for scholars as it does for managers. Hence in our attempts at observing management in organizations what do we see, an objective "other" or an extended perception of ourselves? It is potentially this question that causes the marginal interest of system theoretic researchers—at least as it concerns the authors of this special issue—in impacting communication and decision processes of the organizations they study. Researches strongly focus on emphasizing the contingent nature of systems, of management and of decisions. The transformation of research results could however potentially be done by qualitative system theoretic researchers in a way that they would make sense to organizational members, as their studies provide researchers with the necessary canon of terms and expressions used in organizational communications. Most of the authors of this special issue therefore agree that it would be opportune if both practitioners and researchers would explore means, processes and limitations of such knowledge transformation further.

9

Types of Research Methods

There are an amazing number of types of research methods. This number has increased tenfold in the recent years with the development and honing of technology, in particular the internet. Nearly every topic you can think of can be researched online. There are several basics concerning research methods. Scientific research. This method takes an idea or topic and uses the application of science to determine the answers to questions, typically through experimentation.

This type of research method is very hands on and relies on result over documentation historical research. This method of research relies on the past research results to determine answers to current questions. When discussing scientific methods of research we would talk about such things as formation of topics, followed by a hypothesis or theory of the outcome, conceptual definitions, meaning what the idea of the process is to be, operational definations, meaning how they will get there, then the gathering of date, followed by anlayisis of the data, followed by testing and changing the hypothesis as you go along until you reach a conclusion.

When discussing a historical method of research you talk of identification of the start date of your topic, then evidence of its location and recognition of the originator of the history, followed by analysis of the data. Additional methods of research are Exploratory research, meaning identifies the problems to be researched, Constructive research, which finds solutions to problems, Empirical research which tests solutions to see if the do indeed solve the problems. You can also break research in to two types of research, the primary research and the secondary research. Research is something that has evolved in the manner in which it is done. This having been said the basics of how research is undertaken has remained the same only using the vast technology to make these processes take half the time. When researching a question you will always start with the defining the question, hypothesizing of an answer, gathering of data, testing the answer and redefining your hypothesis until the true answer is reached. This repetitive process applies across the board.

RESEARCH

Research can be defined as the search for knowledge, or as any systematic investigation, with an open mind, to establish novel facts, usually using a scientific method. The primary purpose for applied research (as opposed to basic research) is discovering, interpreting, and the development of methods and systems for the advancement of human knowledge on a wide variety of scientific matters of our world and the universe.

Scientific research relies on the application of the scientific method, a harnessing of curiosity. This research provides scientific information and theories for the explanation of the nature and the properties of the world around us. It makes practical applications possible. Scientific research is funded by public authorities, by charitable organizations and by private groups, including many companies. Scientific research can be subdivided into different classifications according to their academic and application disciplines.

Artistic research, also seen as 'practice-based research', can take form when creative works are considered both the research and the object of research itself. It is the debatable body of thought which offers an alternative to purely scientific methods in research in its search for knowledge and truth.

Historical research is embodied in the scientific method. The phrase *my research* is also used loosely to describe a person's entire collection of information about a particular subject.

Etymology

The word *research* is derived from the French recherche, from rechercher, to search closely where "chercher" means "to look for or to search".

Research Processes

Scientific Research

Generally, research is understood to follow a certain structural process. Though step order may vary depending on the subject matter and researcher, the following steps are usually part of most formal research, both basic and applied:

- Formation of the topic
- Hypothesis
- Conceptual definitions
- Operational definition
- Gathering of data
- Analysis of data
- Test, revising of hypothesis
- Conclusion, iteration if necessary.

A common misunderstanding is that by this method a hypothesis could be proven or tested. Generally a hypothesis is used to make predictions that can be tested by observing the outcome of an experiment. If the outcome is inconsistent with the hypothesis, then the hypothesis is rejected. However, if the outcome is consistent with the hypothesis, the experiment is said to support the hypothesis.

This careful language is used because researchers recognize that alternative hypotheses may also be consistent with the observations. In this sense, a hypothesis can never be proven, but rather only supported by surviving rounds of scientific testing and, eventually, becoming widely thought of as true (or better, predictive), but this is not the same as it having been proven. A useful hypothesis allows prediction and within the accuracy of observation of the time, the prediction will be verified. As the accuracy of observation improves with time, the hypothesis may no longer provide an accurate prediction. In this case a new hypothesis will arise to challenge the old, and to the extent that the new hypothesis makes more accurate predictions than the old, the new will supplant it.

Artistic Research

One of the characteristics of artistic research is that it must accept subjectivity as opposed to the classical scientific methods. As such, it is similar to the social sciences in using qualitative research and intersubjectivity as tools to apply measurement and critical analysis.

Historical Method

The historical method comprises the techniques and guidelines by which historians use historical sources and other evidence to research and then to write history. There are various history guidelines commonly used by historians in their work, under the headings of external criticism, internal criticism, and synthesis.

This includes higher criticism and textual criticism. Though items may vary depending on the subject matter and researcher, the following concepts are usually part of most formal historical research:

- Identification of origin date
- Evidence of localization
- Recognition of authorship
- Analysis of data
- Identification of integrity
- Attribution of credibility.

Research Methods

The goal of the research process is to produce new knowledge. This process takes three main forms (although, as previously discussed, the boundaries between them may be obscure.):

- Exploratory research, which structures and identifies new problems

- Constructive research, which develops solutions to a problem
- Empirical research, which tests the feasibility of a solution using empirical evidence.

Research can also fall into two distinct types:

- Primary research (collection of data that does not yet exist)
- Secondary research (summary, collation and/or synthesis of existing research).

In social sciences and later in other disciplines, the following two research methods can be applied, depending on the properties of the subject matter and on the objective of the research:

- Qualitative research (understanding of human behaviour and the reasons that govern such behaviour)
- Quantitative research (systematic empirical investigation of quantitative properties and phenomena and their relationships).

Research is often conducted using the hourglass model Structure of Research. The hourglass model starts with a broad spectrum for research, focusing in on the required information through the methodology of the project (like the neck of the hourglass), then expands the research in the form of discussion and results.

Publishing

Academic publishing describes a system that is necessary in order for academic scholars to peer review the work and make it available for a wider audience. The 'system', which is probably disorganized enough not to merit the title, varies widely by field, and is also always changing, if often slowly. Most academic work is published in journal article or book form. In publishing, STM publishing is an abbreviation for academic publications in science, technology, and medicine.

Most established academic fields have their own journals and other outlets for publication, though many academic journals are somewhat interdisciplinary, and publish work from several distinct fields or subfields.

The kinds of publications that are accepted as contributions of knowledge or research vary greatly between fields; from the print to the electronic format. Business models are different in the electronic environment.

Since about the early 1990s, licensing of electronic resources, particularly journals, has been very common. Presently, a major trend, particularly with respect to scholarly journals, is open access. There are two main forms of open access: open access publishing, in which the articles or the whole journal is freely available from the time of publication, and self-archiving, where the author makes a copy of their own work freely available on the web.

Research Funding

Most funding for scientific research comes from two major sources: Corporate research and development departments; and government research councils such as the National Institutes of Health in the USA and the Medical Research Council in the UK. These are managed primarily through universities and in some cases through military contractors. Many senior researchers (such as group leaders) spend a significant amount of their time applying for grants for research funds. These grants are necessary not only for researchers to carry out their research, but also as a source of merit.

DIFFERENT TYPES OF RESEARCH

Behavioural research is conducted by scientists who are interested in understanding the behaviour of human beings and animals. These scientists believe that knowledge gained through personal intuition or the claims of others is not a sufficient basis for drawing conclusions about behaviour. They demand that knowledge be gained through the accumulation of empirical data, as prescribed by the scientific method. Behavioural scientists understand that the scientific approach is not perfect, but it is better than any other known way of drawing conclusions about behaviour.

Although science is designed to create a collection of facts, it is not entirely free of values. The values of scientists influence how they interpret their data, what and whom they study, and how they report their research. For instance, some scientists conduct basic research, whereas others conduct applied research. One of the important goals of the scientific method is to make clear to others which aspects of the research process are based on facts and which are based on values. There are three major research designs in behavioural research. There are advantages and disadvantages to each of the approaches, and each provides an essential avenue of scientific investigation. Descriptive research, such as surveys and naturalistic observation, is designed to provide a snapshot of the current state of affairs.

Descriptive research may be either qualitative or quantitative in orientation. Correlational research is designed to discover relationships among variables and to allow the prediction of future events from present knowledge. The relationships among variables are frequently described using the Pearson correlation coefficient. Because correlational research cannot provide evidence about causal relationships between variables, experimental research is often employed to do so. Experiments involve the creation of equivalence among research participants in more than one group, followed by an active manipulation of a given experience for these groups and a measurement of the influence of the manipulation. The goal is to assess the causal impact of the manipulation. Because each of the three types of research designs has both strengths and limitations, it is very important to learn to think critically about research. Such critical evaluation will allow you to select the appropriate research design and to determine what conclusions can and cannot be drawn from research.

DEVELOPING THE RESEARCH HYPOTHESIS

The first stage in a research project is developing an idea. These ideas can come through an interest in solving important social problems, through the use of the inductive method to organize existing facts, and through the exercise of the deductive method to derive predictions from existing theories. The last approach is perhaps the most useful because it ensures that the new research is related to existing research and thus contributes to the accumulation of scientific knowledge.

Before beginning a research project the scientist conducts a literature search, usually by using computer databases to locate abstracts of relevant articles. The literature search involves locating both secondary-and primary-source material. Being knowledgeable about previous research from other research laboratories is essential to the development of effective research. The literature search frequently leads the scientist to modify and refine his/her original research ideas. One of the goals of science is to organize relationships into explanatory principles such as laws and theories. Laws are general principles that apply to all situations. Theories are integrated set of principles that explain and predict many observed events within a given domain. Good theories are both general and parsimonious, they form the basis of future scientific research, and they make predictions that can be tested and falsified.

Theories are tested in the form of research hypotheses—specific and testable predictions regarding the relationship between or among two or more variables. Once a scientist develops a research hypothesis, she or he tests it using either a correlational or an experimental research design.

ETHICS IN RESEARCH

Because research using humans and animals has the potential to both benefit and harm those participants, the ethics of conducting versus not conducting a research project must be carefully evaluated before it is begun. There are no clear-cut right or wrong answers to questions about research ethics, but there are a set of ethical principles, developed by scientific organizations and regulatory agencies, that must be adhered to by those conducting behavioural research.

Conducting ethical research with human participants involves avoiding psychological and physical harm to research participants, providing freedom of choice, treating participants with respect, and honestly describing the nature and use of the research. Behavioural research with animals must be conducted such that the animals are treated humanely at all times. Decisions about what research is appropriate and ethical are based on careful consideration of the potential costs and benefits to both the participants in the research and the advancement of science. The procedures that are followed to ensure that no harm is done to the participants include the use of informed consent before the experiment begins and a thorough debriefing in which the purposes and procedures of the research are explained in detail to the participants. In most cases the institutional review board (IRB) at the institution where the research is being conducted will help the scientist determine whether his or her research is ethical.

MEASURES

Before any research hypothesis can be tested, the conceptual variables must be turned into measured variables through the use of operational definitions. This process is known as measurement. The relationship between the conceptual variables and their measures forms the basis of the testing of research hypotheses because the conceptual variables can be understood only through their operationalizations. Measured variables can be nominal or quantitative. The mapping, or scaling, of quantitative measured variables onto conceptual variables in the behavioural sciences is generally achieved through the use of ordinal, rather than interval or ratio, scales. Self-report measures are those in which the person indicates his or her thoughts or feelings verbally in answer to posed questions. In freeformat measures the participant can express whatever thoughts or feelings come to mind, whereas in fixed-format measures the participant responds to specific preselected questions. Fixed-format measures such as Likert, semantic differential, and Guttman scales contain a number of items, each using the same response format, designed to assess the conceptual variable of interest.

In contrast to self-report measures, behavioural measures can be more unobtrusive and thus are often less influenced by reactivity, such as acquiescent responding and self-promotion. One example of such nonreactive behavioural measures are those designed to assess physiological responding. However, behavioural measures may be difficult to operationalize and code, and the meaning of some behaviours may be difficult to interpret.

RELIABILITY AND VALIDITY

Assessing the effectiveness of a measured variable involves determining the extent to which the measure is free of both random error and systematic error. These determinations are made through examination of correlations among measures of the same and different conceptual variables.

Reliability refers to the extent to which a measure is free from random error. In some cases reliability can be assessed through administration of the same or similar tests more than one time (testretest and equivalent-forms reliability).

However, because such procedures can assess only the reliability of traits, and not states, and because they involve two different testing sessions, reliability is more often assessed in terms of the internal consistency of the items on a single scale using split-half reliability or Cronbach's coefficient alpha

Interrater reliability refers to the reliability of a set of judges or coders. Construct validity is the extent to which a measure is free from systematic error and thus measures what it is intended to measure.

Face validity and *content validity* refer to the extent to which a measured variable appears to measure the conceptual variable of interest and to which it samples from a broad domain of items, respectively. *Convergent validity* refers to the extent to which a measured variable correlates with other measured variables designed to measure the same conceptual variable, whereas *discriminant validity* refers to the extent to which a measured variable does not correlate with other measured variables designed to assess other conceptual variables. In some cases the goal of a research project is to test whether a measure given at one time can predict behavioural measures assessed either at the same time (concurrent validity) or in the future (predictive validity).

SURVEYS AND SAMPLING

Surveys are self-report descriptive research designs that attempt to capture the current opinions, attitudes, or behaviours of a group of people. Surveys can use either unstructured or structured formats and can be administered in the form of in-person or telephone interviews or as written questionnaires.

Surveys are designed to draw conclusions about a population of individuals, but because it is not possible to measure each person in the population, data are collected from a smaller sample of people drawn from the population. This procedure is known as sampling. Probability sampling techniques, including simple random sampling, systematic random sampling, stratified sampling, and cluster sampling, are used to ensure that the sample is representative of the population, thus allowing the researcher to use the sample to draw conclusions about the population.

When nonprobability sampling techniques are used, either because they are convenient or because probability methods are not feasible, they are subject to sampling bias, and they cannot be used to generalize from the sample to the population.

The raw data from a survey are summarized through frequency distributions and descriptive statistics. The distribution of a variable is summarized in terms of its central tendency using the mean, the mode, or the median, as well as its dispersion, summarized in terms of the variance and standard deviation.

The extent to which the sample provides an accurate picture of the population depends to a great extent on the sample size (N). In general, larger samples will produce a more accurate picture and thus have a lower margin of error.

NATURALISTIC METHODS

Naturalistic research designs involve the study of everyday behaviour through the use of both observational and archival data. In many cases a large amount of information can be collected very quickly using naturalistic approaches, and this information can provide basic knowledge about the phenomena of interest as well as provide ideas for future research. Naturalistic data have high ecological validity because they involve people in their everyday lives. However, although the data can be rich and colorful, naturalistic research often does not provide much information about why behaviour occurs or what would have happened to the same people in different situations.

Observational research can involve either participant or nonparticipant observers, who are either acknowledged or unacknowledged to the individuals being observed. Which approach an observer uses depends on considerations of ethics and practicality. A case study is an investigation of a single individual in which unusual, unexpected, or unexplained behaviours become the focus of the research. Archival research uses existing records of public behaviour as data. Conclusions can be drawn from naturalistic data when they have been systematically collected and coded. In observational research various sampling techniques are used to focus in on the data of interest. In archival research the data are coded through content analysis. In systematic observation and content coding the reliability and validity of the measures are enhanced by having more than one trained researcher make the ratings.

HYPOTHESIS TESTING AND INFERENTIAL STATISTICS

Hypothesis testing is accomplished through a set of procedures designed to determine whether observed data can be interpreted as providing support for the research hypothesis. These procedures, based on inferential statistics, are specified by the scientific method and are set in place before the scientist begins to collect data. Because it is not possible to directly test the research hypothesis, observed data are compared to what is expected under the null hypothesis, as specified by the sampling distribution of the statistic.

Because all data have random error, scientists can never be certain that the data they have observed actually support their hypotheses. Statistical significance is used to test whether data can be interpreted as supporting the research hypothesis. The probability of incorrectly rejecting the null hypothesis (known as a Type 1 error) is constrained by setting alpha to a known value such as.05 and only rejecting the null hypothesis if the likelihood that the observed data occurred by chance (the p-value) is less than alpha. The probability of incorrectly failing to reject a false null hypothesis (a Type 2 error) can only be estimated. The power of a statistical test refers to the likelihood of correctly rejecting a false null hypothesis.

The effect size statistic is often used as a measure of the magnitude of a relationship between variables because it is not influenced by the sample size in the research design. The strength of a relationship may also be considered in terms of the proportion of variance in the dependent measure that is explained by the independent variable. The effect size of many relationships in scientific research is small, which makes them difficult to discover.

CORRELATIONAL RESEARCH DESIGNS

Correlational research is designed to test research hypotheses in cases where it is not possible or desirable to experimentally manipulate the independent variable of interest. It is also desirable because it allows the investigation of behaviour in naturally occurring situations. Correlational methods range from analysis of correlations between a predictor and an outcome variable to multiple regression and path analyses assessing the patterns of relationships among many measured variables.

Two quantitative variables can be found to be related in either linear or nonlinear patterns. The type of relationship can be ascertained graphically with a scatterplot. If the relationships are linear, they can be statistically measured with the Pearson correlation coefficient (r). Associations between two nominal variables are assessed with the x2 test of independence.

Multiple regression uses more than one predictor variable to predict a single outcome variable. The analysis includes a test of the statistical significance between the predictor and outcome variables collectively (the multiple R) and individually (the regression coefficients).

Correlational research can in some cases be used to make at least some inferences about the likely causal relationships among variables if reverse causation and the presence of common-causal variables can be ruled out. In general, the approach is to examine the pattern of correlations among the variables using either multiple regression or structural equation analysis. Correlational data can also be used to assess whether hypotheses about proposed mediating variables are likely to be valid. However, because even the most sophisticated path analyses cannot be used to make definitive statements about causal relations, researchers often rely, at least in part, on experimental research designs.

EXPERIMENTAL RESEARCH: ONE-WAY DESIGNS

Experimental research designs enable the researcher to draw conclusions about the causal relationship between the independent variable and the dependent variable. The researcher accomplishes this by manipulating, rather than measuring, the independent variable. The manipulation guarantees that the independent variable occurs prior to the dependent variable.

The creation of equivalence among the conditions in experiments rules out the possibility of a spurious relationship. In between participants research designs, equivalence is created through random assignment to conditions, whereas in repeated-measures designs equivalence is created through the presence of the same participants in each of the experimental conditions. In experiments we can be more confident that the relationship between the independent and dependent variables is not due to common-causal variables than we can in correlational designs because equivalence makes it unlikely that there are any differences among the participants in the different conditions before the experimental manipulation occurred.

Repeated-measures designs have the advantages of increased statistical power and economy of participants, but these designs can be influenced by carryover, practice, and fatigue. These difficulties can, however, be eliminated to some extent through counterbalancing. When there are many conditions to be counterbalanced, a Latin square design may be used. The Analysis of Variance tests whether the mean scores on the dependent variable are different in the different levels of the independent variable, and the results of the ANOVA are presented in the ANOVA summary table.

Although experiments do allow researchers to make inferences about causality, they also have limitations. Perhaps the most important of these is that many of the most interesting behavioural variables cannot, for ethical or practical reasons, be experimentally manipulated.

EXPERIMENTAL RESEARCH: FACTORIAL DESIGNS

In most cases one-way experimental designs are too limited because they do not capture much of the complexity of real-world behaviour. Factorial experimental designs are usually preferable because they assess the simultaneous impact of more than one manipulated independent variable on the dependent variable of interest. Each of the factors in a factorial experimental design may be either between participants or repeated measures. Mixed experimental designs are those that contain both between-participants and repeated-measures factors.

In factorial experimental designs the independent variables are usually crossed with each other such that each level of each variable occurs with each level of each other independent variable. This is economical because it allows tests, conducted with the Analysis of Variance, of the influence of each of the independent variables separately (main effects), as well as tests of the interaction between or among the independent variables.

All of the main effect and interaction significance tests are completely independent of each other, and an accurate interpretation of the observed pattern of means must consider all the tests together. It is useful to create a schematic diagram of the condition means to help in this regard. In many cases it is desirable to use means comparisons to compare specific sets of condition means with each other within the experimental design. These comparisons can be either planned before the experiment is conducted (a priori comparisons) or chosen after the data are collected (post hoc comparisons).

EXPERIMENTAL CONTROL AND INTERNAL VALIDITY

Although experimental research designs are used to maximize the experimenter's ability to draw conclusions about the causal effects of the independent variable on the dependent variable, even experimental research contains threats to validity and thus the possibility of the experimenter drawing invalid conclusions about these relationships. One potential problem is that the presence of extraneous variables may threaten the statistical conclusion validity of the research because these variables make it more difficult to find associations between the independent and dependent variables. Researchers therefore attempt to reduce extraneous variables within the experimental conditions through the use of such techniques as limited-population, before-after, or matchedgroup designs, as well as through standardization of conditions.

Although extraneous variables may lead to Type 2 errors, the presence of confounding variables leads to internal invalidity, in which it is no longer possible to be certain whether the independent variable or the other confounding variables produced observed differences in the dependent measure. To avoid internal invalidity, researchers use appropriate control groups, cover stories, and blocked random assignment to conditions. Some of the most common threats to the internal validity of experiments include placebo effects, demand characteristics, and experimenter bias. Creating valid experiments involves thinking carefully about these potential threats to internal validity and designing experiments that take them into consideration. Blocked random assignment is used to avoid artifacts when assigning participants to conditions in an experiment.

EXTERNAL VALIDITY

External validity refers to the extent to which relationships between independent and dependent variables that are found in a test of a research hypothesis can be expected to be found again when tested with other research designs, other operationalizations of the variables, other participants, other experimenters, or other times and settings. A research design has high external validity if the results can be expected to generalize to other participants and to other tests of the relationship. External validity can be enhanced by increasing the ecological validity of an experiment by making it similar to what might occur in everyday life or by conducting field experiments.

Science relies primarily on replications to test the external validity of research findings. Sometimes the original research is replicated exactly, but more often conceptual replications with new operationalizations of the independent or dependent variables, or constructive replications with new conditions added to the original design, are employed. Replication allows scientists to test both the generalization and the limitations of research findings.

Because each individual research project is limited in some way, scientists conduct research programs in which many different studies are conducted. These programs are often summarized in review papers. Meta-analysis represents a relatively objective method of summarizing the results of existing research that involves a systematic method of selecting studies for review and coding and analysing their results.

QUASI-EXPERIMENTAL RESEARCH DESIGNS

Quasi-experimental research designs are used when it is not possible to randomly assign individuals to groups. Such studies are common in program evaluation research, which involves assessing the effects of training and therapy programs. In other cases the research involves comparisons among individuals who differ on demographic or personality variables.

There are several common quasi-experimental research designs, including the single-group design, the comparison-group design, the before-after design, and the comparison-group before-after design. In general, because participants have not been randomly assigned to the groups, quasi-experimental research has more threats to internal validity than do true experiments. Since the participants select whether to participate in a given treatment, the individuals in the different groups are not equivalent before the differences in the independent variable occur. Furthermore, the participants may decide to drop out of the research before it is over. Other threats result from the presence of extraneous variables, such as changes in the individuals (maturation) or in the experimental setting (history) that occur over time and that influence the dependent measure.

Time-series designs involve the measurement of behaviour more than twice over a period of time. Such designs allow the researcher to get a good idea about what changes occur over the time period being studied. When the initial rate of a behaviour is very stable, it is sometimes possible to draw inferences about the behaviour of a single participant by observing him or her over time.

Reporting Research Results

Communicating scientific ideas and research findings is one of the most important aspects of scientific progress because it contributes to the accumulation of scientific knowledge. Scientists share information with each other in person at scientific conventions, through electronic communication such as fax and e-mail, and through the publication of written research reports.

Research reports, many of which are eventually published in a scientific journal, are the definitive descriptions of a research project. The research report is prepared according to a formal set of guidelines, such as that provided by the American Psychological Association. The goals for writing the research report include being organized, precise, concise, compulsive, interesting, and fair.

There are five major sections within the APA format: Abstract, Introduction, Methods, Results, and Discussion, as well as other sections that contain supplementary information. Each section contains important information about the research, but only the information appropriate to that section. Although constrained to follow a specific format, the research report must also read smoothly and be interesting to the reader. Creating a research report that is both technically informative and easy to read takes a substantial amount of work and will generally require much rewriting.

Data Preparation and Univariate Statistics

Once the data from a research project have been collected, they must be prepared for statistical analysis. Normally this is accomplished by the user entering the data into a computer software program. Once they are entered and saved, the data are checked for accuracy. Decisions must also be made about how to deal with any missing values and whether it is appropriate to delete any of the data.

Statistical analyses of the sample data are based on descriptive statistics, whereas population parameters are estimated using inferential statistics. Frequency distributions are normally used to summarize nominal variables, whereas measures of central tendency and dispersion are normally used to summarize quantitative variables.

Use of inferential statistics involves making estimates about the values of population parameters based on the sampling distribution of the sample statistics. Although the sample mean (*X*—) is an unbiased estimator of the population mean (m), the sample standard deviation (*s*) must be corrected to provide an unbiased estimator of the population mean (s).

The ability to accurately predict population parameters is based to a large extent on the size of the sample that has been collected, since larger samples provide more precise estimates. Statistics such as the standard error of the mean and confidence intervals around the mean are used to specify how precisely the parameters have been estimated.

ARCHIVAL RESEARCH

Basic Definition

An archive is a way of sorting and organizing older documents, whether it be digitally (photographs online, Emails, etc.) or manually (putting it in folders, photo albums, etc.). Archiving is one part of the curating process which is typically carried out by a curator. The art of searching for archives consists of four main step:

1. Thinking about questions to find the archive in mind. Ask oneself:
   * What is my topic of interest?
2. Get the basic facts about the topic of interest.
3. Use websites associated with the particular archive building to search for the archive.
4. Decide if one should visit the archive building for further assistance.

History of Archival Research

Many archives have been around for multiple hundreds of years. For instance Vatican Secret Archives was started in the 17th century AD and contains state papers, papal account books, and papal correspondence dating back to the 8th century. Most archives that are still in existence do not claim collections that date back quite as far as the Vatican Archive.

However, many national archives were established over one hundred years ago and contain collections going back three or four hundred years ago. The United States National Archives and Records Administration was established originally in 1934. The NARA contains records and collections dating back to the founding of the United States in the 18th century. Among the collections of the NARA are the Declaration of Independence, the Constitution of the United States, and an original copy of the Magna Carta. Similarly, the Archives nationales in France was founded in 1790 during the French Revolution and has holdings that date back to AD 625.

Universities are another historic venue for archival holdings. Most universities have archival holdings that chronicle the business of the university. Some universities also have cultural archives that focus on one aspect or another of the culture of the state or country in which the university is located. The University of North Carolina at Chapel Hill has archival collections on the subjects of Southern History and Southern Folklife. Boston University's Howard Gottlieb Archival Research Library has collections dedicated to chronicling advances and famous moments in American art, drama, and public/political life.

The reason for highlighting the breadth and depth of historical archives is to give some idea of the difficulties facing archival researchers in the pre-digital age. Some of these archives were dauntingly vast in the amount of records they held. For example, The Vatican Secret Archive had upwards of 52 miles of archival shelving. In an age where you could not simply enter your query into a search bar complete with Boolean operators the task of finding material that pertained to your topic would have been difficult at the least. The Finding aid made the work of sifting through these vast archives much more manageable. A finding aid is a document that is put together by an archivist or librarian that contains information about the individual documents in a specific collection in an archive. These documents can be used to determine if the collection is relevant to a designated topic. Finding aids made it so a researcher did not have to blindly search through collection after collection hoping to find pertinent information. However, in the pre-digital age a researcher still had to travel to the physical location of the archive and search through a card catalog of finding aids.

Pre-Internet Data Storage

Organizing, collecting, and archiving information using physical documents without the use of electronics is a daunting task. Magnetic storage devices provided the first means of storing electronic data. As technology has progressed over the years, so too has the ability to archive data using electronics. Long before the internet, means of using technology to help archive information were in the works. The early forms of magnetic storage devices that would later be used to archive information were invented as early as the late 19th century, but were not used for organizing information until 1951 with the invention of the UNIVAC I.

UNIVAC I, which stands for Universal Automatic Computer 1, used magnetic tape to store data and was also was the first commercial computer produced in the United States. Early computers such as UNIVAC I were enormous and sometimes took up entire rooms, rendering them completely obsolete in today's technological society. But the central idea of using magnetic tape to store information is a concept that is still in use today.

While most magnetic storage devices have been replaced by optical storage devices such as CDs, USB flash drives DVDs, some are still in use today. In fact, the floppy drive is one example of a magnetic storage device that became extremely popular in the 1970s through the 1990s. Older 5.25" floppy discs have not been used for quite some time but the smaller 3.5" floppy discs aren't obsolete yet. The 3.5" discs hold approximately 1.44 mgs of data and for years have been used by millions of people to back up the information on their hard drives.

Magnetic tape has proven to be a very effective means of archiving data as large amounts of data that don't need to be quickly accessed can be found on magnetic tape. That is especially true of aging data that may not need to be accessed again at all, but for different reasons still needs to be stored "just in case".

Internet Age Archiving

With the explosion of the internet over the past couple decades, archiving has begun to make its way online. The days of using electronic devices such as magnetic tape are coming to an end as people start to use the internet to archive their information.

Internet archiving has become extremely popular for several reasons. As mentioned earlier, the attempt to have as much information take up as little space a possible is very helpful for many archivers. Using the internet to archive allows for this to be possible as well many other benefits. There is no limit to how much information one can store online in their archive. Internet archiving can be used to store as little information needed for a single person, or for as much information needed for a major company. Internet archives can contain large-scale digitization as well as provide long term management and preservation of the digital resources similarly to the electronics used in the pre-internet data storage era. Along with the idea of storage benefits, archiving via Internet ensures that ones information is safe. There is risk of misplacing your information, or having it get destroyed by water or fire etc. Those are problems that may occur when archiving using floppy discs, hard drives, and computers Lastly, the ability to access the information from almost anywhere is one of the main attractions to online archiving. As long as one has access to the internet they can edit and retrieve the information they are looking for.

Most institutions with physical archives have begun to digitize their holdings and make them available on the internet. Notably the National Archive and Records Administration in Washington, D.C. has a clearly defined initiative that was started in 1998 in an attempt to digitize many of their holdings and make them available on the internet.

American Archives Month

October is officially noticed throughout the United States as American Archives month, with the United Kingdom and Republic of Ireland noticing the event as well. The month was founded in 1969 by the Michigan State University Archives & Historical Collections, but now Archives Month is a collaborative effort by professional organizations and repositories. Their main point of American Archives month was and is to celebrate the importance of archives and to raise awareness about the value of archives. Lessons of how to preserve certain photographs and documents are also provided for each state. Each state normally celebrates the affair through a series of week-long events. The majority of the states get involved and plan out different sorts of activities that pertain to archiving. There is also a guide that goes into detail about planning for the event. For the most part, each state coins a phrase each year to describe their interest in archiving. For example:

- Georgia: "Quench your thirst for History."

- North Dakota: "That's Entertainment."
- North Carolina: "Celebrating the NC Record."

Wisconsin was the most recent state to join National Archive Month, joining in 2009, coining the phrase "Scrapbook Wisconsin."

One of the major events is hosted by the staff at the University Archives & Historical Collections. They contribute to American Archives month by hosting a contest about trivia questions pertaining to archives, but it is only open to MSU faculty, staff and students, MSU alumni, and the greater Lansing community.

CONTENT ANALYSIS

Content analysis is a methodology in the social sciences for studying the content of communication. Earl Babbie defines it as "the study of recorded human communications, such as books, websites, paintings and laws." It is most commonly used by researchers in the social sciences to analyse recorded transcripts of interviews with participants.

Content analysis is also considered a scholarly methodology in the humanities by which texts are studied as to authorship, authenticity, or meaning. This latter subject include philology, hermeneutics, and semiotics.

Harold Lasswell formulated the core questions of content analysis: "Who says what, to whom, why, to what extent and with what effect?." Ole Holsti (1969) offers a broad definition of content analysis as "any technique for making inferences by objectively and systematically identifying specified characteristics of messages." Kimberly A. Neuendorf (2002, p. 10) offers a six-part definition of content analysis:

"Content analysis is a summarising, quantitative analysis of messages that relies on the scientific method (including attention to objectivity, intersubjectivity, a priori design, reliability, validity, generalisability, replicability, and hypothesis testing) and is not limited as to the types of variables that may be measured or the context in which the messages are created or presented."

Description

In 1931, Alfred R Lindesmith developed a methodology to refute existing hypotheses, which became known as a content analysis technique, and it gained popularity in the 1960s by Glaser and is referred to as "The Constant Comparative Method of Qualitative Analysis" in an article published in 1964-65. Glaser and Strauss (1967) referred to their adaptation of it as "Grounded Theory." The method of *content analysis* enables the researcher to include large amounts of textual information and systematically identify its properties, e.g. the frequencies of most used keywords (KWIC meaning "Key Word in Context") by locating the more important structures of its communication content. Yet such amounts of textual information must be categorised analysis, providing at the end a meaningful reading of content under scrutiny. David Robertson (1976:73-75) for example created a coding frame for a comparison of modes of party competition between British and American parties. It was developed further in 1979 by the *Manifesto Research Group* aiming at a comparative content-analytic approach on the policy positions of political parties.

Since the 1980s, content analysis has become an increasingly important tool in the measurement of success in public relations (notably media relations) programs and the assessment of media profiles. In these circumstances, content analysis is an element of media evaluation or media analysis. In analyses of this type, data from content analysis is usually combined with media data (circulation, readership, number of viewers and listeners, frequency of publication). It has also been used by futurists to identify trends. In 1982, John Naisbitt published his popular *Megatrends*, based on content analysis in the US media.

The creation of coding frames is intrinsically related to a creative approach to variables that exert an influence over textual content. In political analysis, these variables could be political scandals, the impact of public opinion polls, sudden events in external politics, inflation etc. *Mimetic Convergence*, created by F. Lampreia Carvalho for the comparative analysis of electoral proclamations on free-to-air television is an example of creative articulation of variables in content analysis. The methodology describes the construction of party identities during long-term party competitions on TV, from a dynamic perspective, governed by the logic of the contingent. This method aims to capture the contingent logic observed in electoral campaigns by focusing on the repetition and innovation of themes sustained in party broadcasts. According to such post-structuralist perspective from which electoral competition is analysed, the party identities, 'the real' cannot speak without mediations because there is not a natural centre fixing the meaning of a party structure, it rather depends on ad-hoc articulations. There is no empirical reality outside articulations of meaning. Reality is an outcome of power struggles that unify ideas of social structure as a result of contingent interventions. In Brazil, these contingent interventions have proven to be mimetic and convergent rather than divergent and polarised, being integral to the repetition of dichotomised worldviews.

Mimetic Convergence thus aims to show the process of fixation of meaning through discursive articulations that repeat, alter and subvert political issues that come into play. For this reason, parties are not taken as the pure expression of conflicts for the representation of interests (of different classes, religions, ethnic groups but attempts to recompose and re-articulate ideas of an absent totality around *signifiers* gaining positivity.

Every content analysis should depart from a hypothesis. The hypothesis of *Mimetic Convergence* supports the Downsian interpretation that in general, rational voters converge in the direction of uniform positions in most thematic dimensions. The hypothesis guiding the analysis of *Mimetic Convergence* between political parties' broadcasts is: 'public opinion polls on vote intention, published throughout campaigns on TV will contribute to successive revisions of candidates' discourses. Candidates re-orient their arguments and thematic selections in part by the signals sent by voters. One must also consider the interference of other kinds of input on electoral propaganda such as internal and external political crises and the arbitrary interference of private interests on the dispute. Moments of internal crisis in disputes between candidates might result from the *exhaustion* of a certain strategy. The moments of *exhaustion* might consequently precipitate an inversion in the thematic flux.

As an evaluation approach, content analysis is considered by some to be quasi-evaluation because content analysis judgments need not be based on value statements if the research objective is aimed at presenting subjective experiences. Thus, they can be based on knowledge of everyday lived experiences. Such content analyses are not evaluations. On the other hand, when content analysis judgments are based on values, such studies are evaluations.

As demonstrated above, only a good scientific hypothesis can lead to the development of a methodology that will allow the empirical description, be it dynamic or static.

Content analysis. This is a closely related if not overlapping kind, often included under the general rubric of "qualitative analysis," and used primarily in the social sciences. It is "a systematic, replicable technique for compressing many words of text into fewer content categories based on explicit rules of coding" (Stemler 2001). It often involves building and applying a "concept dictionary" or fixed vocabulary of terms on the basis of which words are extracted from the textual data for concording or statistical computation.

Uses of Content Analysis

Ole Holsti (1969) groups 15 uses of content analysis into three basic categories:

- make inferences about the antecedents of a communication
- describe and make inferences about characteristics of a communication
- make inferences about the effects of a communication.

COMPARATIVE RESEARCH METHODS

The comparative approach to the study of society has a long tradition dating back to Ancient Greece. Since the nineteenth century, philosophers, anthropologists, political scientists and sociologists have used cross-cultural comparisons to achieve various objectives. For researchers adopting a normative perspective, comparisons have served as a tool for developing classifications of social phenomena and for establishing whether shared phenomena can be explained by the same causes. For many sociologists, comparisons have provided an analytical framework for examining (and explaining) social and cultural differences and specificity. More recently, as greater emphasis has been placed on contextualisation, cross-national comparisons have served increasingly as a means of gaining a better understanding of different societies, their structures and institutions.

The development of this third approach has coincided with the growth in interdisciplinary and international collaboration and networking in the social sciences, which has been encouraged since the 1970s by a number of European-wide initiatives. The European Commission has established several large-scale programmes, and observatories and networks have been set up to monitor and report on social and economic developments in member states. At the same time, government departments and research funding bodies have shown a growing interest in international comparisons, particularly in the social policy area, often as a means of evaluating the solutions adopted for dealing with common problems or to assess the transferability of policies between member states.

Yet, relatively few social scientists feel they are well equipped to conduct studies that seek to cross national boundaries, or to work in international teams. This reluctance may be explained not only by a lack of knowledge or understanding of different cultures and languages but also by insufficient awareness of the research traditions and processes operating in different national contexts.

APPROACHES TO CROSS-NATIONAL RESEARCH

For the purposes of this chapter, a study is held to be cross-national and comparative, when individuals or teams set out to examine particular issues or phenomena in two or more countries with the express intention of comparing their manifestations in different socio-cultural settings (institutions, customs, traditions, value systems, lifestyles, language, thought patterns), using the same research instruments either to carry out secondary analysis of national data or to conduct new empirical work. The aim may be to seek explanations for similarities and differences, to generalise from them or to gain a greater awareness and a deeper understanding of social reality in different national contexts.

In many respects, the methods adopted in cross-national comparative research are no different from those used for within-nation comparisons or for other areas of sociological research. The descriptive or survey method, which will usually result in a state of the art review, is generally the first stage in any large-scale international comparative project, such as those carried out by the European observatories and networks. A juxtaposition approach is often adopted at this stage: data gathered by individuals or teams, according to agreed criteria, and derived either from existing materials or new empirical work, are presented side by side frequently without being systematically compared.

Some large-scale projects are intended to be explanatory from the outset and therefore focus on the degree of variability observed from one national sample to another. Such projects may draw on several methods: the inductive method, starting from loosely defined hypotheses and moving towards their verification; the deductive method, applying a general theory to a specific case in order to interpret certain aspects; and the demonstrative method, designed to confirm and refine a theory.

Rather than each researcher or group of researchers investigating their own national context and then pooling information, a single researcher or single-nation team of researchers - the 'safari' approach - may formulate the problem and research hypotheses and carry out studies in more than one country, using replication of the experimental design, generally to collect and analyse new data. The method is often adopted when a smaller number of countries is involved and for more qualitative studies, where researchers are looking at a well-defined issue in two or more national contexts and are required to have intimate knowledge of all the countries under study. The approach may combine surveys, secondary analysis of national data, and also personal observation and an interpretation of the findings in relation to their wider social contexts.

Irrespective of the organisational structure of the research, a shift is occurring in emphasis away from descriptive, universalist and 'culture-free' approaches to social phenomena. The societal approach, which has perhaps been most fully explicated in relation to industrial sociology (Maurice et al., 1986), implies that the researcher sets out to identify the specificity of social forms and institutional structures in different societies and to look for explanations of differences by referring to the wider social context. Another result of the greater emphasis on contextualisation in comparative studies is their increasingly interdisciplinary and multidisciplinary character, since a wide range of factors must be considered at the lowest possible level of disaggregation.

PROBLEMS IN CROSS-NATIONAL COMPARATIVE RESEARCH

The shift in orientation towards a more interpretative, culture-bound approach means that linguistic and cultural factors, together with differences in research traditions and administrative structures cannot be ignored. If these problems go unresolved, they are likely to affect the quality of the results of the whole project, since the researcher runs the risk of losing control over the construction and analysis of key variables.

Managing and Funding Cross-national Projects

The mix of countries selected in comparative studies affects the quality and comparability of the data as well as the nature of the collaboration between researchers. In ideal conditions, a project team manager will be able to select the countries to be included in the study and researchers with appropriate knowledge and expertise to undertake the work. In small-scale bilateral comparisons, this may be feasible, but more often the reality is different, and participation may be determined by factors (sometimes political) which do not make for easy relationships between team members. European programmes often include all EU member states, although the countries concerned may represent very different stages of economic and social development and be influenced by different cultural value systems, assumptions and thought patterns.

The financial resources available for the research differ considerably from one national context to another. Funding bodies have their own agenda: a topic that may attract interest in one country may not obtain funding elsewhere.

The amount of time that can be allocated to the research, the ease with which reliable data can be obtained and the relative expense involved are also likely to affect the quality of the material for comparisons.

The problems of organising meetings which all participants in a project can attend, of negotiating a research agenda, of reaching agreement on approaches and definitions and of ensuring that they are observed are not to be underestimated. Linguistic and cultural affinity is central to an understanding of why researchers from some national groups find it easier to work together and to reach agreement on research topics, design and instruments. Even within a single discipline, differences in the research traditions of participating countries may affect the results of a collaborative project and the quality of any joint publications.

Accessing Comparable Data

In many European projects, national experts are required to provide descriptive accounts of selected trends and developments derived from national data sources. The co-ordinators then synthesise information on key themes and issues. Since much of the international work carried out at European level is not strictly comparative at the design and data collection stages, the findings cannot then be compared systematically. Data collection is strongly influenced by national conventions. Their source, the purpose for which they were gathered, the criteria used and the method of collection may vary considerably from one country to another, and the criteria adopted for coding data may change over time.

In some areas, national records may be non-existent or may not go back very far. For certain topics, information may be routinely collected in tailor-made surveys in a number of the participating countries, whereas in others it may be more limited because the topic has attracted less attention among policy-makers. Official statistics may be produced in too highly aggregated a form and may not have been collected systematically over time. In many multinational studies, much time and effort is expended on trying to reduce classifications to a common base.

Concepts and Research Parameters

Despite considerable progress in the development of large-scale harmonised international databases, such as Eurostat, which tend to give the impression that quantitative comparisons are unproblematic, attempts at cross-national comparisons are still too often rendered ineffectual by the lack of a common understanding of central concepts and the societal contexts within which phenomena are located. Agreement is therefore difficult to reach over research parameters and units of comparison. For example, the demographic and employment statistics compiled at European level are socially constructed and often conceal quite different national situations. Even the definition of a country or society can be problematic, since there is no single identifiable, durable and relatively stable sociological unit equivalent to the total geographical territory of a nation.

Language can present a major obstacle to effective international collaboration, since it is not simply a medium for conveying concepts, but part of the conceptual system, reflecting institutions, thought processes, values and ideology, and implying that the approach to a topic and interpretations of it will differ according to the language of expression.

Although defining a time span may appear to be a simple matter for a longitudinal study, innumerable problems can arise when national datasets are being used. These problems are compounded when comparisons are based on secondary analysis of existing national datasets, since it may not always be possible to apply agreed criteria uniformly.

SOLUTIONS TO THE PROBLEMS OF CROSS-NATIONAL COMPARISONS

Most researchers engaged in cross-national comparative work admit that such research, by its very nature, demands greater compromises in methods than a single-country focus.

The problems of building and managing a research team can often be resolved only by a process of trial and error, and the quality of the contributions to multinational projects may be very uneven. The managerial skills and experience of the co-ordinators are, therefore, critical in holding the team together, in obtaining material and providing the comparative framework for the research, which also requires a sound knowledge and understanding of other national contexts, their languages and intellectual traditions.

When existing large-scale data are being re-analysed, the solution is not to disregard major demographic variables, since they may indicate greater intranational than international differences. An attempt has to be made to establish comparable groupings from the most detailed information available - the raw data - and to focus on the broader characteristics of the sample.

The solution to the problem of defining the unit of observation may be to carry out research into specific organisational, structural fields or sectors and to look at subsocietal units rather than whole societies.

Where new studies are being carried out, it should, theoretically, be possible to replicate the research design and use the same concepts and parameters simultaneously in two or more countries on matched groups.

Whatever the method adopted, the researcher needs to remain alert to the dangers of cultural interference, to ensure that discrepancies are not forgotten or ignored and to be wary of using what may be a sampling bias as an explanatory factor. In interpreting the results, wherever possible, findings should be examined in relation to their wider societal context and with regard to the limitations of the original research parameters.

Why Undertake Cross-national Comparisons?

Although the obstacles to successful cross-national comparisons may be considerable, so are the benefits:

- When researchers from different backgrounds are brought together on collaborative or cross-national projects, valuable personal contacts can be established, enabling them to capitalise on their experience and knowledge of different intellectual traditions and to compare and evaluate a variety of conceptual approaches.
- Comparisons can lead to fresh, exciting insights and a deeper understanding of issues that are of central concern in different countries. They can lead to the identification of gaps in knowledge and may point to possible directions that could be followed and about which the researcher may not previously have been aware. They may also help to sharpen the focus of analysis of the subject under study by suggesting new perspectives.
- Cross-national projects give researchers a means of confronting findings in an attempt to identify and illuminate similarities and differences, not only in the observed characteristics of particular institutions, systems or practices, but also in the search for possible explanations in terms of national likeness and unlikeness. Cross-national comparativists are forced to attempt to adopt a different cultural perspective, to learn to understand the thought processes of another culture and to see it from the native's viewpoint, while also reconsidering their own country from the perspective of a skilled, external observer.

10

Method of Experimental Survey

Research involving persons with impaired decision-making abilities continues to be a topic of debate among bioethicists, researchers, and policymakers. The study of decisionally impaired persons is critical to developing and improving interventions to treat them; yet, decisional impairment can be an obstacle to informed consent. There is a need for clear policies about how to conduct research with such persons.

Although decisional impairment can be caused by many conditions, including a variety of medical illnesses, recent debates have often focused on the mentally ill. For example, though noting that a policy based on group membership rather than on a "common functional characteristic (ie, questionable decision-making capacity)" can "raise the specter of equating mental disorders with incapacity and thus potentially stigmatize these individuals," the National Bioethics Advisory Commission (NBAC) still focused its attention on "persons with mental disorders".

The NBAC report was criticized for singling out and thereby stigmatizing the mentally ill. Such practices have been perpetuated in some laws that treat incompetent psychiatric patients differently than incompetent persons with other medical problems. Because stigma regarding mental illness remains strong, it seems essential to understand whether and how stigma may affect research ethics policies affecting the mentally ill.

Stigma of mental illness has many dimensions. Persons with psychosis are perceived as more violent and dangerous, although they account for only a small proportion of violence in the population. Research findings consistently demonstrate that the public prefers to maintain social distance from persons with mental health problems. The public has also been shown to attribute more personal responsibility and other specific causal explanations for mental health problems such as psychosis compared to those associated with medical illness. Additionally, society tolerates inequities in the allocation of resources for the treatment of mental illness, and funding remains grossly inadequate for the persistent high levels of need for such services. With regard to research participation, mentally ill patients are seen as incompetent and potentially more easily coerced. Specific research procedures, even when commonly used in other areas of medical research, are treated as riskier when used in mental illness research. How might some of these dimensions of stigma affect how people evaluate research ethics issues?

For the present study we conceptualized stigma as discrimination based on ethically irrelevant factors that has the potential to cause adverse effects. Specifically, stigma in the context of research ethics would be ethically unjustified discrimination that precludes otherwise valuable research intended to benefit the stigmatized population. We tested the hypothesis that there is stigma against mental illness research, specifically, that research involving the mentally ill would be seen as less allowable than research involving the medically ill, even when ethically relevant factors (such as the subject's specified decision-making competency status, risk-benefit factors of the research protocol, or the subject's chronicity of illness, functional level, and level of social support) are similar. We also hypothesized that there would be an interaction between competency status of research subjects and illness type—specifically, that the incompetent mentally ill would be "more protected" than the incompetent medically ill. We also examined various dimensions of mental illness stigma by analysing them as potential mediators and moderators of the primary stigma effect due to illness type.

METHODS

The 7 experimental scenarios described a person (with randomly selected gender, identified as either "John" or "Pam") who was being considered for participation in a research study. Each scenario had the following elements: illness label, illness description, functional level, chronicity of illness, description of social support, description of the research study (in which lumbar puncture would be used to obtain cerebrospinal fluid), including its purpose, procedures, risks, and lack of direct benefit, and a specified competency status. The illness label, illness description, and specified competency status were experimentally manipulated; the other elements were held constant across all 7 scenarios.

Scenarios 1, 2, and 3 described a person with "mental illness" who had delusions and hallucinations. Scenarios 4, 5, 6 described a person with "medical illness" that "affects the kidneys and the brain" who had "difficulty thinking and remembering things."

We varied the stated competency status of the subject. Scenarios 1 and 4 stated, "[John/Pam] is currently doing well. A doctor who is not connected to the research study has examined [John/Pam], and he believes [John/Pam] is able to make [his/her] own decisions about participating in this research study." Scenarios 2 and 5 specified that the portrayed subject was deemed by an independent physician too impaired to make his or her own decision about participating and that a family surrogate would have to consent instead. In scenarios 3 and 6, the competency status was left unspecified.

Scenario 7 was identical to the mental illness scenarios except that the illness was not labelled as medical or mental, and it included a medical causal framework ("affects both the kidneys and the brain, but the main problem has been the effects on the brain") but with symptoms identical to the mental illness scenarios. Like scenarios 3 and 6, the competency status was left unspecified.

The main dependent variable was assessed with the question, "Imagine that you are part of an ethics committee that decides whether certain studies should be allowed. Would you allow researchers to do studies like this with patients like [John/Pam]?" Participants also rated the level of risk involved with the research described in the scenarios, the importance of the research, the vulnerability of the portrayed subject to involuntary participation, and the capacity of the portrayed subject to give consent to research on his or her own.

The respondents also completed two widely used scales to assess stigma, the Social Distance Scale (SDS), which measures willingness to interact socially with the person described in the scenario, and an adapted version of the Perceived Causes measure (originally developed for the 1996 National Opinion Research Centre's General Social Survey), which gauges participants' opinions on possible causes of the illness presented in the scenario.

Participants' attitudes toward biomedical research were measured using the Research Attitudes Questionnaire (RAQ), a scale developed by our group. The internal consistency for this scale was adequate (á = 0.77).

DEMOGRAPHICS OF RESPONDENTS IN THE 7 RANDOMLY ASSIGNED SCENARIO GROUPS

Before fielding the research study, the paper-based version of the survey was circulated among 15 individuals, including social science researchers and laypersons. Any issues concerning the wording of questions and formatting of the survey were discussed among the researchers and resolved. Quality assurance testing was also conducted with the web-based survey to ensure usability, accurate data recording, and comprehension.

This study was deemed exempt from IRB (institutional review board) review by the University of Michigan.

Statistical Analysis

Depending on the nature of the data, comparisons across the 7 scenarios were made using analysis of variance (ANOVA) or chi-square tests. Two group comparisons were made using chi-square tests or *t* tests. The main dependent variable that measured the respondents' willingness to allow the research described in the scenarios was recoded to create a binary variable by combining the "definitely" and "probably" categories. Using this binary outcome variable, logistic regression models were used to examine the primary research questions, namely, the effects of illness (mental versus medical versus unspecified illness) and competency status (competent, not competent, competency unspecified). Specific mediation (perceived capacity, vulnerability, importance, social distance, and causal attributions) and moderation (risk perception) effects were examined using regression models.

We explored the general predictors of willingness to allow research. Controlling for scenario effects, we examined a forward stepwise logistic regression model with willingness to allow as the dependent variable and the following predictors: age, race, ethnicity, gender, financial status, education, perceived capacity, importance of research, total Social Distance score, perceived risk, vulnerability, the 6 causal explanation variables (choice, chemical imbalance, upbringing, stress, genetics, God's will), and Research Attitudes Questionnaire total score.

Results

The 3140 persons were randomized to 1 of 7 scenarios so that each person was presented only 1 scenario. The response rates to questions ranged from 76.4% to 81.5% for demographic questions to 79.9–91.2% for the survey questions. For no item was there a significantly different response rate among the 7 groups ($\div^2$ range = 3.08 to 7.41, *df* = 6, *p* range =.28 to.80).

Summary of Scenario Effects on the Respondents' Willingness to Allow Research

Illness effect was present in the hypothesized direction, with the respondents assigned to medical illness scenarios being more willing to allow the research than those assigned to the mental illness scenarios. This illness effect was present when the competency status was specified as either competent or unspecified but not when it was specified as incompetent. Thus, there was an illness by competence interaction, but opposite the hypothesized direction.

As expected, the effect of specifying that a subject was incompetent made the respondents much less willing to allow the research, regardless of illness. Within the illness groups, scenarios that did not specify competency status elicited responses similar to those resulting from scenarios that did specify that the subject was competent.

Finally, we compared the responses to the unspecified illness scenario (scenario 7) with responses to the analogous mental illness and medical illness scenarios.

The respondents to the mental illness scenario (scenario 3) were less willing to allow the research than the respondents to the unspecified illness scenario. The responses to the medical illness scenario (scenario 6) were not different from responses to the unspecified illness scenario, despite the fact that the illness symptoms were identical to the mental illness scenario.

Mediators and Moderators

The responses to the variables that we had hypothesized as potential mediators or moderators. Perception of risk was examined as a potential moderator but did not prove to be a moderator.

We checked for mediating effects of perceived capacity, vulnerability, importance, social distance, general research attitudes, and causal attributions on the illness effect (using the groups 1–3 versus groups 4–6 comparison on willingness to allow research). Mediation analyses controlled for all other potential mediators of interest.

Only perceived capacity was a mediator of the illness effect on willingness to allow research responses. Specifically, perceived capacity was a strong predictor of willingness to allow research (odds ratio = 2.93, $p < .001$); illness was highly associated with perceived capacity (odds ratio = 1.67, $p < .001$). When both perceived capacity and illness variables were entered into the logistic regression model, illness was no longer a significant predictor (odds ratio = 1.18, $p = 0.138$) of the willingness response, although perceived capacity remained a strong predictor (odds ratio = 2.71, $p < .001$).

Exploratory Analysis of Predictors of Willingness to Allow Research

We conducted an exploratory analysis of predictors of willingness to allow research using multiple logistic regression models. We controlled for scenario effects in order to ascertain an overall sense of which variables are independently associated with willingness to allow the kind of nontherapeutic research portrayed in our scenarios.

Older respondents were slightly less willing to allow the research study portrayed in the scenario. Women were less willing to allow than men; blacks and Asians were less willing than whites to allow the research study. Education, ethnicity, and financial status were not significant predictors of willingness to allow research. There were no interaction effects involving scenario and any of the demographic variables.

As expected, perceived capacity was a strong predictor. The strongest predictor was the perceived risk of the research procedure portrayed in the scenarios. General attitude toward research, as measured by the Research Attitudes Questionnaire, was a significant predictor. For every 10-point increase in the total score (which is approximately equal to a 1-point change per item that has 5 response categories), the adjusted odds ratio was 2.03. Of the 6 possible causal explanations for the illnesses portrayed in the scenarios, none independently predicted willingness to allow research except "chemical imbalance in the brain," which was associated with higher willingness to allow. The social distance variable was not a predictor. Not surprisingly, vulnerability was associated with lower willingness to allow research, while importance of the research was associated with greater willingness to allow.

DISCUSSION

There is an extensive literature on the stigma of mental illness. This is the first study to clearly demonstrate that research involving the mentally ill (here portrayed as people with a chronic psychotic illness) is stigmatized. For the present study stigma was understood as discrimination that serves no ethically justifiable purpose while having the potential to cause adverse effects, in this case by precluding research that would benefit the stigmatized population. Key features of this randomized, experimental survey support this interpretation. The ethically relevant parameters—those factors that ought to affect one's responses regarding whether to allow a research study—were kept constant across all of our scenarios: degree and duration of disability, level of functioning, level of social support, the nature and purpose of the research procedures, and the risk-benefit description of the research procedures. Each participant responded to a single scenario in order to minimize the socially desirable answers that may occur when participants are invited to compare medical versus psychiatric scenarios. By manipulating the specified competency status within illness groups, we were able to demonstrate that the respondents were sensitive to the ethically relevant issue of decision-making competence. By using a scenario (scenario 7) that contained a generic disease label (with a medical causal framework) along with a symptom picture identical to the mentally ill scenarios, we demonstrated that it is not necessarily the symptoms of mental illness but rather the designation of an illness as "mental," or the lack of a medical causal framework, that elicits the stigma.

We were surprised by the nature of the interaction between the competency status and illness type. We had hypothesized that the "most protected" group would be the mentally ill persons who were specified as incompetent. Instead, our respondents discriminated between the mentally ill and the medically ill not when the research subjects' competence status was specified as incompetent but rather when that status was either unspecified or specified as competent.

The results of the mediation analyses are important because they confirm that the tendency to discriminate against psychiatric research is mediated by the specific belief that persons with mental illness are less capable of making decisions, even when it is made explicit to the respondents that the mentally ill person has been deemed competent by an independent physician. Of the respondents, 32% felt that the mentally ill subject described as competent was in fact "probably or definitely not capable," compared with 18% for the medically ill subject. It appears that laypersons are affected by an older model of diagnosis-driven definitions of competence that has now been deemed ethically unacceptable, even when they are told that the persons have been independently determined to be competent.

The illness effect was not mediated by the respondents' feeling that research into mental illness is less important or that psychiatric patients are, in comparison to the medically ill, more prone to being enrolled in research against their wishes. While general attitude toward research (RAQ) significantly predicted willingness to allow research, it did not mediate the differential responses between psychiatric and medical scenarios.

We confirmed the existence of certain aspects of stigma, but they were not associated with willingness to allow research. For example, the desire to remain socially distant from persons with mental illness did not affect responses regarding willingness to allow participation in research.

Finally, perceived risk of the research procedure portrayed in the scenario was a very strong predictor of willingness to allow research; however, it did not interact with type of illness. The perception of risk of research with the mentally ill as compared to medically ill patients was about the same, despite NBAC's concerns that psychiatric research involves greater risk than medical research.

Limitations

Analogous to the distinction between efficacy (internal validity) and effectiveness (external validity) in randomized clinical trials, our study has stronger internal validity than external validity. The survey's experimental between-subjects design with random assignment of large numbers of respondents to each cell ensures that the primary stigma effect (ie, illness effect) is real. The exploratory analysis of the predictors of willingness to allow research also supports the internal validity of the study; our respondents' perception of risk, their perception of vulnerability of the subjects, their sense of importance of research, and so on all predicted their response in the expected directions, which shows that they were answering the questions as intended.

Although the sample frame was not a probabilistic sample of the US population, this study may still provide good evidence for the external validity of the stigma effect. We were able to recruit and randomize a highly heterogeneous group of respondents in terms of race, ethnicity, age, gender, financial status, and education. None of these demographic variables moderated the stigma effect (ie, illness effect), so it is highly unlikely that the main results are due to biased sample selection. It is true, however, that the point estimates of frequency of responses need to be interpreted with caution.

Finally, it is possible that we did not control for all the ethically relevant variables across the 7 scenarios and that our respondents were discriminating between illnesses based on this unidentified, yet ethically relevant, variable. Although this seems unlikely, it is important that future research continue to unearth potential determinants of research stigma.

There are 3 main findings of this study. Even when ethically relevant factors are similar between medical and mental illness research, there is a tendency to restrict mental illness research compared to medical illness research. This restrictive view of mental illness research is largely mediated through the outdated belief that having a mental illness makes a person incapable of making his or her own decisions. Finally, this discriminatory treatment of mental illness research is not so much about biased treatment of the incompetent mentally ill but rather of the competent mentally ill. Moreover, this stigma is deep enough to override the statement that an independent physician has deemed a mentally ill person competent. This last finding is particularly troubling, as it indicates that the stigmatizing attitude may be influential in spite of "official" statements to the contrary.

This study does not prove that policies singling out the decisionally impaired mentally ill are driven by stigma. However, it does show that such policies are consistent with deeply ingrained stigma regarding the mentally ill. Since there is no reason to think that policymakers and IRB members are exempt from the influence of such stigma, they must be especially careful to guard against it in their own formulation and implementation of research ethics policy regarding the decisionally impaired.

RESEARCH METHODOLOGY EXPLAINED FOR EVERDAY PEOPLE

Research is the foundation of modern organizational science in academics; its goal is to empower individuals and nations alike with growth achieved through acquired empirical wisdom. When done effectively, research can be conducted much like peeling an onion. In the course of each layer shed, new directions, perspectives, and truths are revealed. Similarly, research is like walking through a maze that sometimes takes scholars on roads that seem to lead nowhere, generate new questions for them to pursue, or reward them with the satisfaction of coming to the end of a journey with new enlightenment that cannot seem to be contradicted.

Good scholarly research does not occur quickly or easily. However, modern advances in technology lend to making research more accessible, organized, and easier to assimilate than prior to the development of word processors and computer databases. Modern research efforts depict a plethora of methodologies, literature, and themes to research abundantly and thoroughly, though with as many varieties in underlying assumptions and orientations as to what exactly constitutes knowledge. Still, diversity in the science of research methodology paves roads to discovery, growth, and empowerment. It is the research itself that should, however, determine the method of research.

OVERVIEW

This chapter discusses the processes of modern research methodology and focuses, primarily, on qualitative and quantitative approaches. Definitions of research concepts are provided to paint a picture of the strengths and weaknesses commonly attributed to each method, especially as they pertain to conducting survey research.

Pursuing a better understanding of research methods through examining methods of investigative study are influenced by trends in both science and society, which make research challenging and debated, though rewarding and rich. Although scholarly journals reveal just how challenging research itself can be conducted reliably and with validity, this chapter aims to translate terminology found in advanced research literature to accessible terms for ease of understanding and applicability. With a better understanding of research terms and processes, research can be more rewarding and less taxing.

Research results do not always reflect a definitive answer with clearly revealed conclusions and, in fact, often seem to generate more questions than they answer. Sometimes, research proves that more investigation or information is necessary to draw definitive or precise conclusions or to develop theory or new hypotheses. In addition, further research may only reveal that there is more than one correct answer to the research questions. However, a thorough study that is conducted properly may indeed reward investigators with the answers they sought. In order to study life processes, access to the information must be obtained. The nature of the research and questions help establish the types of access required. Remenyi, Williams, Money, and Swartz (1998) argue that promising research sites should have an entrance where trust can be established and possibilities for gathering credible, quality, and suitable evidence are available.

Interpretation of information is often not so straightforward or will take multiple forms. It is through varying methods or integrating quantitative and qualitative methods that information can be interpreted and derived in its complexity. Becker (1998), Davies (2003), Creswell (2003), as well as many others, suggest that research requires either qualitative, quantitative, or both types of data. As this chapter will show, the research purposes and questions should direct what approach to take as researchers look for where and how to pursue more data. For instance, research questions directing qualitative studies often inquire into processes associated with change or individuals' meaning-making, seeking knowledge in variation and diverse perspectives, while quantitative studies are typically geared towards revealing relationships between variables, as measured by central tendencies in a data set. In fact, variations of data collection and analysis methods will be naturally called for when designing and drawing conclusions in a study.

The Process

The process of research is best done with knowledge of some basic guidelines. Creswell (2003) recommends that researchers reduce their entire study to a single, overarching question and several sub-questions. Qualitative researchers should state the broadest question they can possibly pose and glean data from any of six sources: archival records, direct observation, documents, interviews, participant observation, and physical artifacts (Yin, 1989). Of course, interviewing and observing are natural sources of direct data collection.

Recording data may best be done with a pre-designed log where both observations and interview data can be viewed. Established interview protocols are also wise to structure the research and guide discussion. Such protocols will also enable the interviewer to take notes on the responses of the participant during the interview. They also assist researchers in organizing thoughts on items such as headings, ways for starting the interview, and concluding ideas in a conversation with time constraints. Audio recordings are a valuable tool in research for validity reasons, because they allow answers to be document verbatim.

COMPARING AND CONTRASTING QUALITATIVE AND QUANTITATIVE RESEARCH METHODS

Extensive debate between the merits of qualitative and quantitative research has occurred for many years. As Strauss and Corbin (1990) wrote, qualitative research is any kind of research that produces findings not arrived at by means of statistical procedures or other means of quantification. On the other hand, Creswell (2003) explained, quantitative methods are used chiefly to test or verify theories or explanations, identify variables to study, relate variables in questions or hypotheses, use statistical standards of validity and reliability, and employ statistical procedures for analysis.

Certainly, both qualitative and quantitative research methods have individual strengths and weaknesses. Evaluating the strengths and weaknesses of each approach involves a form of qualitative research in itself. Importantly, employing properly designed research strategies (e.g., in data collection and analysis), while meeting the needs of each research project, often determines whether the research will be fruitful. In fact, qualitative data often needs to be supplemented with quantitative methods, and vice versa, in order to reveal different learnings from the research. Clearly, there is a need for both quantitative and qualitative research, as their relative strengths complement the weaknesses of the other.

Academic and social researchers have typically been educated to show favour to quantitative over qualitative methods due to the ability to show validity on a numeric scale with the aid of statistical tools. Even so, the use of statistics and statistical tools can be clearly assessed in terms of whether certain tests were properly selected and implemented. Quantitative research papers identify a problem and can generally be are characterized by: (1) discussing the purpose of the study; (2) identifying the sample population and instruments used, and (3) discussing the relationship between variables, research questions, steps taken in the analysis of the data, and outcomes. Moreover, qualitative research is usually presented in the same way with its purposes, methods for data collection, analysis and findings for answering them. It is their results that differ.

Horna (1994) asserts that quantitative research designs are best used to depict and explain social facts that can be investigated through the employment of methodologies of deductive logic which is common to natural sciences and Western civilization values. In addition, "a quantitative approach is one in which the researcher primarily uses postpositivist claims for developing knowledge...and collects data on predetermined instruments that yield statistical data". When data is quantifiable, validity and verification or rejection of a hypothesis are conducted through measurement, resulting in a conclusion of acceptance or refutation. Qualitative data, while also addressing issues of validity, typically does so with acceptance of the plurality of truth, thus characterizing validity as the presence of a coherent and traceable logic of analysis and interpretation, versus a measurement of statistical power. When data is quantifiable, the length of the research paper can be considerably shorter in size, due to its numerical depictions of new understanding. Statistical analysis and quantitative data should not be discounted, however, and should instead be valued because of their usefulness in making comparisons across relatively large numbers of people, events, or objects. Likewise, distributions, central tendencies, aggregate patterns, probabilities, and correlations are best researched with quantitative analysis, and qualitative research must often stop short of generalizing outside the sample studied.

On the other hand, qualitative research is often deemed successful when it is triangulated, able to be replicated, and is expressed with thick description. Qualitative research is seen as especially important because it is useful in exploring real organizational goals, processes, failures, and links, focusing on "understanding particulars" rather than "generalizing to universals," as quantitative research is said to do. As opposed to the breadth of quantitative approaches, qualitative research is valuable in its depth and its ability to uncover and interpret mechanisms behind behaviours and meaning-making.

Unlike the focus on textual interpretation in qualitative studies, quantitative research focuses on measurement "using predetermined categories that can be treated as internal or ordinal data and subjected to statistical analysis". Researchers often assume quantitative research to be precise and easily comparable because it is grounded in "hard" evidence, which is usually acquired through tests, questionnaires, and surveys. Moreover, quantitative research is considered more useful for measuring outcomes of processes that are best understood by qualitative means.

On the other hand, qualitative research provides a more holistic examination of research, is usually based on interviews, observations, or focus groups, and focuses primarily on life experiences, social processes, and organizational structures and settings. Information is collected based upon spoken and written text and is not inhibited or constrained by predetermined standardized categories, thus allowing the resulting theory to be inductive and "grounded" in the data. Human perceptions and understandings are recorded in qualitative studies to show situations as participants perceive them. In fact, Ulmer and Wilson (2003) believe that qualitative research has advantages over quantitative research because quantitative research cannot accurately quantify "abstract concepts—emotions, culture, social organization, social relationships..." with validity. Life experiences and social processes, they imply, are difficult to quantify.

As with quantitative methods, there are limitations in qualitative research, as Creswell (2003) noted, including:

Researcher may be seen as intrusive. Private information may be observed that the researcher cannot report. Researcher may not have good attending and observation skills. Certain participants may present special problems in gaining rapport. Interviews provide indirect information filtered through the views of interviewees. Interviews provide information in a designated 'place' rather than the natural field setting. Researcher's presence may bias responses. People are not equally articulate and perceptive.

Skinner, Tagg, and Holloway (2000) conveyed several concerns for qualitative research, too. First, they question whether or not qualitative data can stand up to intense examination, a doubt that stems from the common presumption that either participants or interpretations of data are biased by the researcher. Bias is something that qualitative research acknowledges via the "subjective-I" approach; replication can be a problem, but qualitative research does not posit that this can be done. In fact, qualitative research rejects the idea of objectivity almost altogether. However, it should be noted that there are also biases in quantitative measures too, as found in the design and wording of survey questions, which are rarely questioned. In the case of researcher bias, generalization of ideas to all participants impacts validity. The second concern involves time considerations and resources for collection and analysing data, which occurs by relying on diaries, logs, and audio recordings. These resources may be incomplete when amassed during a short time allotted for data collection, such that additional information could be unknown at the time the research is taking place. Third, whether the information is recorded and interpreted accurately is a factor of concern as well, and data often goes missing or is difficult to obtain. Obtaining this type of information is compounded if the environment does not support a qualitative approach for one reason or another. An example of this type of qualitative environment may be in an environment that does not give sufficient time during a survey.

UNDERSTANDING QUALITATIVE RESEARCH: DEFINITIONS AND PROCESSES

Strauss and Corbin (1990) believe that qualitative research requires certain essential skills typified by the ability to recognize and avoid bias, while being able to think abstractly and critically analyse situations. One approach to qualitative research is "interpretive" or "hermeneutic," a perspective that assumes truth is socially constructed. Its primary goal is to discover or generate meanings held by respondents through transcending facts and causal analyses in order to investigate how they are constructed. Included in interpretive research are ethnography, grounded theory, ethnomethodology, interpretive biography, and phenomenology, as well as others.

Interpretive research usually begins with observation or intuition, followed by searching for data that supports, contradicts, or leads other directions. This search for supporting or incongruous data better equips a researcher to defend a position or further examine processes.

Interpretive research is often a rejection of postpositivist perspectives, which are typically identified in quantitative studies. Characterized by fixed and stable measures, postpositivist perspectives are identified through scientific experimental research. The postpositivist perspective is value-free and is usually found in descriptive, correlational, and experimental research, with an emphasis on coming from an objective stance (Capella, 2003). In order to meet an objective position, the researcher must have "the ability to maintain analytical distance while at the same time being able to draw on past experience and theoretical knowledge to interpret what is seen; astute powers of observation and good interactional skills" (Strauss and Corbin,1990). As with quantitative approaches, valid and reliable data is also important to qualitative researchers.

Interpretive research usually begins with observation or with intuition. The second usual phase is searching for data that supports, contradicts or leads other directions. By doing so, researchers will be better equipped to defend a position or further examine processes.

Validity

Derived from the Latin term validitas, meaning "strength," *validity* is a term used in both qualitative and quantitative research, asserting that a finding can never truly be proven, only argued. Cook and Campbell (1979) believe that "validity is the best available approximation to the truth or falsity of propositions, including propositions about cause...at best; one can know what has not yet been ruled out as false". Therefore, conclusions that claim validity must be considered by researchers and academics alike as approximate or tentative.

There are two types of validity in research: internal and external. External validity describes how well a research finding can be applied to the population from which a sample is drawn, while internal validity speaks to factors that impact the estimation of accuracy in terms of conclusions drawn about the sample itself. Transferability deals with external validity and can be described by the range of limitations on application of study findings beyond the context in which the study was done. For instance, factors that affect transferability in a study include the presence of an adequate and sufficiently varied sample.

Researchers must consider who and what the findings concern in order to assess transferability.

Validity in qualitative research is distinct from usage of the same term in quantitative studies; the second is discussed further below in the section on quantitative research. Qualitative researchers assert that validity in their work expresses the credibility of a finding or interpretation, assessed in relationship to the purposes and circumstances of the study, rather than being a context-independent property of methods or conclusions. Validity threats characterize the ways in which a researcher can be incorrect about her interpretations or other explanations for the findings she shares. The use of triangulation, as described in the next section will prove useful in such situations.

Two particular issues are common: the first are validity threats in qualitative research, and bias and reactivity. Bias refers to the selection of data that will confirm a researcher's thoughts and ideas. Reactivity describes the influence a researcher has and uses over those he is studying. Several approaches are commonly used by qualitative researchers in striving to conduct valid research. These include the search for evidence that will discredit their interpretations, triangulation (explained above), soliciting feedback from colleagues on their analyses to ascertain the reason behind their conclusions, and conducting member checks with participants to determine if interpretations ring true for them.

Another way of demonstrating validity is to record detailed information about the actual survey instrument used, if one was actually utilized in the study. Recording the process of data collection and how the information was analyzed enhances the final product and the credibility of the research. However, it is important to note that when a researcher modifies an instrument or combines instruments in a study, the original validity may not hold for the new instrument, and it becomes imperative to re-establish validity during data analysis with any of the techniques identified above. It is also important to note that it is more likely that research results will be deemed valid if there are no conflicting perspectives on the information.

Triangulation

Triangulation is another term used in qualitative research and was originally developed by land surveyors seeking to increase validity of maps by incorporating measures from differing angles. These varieties of angles gave diverse perspectives and helped enrich the cartographers' vantage points. Triangulation of data collection and analytic methods is used by researchers to address credibility and validity concerns by incorporating multiple sources for data and/or several methods of analysis. With the aid of multiple sources of information, a study's validity is supported. In research, triangulation assists researchers in increasing their understanding of complex subject matter and can vary data collection by time, location, respondents, and the information being accumulated.

Howe & Eisenhart (1990) show that time variation in an effort to triangulate data analyses same, similar, or differing subjects at different points in time. Only when information continually appears to be consistent in future analysis can unwavering conclusions be drawn. In a qualitative study, conclusions can also be drawn with regard to the influence of time on the form and content of the data. By comparing differing sets of data using triangulation, the researcher can gain enhanced understanding and new perspectives that will strengthen their conclusions through a refinement of their emerging theories.

Triangulation of research is a valuable tool for compensating missing information that was not gathered in surveys during a single round of questioning because it requires multiple rounds of surveys from the same or different respondents. This process creates varying sample groups and varying questions, which will yield more accurate conclusions because a larger sample would be used than in a study using grounded theory with one round of data collection from a single sample. When analysing the data, the researcher should consider whether or not the characteristics of the sample are understood in enough depth to draw conclusions.

With these definitions and processes in mind, it makes it easier to understand how they may be applied within the many varieties of qualitative approaches to research. A number of qualitative research designs and strategies will be discussed in the next section of this chapter.

Grounded Theory

A form of interpretive research, grounded theory takes an inductive approach to developing theory from interviews that are transcribed verbatim and coded to see relevant trends, explore unanticipated themes, or reveal that there is no evidence to answer a research question. Glaser and Strauss (1967) show how grounded theory was developed and how it works.

There are several important distinctions between grounded theory and quantitative methods. For example, quantitative research usually begins with a hypothesis, which is tested by running data through statistical analyses, leading to the development of a theory that either refutes or confirms the hypothesis. Conversely, grounded theory starts with data in the form of observations or interviews, from which the researcher searches for patterns, similarities, and differences to develop a theory—without a preset hypothesis. Data collection in grounded theory research comes from any of many different textual resources, including journal articles, interviews, observations documented with field notes, government research, or other academic research. This form of research is valuable because of its use of personal experiences and interviews.

The processes of grounded theory are performed in a parallel format, beginning immediately after the data is gathered, so that the researcher can identify what path will be taken to obtain more information. This is known as a reactive process and is characterized by dynamic analysis of the information, while modification of the collection process takes place to adapt to emerging findings and processing of the information. Dynamic analysis can be described as the way a researcher looks at every piece of information collected, as it is collected during simultaneously. Each concept uncovered in the research becomes part of the theory as it shows up consistently and with significance for participants. When themes do not continually appear and reappear during data collection, researchers must determine whether their absence is a deficiency in defining the concept or there is an influencing factor that is changing the results of the research.

Data collection used in grounded theory research comes from any of many different resources including: journal articles, interviews, observations, government research, or other academic research. The process of grounded theory is characterized by dynamic analysis of the information, while modification of the collection process takes place to test for accuracy of collection and processing of the information.

This process of gathering, testing and processing may include the use of quantitative statistical hypothesis testing or by comparing data sets with other various samples and tests that may confirm that patterns of consistency exist. Conclusions may be drawn by an elimination process using individually chosen variables using variations of this technique. Grounded theory works well in gathering and processing survey research information, though it should be noted that the designing of surveys and highly structured interviews can be antithetical to grounded theory when they orient the respondent to reply in a certain way. In the process of using grounded theory, survey research questions unsystematically change and become less uncertain. This process of refinement results in clarity and more accurate responses from which to draw conclusions and build theory.

Reflexivity

Reflexivity is a research strategy and term that can be metaphorically compared to a knower's mirror. Malterud, (2001) describes reflexivity as "an attitude of attending systematically to the context of knowledge construction, especially to the effect of the researcher, at every step of the research process". Reflexivity acknowledges that the researcher is inextricable from the material she is studying, and one question asked by a reflexive approach is if the researchers' motives, perspectives, background, and preliminary hypotheses have been sufficiently addressed in a study. Reflexivity is simply a self-reflection by the researcher of his or her biases and predispositions. Reflexivity is useful in research because it helps check potential research biases that may occur. Biases should be checked while doing qualitative research because the researcher is the instrument and means of the data collection.

Researchers that use a reflexive strategy understand they are a part of their research through the relationships they have with participants and the unavoidable presuppositions they bring to their work. Rossman and Rallis (1998) add that reflexivity also implicates those a researcher is studying because they react to the researcher. It is important for researchers to examine and test their reflexive influence throughout a study, from data collection through analysis and interpretation. In addition, reflexivity can be addressed by accepting rather than rejecting the idea that a study takes place in relationships as well as in a cultural and historical context.

Phenomenology

Phenomenology is a qualitative research design that assesses information based on the principle that reality is made up of independently perceivable and understandable objects and events and not of anything dependent on human consciousness or interpretation. Phenomenology is said to give information a more humanistic perspective. It is used to discover the context of events in organizations under study while evaluating information extrapolated from grounded theory.

Phenomenologists believe that the world is a social construct and that the observer is a part of what is being observed. Their research is developed through inductive reasoning and focuses on understanding complexity, meaning, and specific contexts, or as Easterby-Smith, Thorpe, and Lowe (1994) describe, "to appreciate different constructions and meanings that people place upon their experience".

Researchers use focus groups and phenomenology in order to facilitate a shared conversation for a group of people who will develop a mutual understanding. Discussions are the primary tool used to assess the true feelings of those being studied and occur between researcher and participants, as well as among participants in the focus group. Researchers conducting focus groups with the use of phenomenology also typically attempt to experience the world from the perspectives of the research group.

Phenomenology has its limitations in the eyes of many academics and researchers. For example, researchers often assert that phenomenologically-based information is limited in its transferability, arguing that research is perceived better generalized through quantitative than phenomenological means. Phenomenology in qualitative research allows researchers to share the question the lived experiences of the subjects. One may not be able to generalize a situation, but it can describe what people believe happened in a certain instance.

Preconceptions in Research

Preconceptions are another component of qualitative research that must be considered. Described as previous and professional experiences, motivation, and qualifications for exploration of the topic, these beliefs constitute subjectivity in terms of how things are and what is to be investigated, or, metaphorically speaking, a researcher's backpack of expectations.

Preconceptions are closely tied to one's theoretical frame of reference, and, thus, they are not always perceived as a detriment to qualitative research. Instead, preconceptions are viewed as a natural cognitive process and not necessarily determinants of research outcomes. They can be reshaped with counter-evidence, providing the researcher engages in reflective consideration of them and is willing to be wrong when preconceptions are challenged by evidence.

Theoretical Frame

The analyst's theoretical frame of reference is her pair of reading glasses, the lens through which she will view and interpret her results. A theoretical frame of reference represents the models and ideas applied to the data in order to assist in understanding it. Given that it frames interpretations, qualitative researchers must ask themselves whether or not the perspectives constituting their theoretical orientation are evident in the data and their interpretations. In addition, the researcher must analyse his framework to make sure it is adequate for the study and should account for the extent of the role given to the theoretical framework during the investigation.

Reliability

Reliability is another term often used in conjunction with validity in qualitative research and is understood by qualitative researchers as the degree to which a finding will be attained repeatedly over time. Maines (1993) points out that all sociological data is already interpreted. They are fact interpretations represented by numbers. They are no less representational in nature than words. Therefore, researchers must ascertain whether the interpretations they make are reliable.

Importantly, some qualitative researchers reject the notion of reliability when studying cognitive and emotional processes because, they assert, human meaning-making naturally changes over time and varies by context. The setting, time of day, current events in the life of the participant, and rapport with the researcher are all factors that will influence the data that is collected. In essence, the manner in which the data is collected will be a reflection of the lived experiences of those interviewed. It should be noted that those lived experiences may vary greatly among each individual interviewed.

UNDERSTANDING QUANTITATIVE DEFINITIONS AND METHODOLOGIES

One purpose of this chapter is to analyse research methodology in order to allow the researcher of this chapter and others to understand the processes of qualitative and quantitative research. Language common to these two types of research is generally not used in everyday conversation. Therefore, to balance the previous section on qualitative approaches, this section will define terminology that is common in discussions of quantitative research.

Positivism

Positivism, which typically focuses on cause and effect and the determination of facts, or as Davies (2003) explains, "seeking one unambiguous truth". Positivism refers to the traditional scientific method for conducting research and interpreting results, using the following steps:

1. Develop a hypothesis to be proven or disproven.
2. Use a predetermined and set method to measure the relationship between variables in the data.
3. Collect data through surveys, experiments, or observations.
4. Employ a quantitative analytic approach to draw a conclusion that accepts or rejects the hypothesis.

In positivism (usually distinguished from the flexibility of qualitative research), the researcher presumes his objectivity and takes a stance outside of the events being studied. The objective is to measure a theory in order to address practical issues, while assuming an absolute truth can be attained through analysis rooted in provable principles. Consequently, assumptions lead to logical deductions in which conclusions are drawn from predictions of observable matter. "It is the insistence on explanation, prediction, and proof that are the hallmarks of positivism". However in the case of the null hypothesis, researchers seek not to prove an hypothesis, but reject the null hypothesis and support the hypothesis. This yields a small but determining difference.

One drawback in a positivistic approach is that it assumes structures do not change or evolve. Another criticism of this paradigm is that it functions hierarchically and oversimplifies the contexts in which people live, falsely assuming that an objective stance can be taken.

Variables

Variables are understood as characteristics that can take on different values, such as situational conditions, constraints, opportunities, identity markers, relationships, and events. According to Ulmer and Wilson (2003), "Statistical analysis can enable a researcher to engage in analysis of how outcomes may vary according to the contingencies and conditions of situations". There are two types of variables in quantitative research: dependent and independent.

An independent variable is manipulated by the researcher in some way in order to measure the effect of the manipulation on the dependent variable. For instance, in a study of the effect of bonuses on employee tenure at a company, the independent variable, bonuses, would be manipulated to determine if the presence or absence of an annual bonus makes a difference in the length of time employees stay with a company. Therefore, multivariate statistical techniques can be utilized to allow researchers to examine how a dependent variable will vary according to the situation and contingencies represented by an individual variable.

Realism

One cannot discuss definitions of research terms without addressing what is known as the "realist approach." Harlos, Mallon, Stablein, and Jones (2003) describe writing from the realist approach as that which "holds that there are factual truths that can be fashioned into empirical realities with enough diligence, perseverance, and penetration into underlying fabrics of settings.

In this way, it defines itself in relation to hard science". They also assert that realists hold a belief that there is an identifiable truth and warn researchers to guard themselves against biases that lead them to sway participants, either intentionally or unintentionally. The realist approach involves setting aside presuppositions and refusing immersion in research settings while keeping systematic notes, in order to maintain a presumably objective stance. Triangulation occurs between observation, views of reality as reported by respondents, and reports of numerous informants.

The opposition to the realist approach asserts that realists fail to accept inherent limitations on discovering singular, universal truths, though the realist approach is still being used and is widely accepted in organizational studies.

Validity

In quantitative research, there are several ways to establish validity. Validity takes on a different meaning than when used in qualitative studies. Validity refers to how well an instrument measures what the researcher wants to evaluate. Specifically, a measure has content validity if the items it contains address all of the topics the researcher aims to study and is assessed in terms of face validity or sampling-content validity, in which researchers systematically identify how items on an instrument cover the topics of interest. A more rigorous assessment, construct validity refers to the degree to which a measure actually captures the theoretical construct it aims to cover. It is typically evaluated by testing the measure for applicability under varying circumstances using probabilities, specifically the statistical likelihood that the researcher is wrong.

Now, with a deeper understanding of terminology used in research, this chapter will discuss the benefits of survey data. Although there are many varieties of data, including: in-depth interviews, focus groups, oral histories, descriptive data, and mixed-methods data, to name a few; survey data is being described in this chapter because of the future benefit of its proposed use in upcoming work by the author of this chapter.

Survey data collection is of particular interest and very popular among graduate students who are studying trends and consistent patterns. Whereas, the descriptions and definitions of research methods and designs may be used in a proposed-future dissertation, other data varieties will not. Describing the other varieties of data in this chapter has not been deemed necessary by the author, due to the enormous breadth of information available on each of these data types.

Therefore, by focusing only on describing survey data, it serves a two-fold purpose. First, it enlightens readers and the author of this chapter with an understanding on the specific type of data to be used by the author in a proposed-future dissertation paper. Secondly, because it is known that the other types of data are easily researchable and will not be used by the author in the proposed-future dissertation, it is not necessary to use valuable time to describe each data type in a paper used as a foundation for the proposed-future dissertation mentioned.

SURVEY DATA

Survey data can be gathered in many ways, such as with the use of questionnaires administered in person, interviews, and telephone surveys. Information attained through surveys benefits researchers by recording personal behaviours, attitudes, identities, and definitions from a high volume of respondents. Surveys are useful for gaining information that is difficult to discuss or cannot otherwise be calculated by observation, such as risk, fear, religious belief, and racial attitude. Ulmer and Wilson (2003) believe that the strength of using surveys comes from the fact that "the researcher can rely on outside observations. As a result, many scholars believe that surveys, under certain circumstances, provide more valid measures of phenomena than do official records". Moreover, surveys provide a systematic and structured method for acquiring information on the same topic from a large group of people in a relatively short amount of time.

However, survey data does have its limits. Surveys require that respondents answer questions honestly and accurately, and researchers must be aware that questions are subject to interpretation by the respondents. Therefore, it is recommended that researchers check with respondents on their answers to make sure there is as much uniformity in their interpretation as possible, employ surveys with a published record of reliability, and determine that questions asked in the survey accurately represent the study's intentions.

Esposito and Murphy (1999) believe the quantitative data typically acquired through survey responses do not give a very deep interpretation of occurrences, such as open-ended qualitative interviews would provide. These "snapshot", point-in-time measures give a shallow view that fails to give a rich or true assessment of the aspect of life being studied.

In order to study life for research purposes, access must be obtained to the information. The nature of the research and questions asked help establish the types of access required. Remenyi, Williams, Money, and Swartz (1998) believe that good research sites should have an entrance, trust can be established, and possibilities for gathering credible/quality and suitable evidence are available.

Finally, questions concerning data collection should analyse whether the strategy for collection has been clearly stated or not. Without a clearly articulated method for data collection, replications are obstructed and validity and reliability might come into question. These questions should address whether or not the best approach has been chosen for answering the primary research question.

Mixed Methods

Although mixed methods is not within the scope of the question addressed in the beginning of this chapter, it is being briefly described here, because of its apparent utility in survey research which is addressed as the focus of this chapter. Also, it has been included in this piece out of hindsight and necessity for possible usage in a proposed-future dissertation by the author.

Determining whether to use qualitative or quantitative research should become more apparent as the research process unfolds. Hines (2000) believes that multiple methods provide construct validity, as well as internal and external validity, while allowing complex issues to be examined using the respondents' language. Creswell (2003) also indicates that using mixed-methods research will assist in making better interpretations because informants will be providing information that is both measurable and analyzed through rich description. A mixed-methods approach will also aid in reducing researcher bias and allowing documentation to be measured and analyzed more effectively. Likewise, Malterud (2001) states that, "qualitative studies can also be added to quantitative ones, to gain a better understanding of the meaning and implications of the findings".

Qualitative data is what often shapes the body of the research. Furthermore, it depicts the world as having several realities rather than one truth. On the other hand, quantitative research allows the use of data that identifies partial regularities, turnover in numbers, and statistical operations. Quantification shows a mixing and churning in numeric or sequential patterns and also emulates natural science. The practice of gathering and processing qualitative data should include the supplemental use of statistical hypothesis testing or comparing data sets with other samples and tests in order to confirm patterns.

Determining whether or not to use qualitative or quantitative research is not always so cut and dry. When great amounts of data are sought, quantitative research is often the most efficient and cost-effective research method. However, when data analysis and research questions require large amounts of description dealing with human experiences and perceptions, quantitative research could restrict the findings, making a qualitative approach ideal. The study itself should determine the method.

Ulmer and Wilson (2003) argue that "researchers can use qualitative data and statistical analysis without violating pragmatist ontological and epistemological positions" by meeting the following five conditions that serve to incorporate methods:

(a) Using quantification and statistical analysis of outcomes of social processes to sensitize or lay the groundwork for qualitative study of the social processes in question themselves; (b) understanding that quantification should not be seen as synonymous with empiricism; (c) specifying that individual and joint actors, not variables, exercise agency (i.e., variables do not think or do things, people do, and we create variables to represent those things); (d) remembering that social causality lies not in variables or statistical models but in interpretive processes as people individually and jointly define situations and act within them; and (e) striving to keep the conceptual distance between the quantified measures and the phenomena measured as small as possible (i.e., maximizing validity).

As Hines (2000) asserts, there is no one best method for conducting survey research. Qualitative research is valuable for describing events, circumstances, and other areas of human understanding, including people's experiences and meanings in a normal social setting, as well as processes and structures. Similarly, Bryman (1993) believes qualitative research is best defined in studies of the social world; as it analyses and describes human behaviour from the point of view of those being studied. However, quantitative research too has value due to its ability to measure data, generalize findings, and make predictions.

These research strategies should not be thought of as incompatible, but complementary. Their procedures for interpreting data and other types of information are interpreted differently, and they answer different types of questions. Their underlying principle for increasing understanding of a subject, however, is the same, and they can be used to interpret or enhance one another. Mixed-methods research utilizes both qualitative and quantitative methods in order to explore a topic in breadth and depth. Mixed methods lead to a "truer analysis," as Davies (2003) indicates, and quantitative discoveries should lead to a reflection on qualitative decision making in order to get a better understanding of the ideas in the "heads of economic actors and the models they use".

Research should occur through multiple methods of gathering data for the purpose of drawing a robust conclusion. As Davies (2003) explains, incorporation of both qualitative and quantitative designs in research could yield results that would not have been identified through use of one method or the other. Mixed method clearly has their advantages in research and is often the answer to the debate over which type of research is best.

Although not every tool and method in either quantitative or qualitative research was discussed in this chapter, it is clear that each method represents a different paradigm, making no possible answer as to which is conclusively best. One primary conclusion that can be drawn from this chapter is that for any study proposed, one will not know which research method will produce the most accurate conclusions without examining the kind of knowledge sought. Once a survey is initiated and the data is collected, clues to new avenues that researchers should pursue and new questions to be asked will be revealed. During this process, researchers need to be aware of personal biases in collecting and analysing data. They should find ways to keep their own and their respondents' biases in check in order to produce results that accomplish what scholars have yearned to do for centuries—help society grow in knowledge through realized truths.

THE EXPERIMENTAL METHOD

The experimental method is usually taken to be the most scientific of all methods, the 'method of choice'. The main problem with all the non-experimental methods is lack of control over the situation. The experimental method is a means of trying to overcome this problem. The experiment is sometimes described as the cornerstone of psychology: This is partly due to the central role experiments play in many of the physical sciences and also to psychology's historical view of itself as a science. A considerable amount of psychological research uses the experimental method.

An experiment is a study of cause and effect. It differs from non-experimental methods in that it involves the deliberate manipulation of one variable, while trying to keep all other variables constant.

EXPERIMENTS IN THE LABORATORY

In psychological experiments (like experiments in other fields) we try to keep all aspects of the situation constant except one-the one we are looking at. For example, suppose we want to investigate which of two methods is more successful at teaching children to read. The aspect that we vary is called the independent variable (IV) and we change this in a very precise way. In this example the teaching method is the independent variable. We call the factor which we then measure, in our example it would be some measure of the childrens reading ability, the dependent variable (DV), because, if our ideas are correct, it depends on the independent variable. In our example, the childrens reading ability depends on the teaching method used.

The variable which is being manipulated by the researcher is therefore called the independent variable and the dependent variable is the change in behaviour measured by the researcher.

All other variables which might affect the results and therefore give us a false set of results are called confounding variables (also referred to as random variables). Examples of confounding variables in the example given might include the following :

- Differences in the instructions given by an experimenter or in the stimulus materials being used (which could be overcome by standardising instructions and materials foe all those taking part)
- Differences between participants, e.g. in their age (which could be eliminated as a variable by using a single age group, or alternatively it could be made more constant by ensuring that the age structure of each of the groups taking part in the experiment is very similar).

By changing one variable (the IV) while measuring another (the DV) while we control all others, as far as possible, then the experimental method allows us to draw conclusions with far more certainty than any non-experimental method. If the IV is the only thing that is changed then it must be responsible for any change in the dependent variable.

Probably the commonest way to design an experiment in psychology is to divide the participants into 2 groups, the experimental group and the control group, and then introduce a change for the experimental group and not the control group. Suppose we wish to see if people sit at a library table for a shorter time if someone comes and sits at the same table than if they remain alone. First we must measure the average amount of time people sit when they are alone. This is the control condition and it gives us a baseline against which to judge our results. Then we send a confederate to sit at the same table and we measure the average amount of time the person sits there. This is the experimental condition.

A control group, then, is a group for whom the experimenter does not change the IV. The experimental and control groups must be matched on all important characteristics, e.g. age, sex, experience etc.

Advantages of Laboratory Experiments

1. Experiments are the only means by which cause and effect can be established. It has already been noted that an experiment differs from non-experimental methods in that it enables us to study cause and effect because it involves the deliberate manipulation of one variable, while trying to keep all other variables constant. Sometimes the independent variable (IV) is thought of as the cause and the dependent variable (DV) as the effect.
2. It allows for precise control of variables. The purpose of control is to enable the experimenter to isolate the one key variable which has been selected (the IV), in order to observe its effect on some other variable (the DV); control is intended to allow us to conclude that it is the IV, and nothing else, which is influencing the DV.
3. Experiments can be replicated. We cannot generalise from the results of a single experiment. The more often an experiment is repeated, with the same results obtained, the more confident we can be that the theory being tested is valid. The experimental method consists of standardised procedures and measures which allow it to be easily repeated.
4. It is also worth noting that an experiment yields quantitative data (numerical amounts of something) which can be analysed using inferential statistical tests. These tests permit statements to be made about how likely the results are to have occurred through chance.

Limitations of Laboratory Experiments

Artificiality: The experiment is not typical of real life situations. Most experiments are conducted in laboratories-strange and contrived environments in which people are asked to perform unusual or even bizarre tasks. The artificiality of the lab, together with the 'unnatural' things that the subjects may be asked to do, jointly produces a distortion of behaviour. Therefore it should be difficult to generalise findings from experiments because they are not ecologically valid (true to real life).

Behaviour in the laboratory is very narrow in its range. By controlling the situation so precisely, behaviour may be very limited.

A major difficulty with the experimental method is demand characteristics. Some of the many confounding variables in a psychology experiment stem from the fact that a psychology experiment is a social situation in which neither the Subjects or the Experimenters are passive, inanimate objects but are active, thinking human beings. Imagine you've been asked to take part in a psychology experiment. Even if you didn't study psychology, you would be trying to work out what the experimenter expected to find out. Experimenters too have expectations about what their results are likely to be. Demand characteristics are all the cues which convey to the participant the purpose of the experiment.

The experimental method as used in psychology has a history of using biased or unrepresentative sampling. George Miller (1962) estimated that 90% of U.S. experiments have used college students (who are accessible and 'cheap') and yet the results still tend to be generalised to the U.S. population as a whole, and often beyond that to Britain, Western Europe, etc. But there is no reason to believe that U.S. college students are typical of any other group in terms of gender, age, personality, social class background or any other subject variable which can influence how subjects will perform in any experimental situation. What's more, these students are often psychology students who are required to participate in research as a course requirement!

It has already been noted that a strength of the experimental method is the amount of control which experimenters have over variables. However it must also be noted that it is not possible to completely control all variables. There may be other variables at work which the experimenter is unaware of. In particular, it is impossible to completely control the mental world of people taking part in a study.

A very major problem with the experimental method concerns ethics. For example, experiments nearly always involve deceiving participants to some extent and the very term 'subject' implies that the participant is being treated as something less than a person. Recently the use of the experimental method has come under considerable criticism for the way that researchers often break ethical guidelines. It is also important to recognise that there are very many areas of human life which cannot be studied using the experimental method because it would be simply too unethical to do so.

Another issue is to do with normative data. Some researchers consider that an important advantage which experiments have over, say, observational techniques is the random assignment of research participants to experimental conditions. This helps to reduce the problems of analysis caused by systematic differences between people. Other psychologists, however, argue that grouping people together in this way, and trying to cancel out individual differences so that we only look at a group norm, is limited in how much it can tell us because it ignores what is special about people.

Mainly because of the above limitations psychologists are increasingly more likely to use other non-experimental methods- and in particular more qualitative methods.

THE FIELD EXPERIMENT

Sometimes it is possible to carry out experiments in a more natural setting, i.e. in 'the field '. A famous example of this is the series of studies carried out by Piliavin et al (1969) in which they arranged for a person to collapse on an underground train and waited to see how long it was before the person was helped. One of the independent variables they used was the appearance of the 'victim': whether he was carrying a walking stick or whether he appeared to be drunk.

As with the laboratory experiment, the independent variable is still deliberately manipulated by the researcher.

However it is not possible to have such tight control over variables in the field, but it does have the advantage of being far less artificial than the laboratory.

Natural Experiments

In some circumstances, psychologists can take advantage of a natural situation in order to carry out an investigation in circumstances which they cannot themselves manipulate. For example, a primary school may decide to try out a completely new reading scheme and the effects of this could be compared with a similar school using a different reading scheme. A local hospital may decide to have mixed wards rather than separate wards for men and women. The effects on the patients of being in these wards could be compared with those in single-sex wards.

This is not a true experiment because the psychologist is unable to manipulate or control variables. For this reason it is sometimes referred to as a quasi-experiment. It is possible, though to compare two groups, the equivalent of an experimental and a control group. It has the advantage that the participants are unaware that they are taking part in an investigation and it is certainly not as artificial as a laboratory setting.

11

Sampling Methodology

Event sampling methodology (ESM) is a new form of sampling method that allows researchers to study ongoing experiences and events that vary across and within days in its naturally-occurring environment. Because of the frequent sampling of events inherent in ESM, it enables researchers to measure the typology of activity and detect the temporal and dynamic fluctuations of work experiences. Popularity of ESM as a new form of research design increased over the recent years because it addresses the shortcomings of cross-sectional research, where once unable to, researchers can now detect intra-individual variances across time. In ESM, participants are asked to record their experiences and perceptions in a paper or electronic diary.

There are three types of ESM:

1. Signal contingent – random beeping notifies participants to record data. The advantage of this type of ESM is minimization of recall bias.
2. Event contingent – records data when certain events occur
3. Interval contingent – records data according to the passing of a certain period of time.

ESM has several disadvantages. One of the disadvantages of ESM is it can sometimes be perceived as invasive and intrusive by participants. ESM also leads to possible self-selection bias. It may be that only certain types of individuals are willing to participate in this type of study creating a non-random sample. Another concern is related to participant cooperation. Participants may not be actually fill out their diaries at the specified times. Furthermore, ESM may substantively change the phenomenon being studied. Reactivity or priming effects may occur, such that repeated measurement may cause changes in the participants' experiences. This method of sampling data is also highly vulnerable to common method variance.

Further, it is important to think about whether or not an appropriate dependent variable is being used in an ESM design. For example, it might be logical to use ESM in order to answer research questions which involve dependent variables with a great deal of variation throughout the day. Thus, variables such as change in mood, change in stress level, or the immediate impact of particular events may be best studied using ESM methodology. However, it is not likely that utilizing ESM will yield meaningful predictions when measuring someone performing a repetitive task throughout the day or when dependent variables are long-term in nature (coronary heart problems).

REPLACEMENT OF SELECTED UNITS

Sampling schemes may be *without replacement* ('WOR'-no element can be selected more than once in the same sample) or *with replacement* ('WR'-an element may appear multiple times in the one sample). For example, if we catch fish, measure them, and immediately return them to the water before continuing with the sample, this is a WR design, because we might end up catching and measuring the same fish more than once. However, if we do not return the fish to the water (e.g. if we eat the fish), this becomes a WOR design.

Sample Size

Formulas, tables, and power function charts are well known approaches to determine sample size.

Formulas

Where the frame and population are identical, statistical theory yields exact recommendations on sample size. However, where it is not straightforward to define a frame representative of the population, it is more important to understand the cause system of which the population are outcomes and to ensure that all sources of variation are embraced in the frame. Large number of observations are of no value if major sources of variation are neglected in the study. In other words, it is taking a sample group that matches the survey category and is easy to survey. Bartlett, Kotrlik, and Higgins (2001) published a paper titled *Organizational Research: Determining Appropriate Sample Size* in Survey Research Information Technology, Learning, and Performance Journal that provides an explanation of Cochran's (1977) formulas. A discussion and illustration of sample size formulas, including the formula for adjusting the sample size for smaller populations, is included. A table is provided that can be used to select the sample size for a research problem based on three alpha levels and a set error rate.

Steps for Using Sample Size Tables

1. Postulate the effect size of interest, á, and b.
2. Check sample size table
1. Select the table corresponding to the selected á
2. Locate the row corresponding to the desired power
3. Locate the column corresponding to the estimated effect size.
4. The intersection of the column and row is the minimum sample size required.

Sampling and Data Collection

Good data collection involves:

- Following the defined sampling process
- Keeping the data in time order
- Noting comments and other contextual events
- Recording non-responses.

Most sampling books and papers written by non-statisticians focus only in the data collection aspect, which is just a small though important part of the sampling process.

Errors in Sample Surveys

Survey results are typically subject to some error. Total errors can be classified into sampling errors and non-sampling errors. The term "error" here includes systematic biases as well as random errors.

Sampling Errors and Biases

Sampling errors and biases are induced by the sample design. They include:

1. Selection bias: When the true selection probabilities differ from those assumed in calculating the results.
2. Random sampling error: Random variation in the results due to the elements in the sample being selected at random.

Non-sampling Error

Non-sampling errors are caused by other problems in data collection and processing. They include:

1. Overcoverage: Inclusion of data from outside of the population.
2. Undercoverage: Sampling frame does not include elements in the population.
3. Measurement error: E.g. when respondents misunderstand a question, or find it difficult to answer.
4. Processing error: Mistakes in data coding.
5. Non-response: Failure to obtain complete data from all selected individuals.

After sampling, a review should be held of the exact process followed in sampling, rather than that intended, in order to study any effects that any divergences might have on subsequent analysis. A particular problem is that of *non-response*.

Two major types of nonresponse exist: unit nonresponse (referring to lack of completion of any part of the survey) and item nonresponse (submission or participation in survey but failing to complete one or more components/questions of the survey). In survey sampling, many of the individuals identified as part of the sample may be unwilling to participate, not have the time to participate (opportunity cost), or survey administrators may not have been able to contact them. In this case, there is a risk of differences, between respondents and nonrespondents, leading to biased estimates of population parameters.

This is often addressed by improving survey design, offering incentives, and conducting follow-up studies which make a repeated attempt to contact the unresponsive and to characterize their similarities and differences with the rest of the frame. The effects can also be mitigated by weighting the data when population benchmarks are available or by imputing data based on answers to other questions.

Nonresponse is particularly a problem in internet sampling. Reasons for this problem include improperly designed surveys, over-surveying (or survey fatigue), and the fact that potential participants hold multiple e-mail addresses, which they don't use anymore or don't check regularly. Web-based surveys also tend to demonstrate nonresponse bias; for example, studies have shown that females and those from a white/Caucasian background are more likely to respond than their counterparts.

SAMPLING (STATISTICS)

Sampling is that part of statistical practice concerned with the selection of a subset of individual observations within a population of individuals intended to yield some knowledge about the population of concern, especially for the purposes of making predictions based on statistical inference. Sampling is an important aspect of data collection.

Researchers rarely survey the entire population for two reasons : the cost is too high, and the population is dynamic in that the individuals making up the population may change over time.

The three main advantages of sampling are that the cost is lower, data collection is faster, and since the data set is smaller it is possible to ensure homogeneity and to improve the accuracy and quality of the data.

Each observation measures one or more properties (such as weight, location, colour) of observable bodies distinguished as independent objects or individuals. In survey sampling, survey weights can be applied to the data to adjust for the sample design. Results from probability theory and statistical theory are employed to guide practice. In business and medical research, sampling is widely used for gathering information about a population.

Process

The sampling process comprises several stages:

- Defining the population of concern
- Specifying a sampling frame, a set of items or events possible to measure
- Specifying a sampling method for selecting items or events from the frame
- Determining the sample size
- Implementing the sampling plan
- Sampling and data collecting.

Population Definition

Successful statistical practice is based on focused problem definition. In sampling, this includes defining the population from which our sample is drawn. A population can be defined as including all people or items with the characteristic one wishes to understand. Because there is very rarely enough time or money to gather information from everyone or everything in a population, the goal becomes finding a representative sample (or subset) of that population.

Sometimes that which defines a population is obvious. For example, a manufacturer needs to decide whether a batch of material from production is of high enough quality to be released to the customer, or should be sentenced for scrap or rework due to poor quality. In this case, the batch is the population.

Although the population of interest often consists of physical objects, sometimes we need to sample over time, space, or some combination of these dimensions. For instance, an investigation of supermarket staffing could examine checkout line length at various times, or a study on endangered penguins might aim to understand their usage of various hunting grounds over time. For the time dimension, the focus may be on periods or discrete occasions.

In other cases, our 'population' may be even less tangible. For example, Joseph Jagger studied the behaviour of roulette wheels at a casino in Monte Carlo, and used this to identify a biased wheel. In this case, the 'population' Jagger wanted to investigate was the overall behaviour of the wheel (i.e. the probability distribution of its results over infinitely many trials), while his 'sample' was formed from observed results from that wheel. Similar considerations arise when taking repeated measurements of some physical characteristic such as the electrical conductivity of copper.

This situation often arises when we seek knowledge about the cause system of which the *observed* population is an outcome. In such cases, sampling theory may treat the observed population as a sample from a larger 'superpopulation'. For example, a researcher might study the success rate of a new 'quit smoking' program on a test group of 100 patients, in order to predict the effects of the program if it were made available nationwide. Here the superpopulation is "everybody in the country, given access to this treatment"-a group which does not yet exist, since the program isn't yet available to all.

Note also that the population from which the sample is drawn may not be the same as the population about which we actually want information. Often there is large but not complete overlap between these two groups due to frame issues etc. Sometimes they may be entirely separate-for instance, we might study rats in order to get a better understanding of human health, or we might study records from people born in 2008 in order to make predictions about people born in 2009.

Time spent in making the sampled population and population of concern precise is often well spent, because it raises many issues, ambiguities and questions that would otherwise have been overlooked at this stage.

Sampling Frame

In the most straightforward case, such as the sentencing of a batch of material from production (acceptance sampling by lots), it is possible to identify and measure every single item in the population and to include any one of them in our sample. However, in the more general case this is not possible. There is no way to identify all rats in the set of all rats. Where voting is not compulsory, there is no way to identify which people will actually vote at a forthcoming election (in advance of the election). These imprecise populations are not amenable to sampling in any of the ways below and to which we could apply statistical theory. As a remedy, we seek a *sampling frame* which has the property that we can identify every single element and include any in our sample. The most straightforward type of frame is a list of elements of the population (preferably the entire population) with appropriate contact information. For example, in an opinion poll, possible sampling frames include:

- Electoral register
- Telephone directory.

Not all frames explicitly list population elements. For example, a street map can be used as a frame for a door-to-door survey; although it doesn't show individual houses, we can select streets from the map and then visit all houses on those streets.

The sampling frame must be representative of the population and this is a question outside the scope of statistical theory demanding the judgment of experts in the particular subject matter being studied. All the above frames omit some people who will vote at the next election and contain some people who will not; some frames will contain multiple records for the same person. People not in the frame have no prospect of being sampled. Statistical theory tells us about the uncertainties in extrapolating from a sample to the frame. In extrapolating from frame to population, its role is motivational and suggestive.

To the scientist, however, representative sampling is the only justified procedure for choosing individual objects for use as the basis of generalization, and is therefore usually the only acceptable basis for ascertaining truth. —Andrew A. Marino

It is important to understand this difference to steer clear of confusing prescriptions found in many web pages.

In defining the frame, practical, economic, ethical, and technical issues need to be addressed. The need to obtain timely results may prevent extending the frame far into the future.

The difficulties can be extreme when the population and frame are disjoint. This is a particular problem in forecasting where inferences about the future are made from historical data. In fact, in 1703, when Jacob Bernoulli proposed to Gottfried Leibniz the possibility of using historical mortality data to predict the probability of early death of a living man, Gottfried Leibniz recognized the problem in replying:

Nature has established patterns originating in the return of events but only for the most part. New illnesses flood the human race, so that no matter how many experiments you have done on corpses, you have not thereby imposed a limit on the nature of events so that in the future they could not vary. —Gottfried Leibniz

Kish posited four basic problems of sampling frames:

1. Missing elements: Some members of the population are not included in the frame.
2. Foreign elements: The non-members of the population are included in the frame.
3. Duplicate entries: A member of the population is surveyed more than once.
4. Groups or clusters: The frame lists clusters instead of individuals.

A frame may also provide additional 'auxiliary information' about its elements; when this information is related to variables or groups of interest, it may be used to improve survey design. For instance, an electoral register might include name and sex; this information can be used to ensure that a sample taken from that frame covers all demographic categories of interest.

(Sometimes the auxiliary information is less explicit; for instance, a telephone number may provide some information about location.)

Having established the frame, there are a number of ways for organizing it to improve efficiency and effectiveness.

It's at this stage that the researcher should decide whether the sample is in fact to be the whole population and would therefore be a census.

PROBABILITY AND NONPROBABILITY SAMPLING

A probability sampling scheme is one in which every unit in the population has a chance (greater than zero) of being selected in the sample, and this probability can be accurately determined. The combination of these traits makes it possible to produce unbiased estimates of population totals, by weighting sampled units according to their probability of selection.

Example: We want to estimate the total income of adults living in a given street. We visit each household in that street, identify all adults living there, and randomly select one adult from each household. (For example, we can allocate each person a random number, generated from a uniform distribution between 0 and 1, and select the person with the highest number in each household). We then interview the selected person and find their income. People living on their own are certain to be selected, so we simply add their income to our estimate of the total. But a person living in a household of two adults has only a one-in-two chance of selection. To reflect this, when we come to such a household, we would count the selected person's income twice towards the total. (In effect, the person who is selected from that household is taken as representing the person who isn't *selected.)*

In the above example, not everybody has the same probability of selection; what makes it a probability sample is the fact that each person's probability is known. When every element in the population *does* have the same probability of selection, this is known as an 'equal probability of selection' (EPS) design. Such designs are also referred to as 'self-weighting' because all sampled units are given the same weight. Probability sampling includes: Simple Random Sampling, Systematic Sampling, Stratified Sampling, Probability Proportional to Size Sampling, and Cluster or Multistage Sampling. These various ways of probability sampling have two things in common:

1. Every element has a known nonzero probability of being sampled and
2. involves random selection at some point.

Nonprobability sampling is any sampling method where some elements of the population have *no* chance of selection (these are sometimes referred to as 'out of coverage'/ 'undercovered'), or where the probability of selection can't be accurately determined.

It involves the selection of elements based on assumptions regarding the population of interest, which forms the criteria for selection. Hence, because the selection of elements is nonrandom, nonprobability sampling does not allow the estimation of sampling errors. These conditions give rise to exclusion bias, placing limits on how much information a sample can provide about the population. Information about the relationship between sample and population is limited, making it difficult to extrapolate from the sample to the population.

Example: We visit every household in a given street, and interview the first person to answer the door. In any household with more than one occupant, this is a nonprobability sample, because some people are more likely to answer the door (e.g. an unemployed person who spends most of their time at home is more likely to answer than an employed housemate who might be at work when the interviewer calls) and it's not practical to calculate these probabilities.

Nonprobability Sampling includes: Accidental Sampling, Quota Sampling and Purposive Sampling. In addition, nonresponse effects may turn *any* probability design into a nonprobability design if the characteristics of nonresponse are not well understood, since nonresponse effectively modifies each element's probability of being sampled.

Sampling Methods

Within any of the types of frame identified above, a variety of sampling methods can be employed, individually or in combination. Factors commonly influencing the choice between these designs include:

- Nature and quality of the frame
- Availability of auxiliary information about units on the frame
- Accuracy requirements, and the need to measure accuracy
- Whether detailed analysis of the sample is expected
- Cost/operational concerns.

Simple Random Sampling

In a simple random sample ('SRS') of a given size, all such subsets of the frame are given an equal probability. Each element of the frame thus has an equal probability of selection: the frame is not subdivided or partitioned. Furthermore, any given *pair* of elements has the same chance of selection as any other such pair (and similarly for triples, and so on). This minimises bias and simplifies analysis of results. In particular, the variance between individual results within the sample is a good indicator of variance in the overall population, which makes it relatively easy to estimate the accuracy of results.

However, SRS can be vulnerable to sampling error because the randomness of the selection may result in a sample that doesn't reflect the makeup of the population. For instance, a simple random sample of ten people from a given country will *on average* produce five men and five women, but any given trial is likely to overrepresent one sex and underrepresent the other.

SRS may also be cumbersome and tedious when sampling from an unusually large target population. In some cases, investigators are interested in research questions specific to subgroups of the population. For example, researchers might be interested in examining whether cognitive ability as a predictor of job performance is equally applicable across racial groups. SRS cannot accommodate the needs of researchers in this situation because it does not provide subsamples of the population.

Simple random sampling is always an EPS design, but not all EPS designs are simple random sampling.

Systematic Sampling

Systematic sampling relies on arranging the target population according to some ordering scheme and then selecting elements at regular intervals through that ordered list. Systematic sampling involves a random start and then proceeds with the selection of every *k*th element from then onwards. In this case, k=(population size/sample size).

It is important that the starting point is not automatically the first in the list, but is instead randomly chosen from within the first to the *k*th element in the list. A simple example would be to select every 10th name from the telephone directory (an 'every 10th' sample, also referred to as 'sampling with a skip of 10').

As long as the starting point is randomized, systematic sampling is a type of probability sampling. It is easy to implement and the stratification induced can make it efficient, *if* the variable by which the list is ordered is correlated with the variable of interest. 'Every 10th' sampling is especially useful for efficient sampling from databases.

Example: Suppose we wish to sample people from a long street that starts in a poor district (house #1) and ends in an expensive district (house #1000). A simple random selection of addresses from this street could easily end up with too many from the high end and too few from the low end (or vice versa), leading to an unrepresentative sample. Selecting (e.g.) every 10th street number along the street ensures that the sample is spread evenly along the length of the street, representing all of these districts. (Note that if we always start at house #1 and end at #991, the sample is slightly biased towards the low end; by randomly selecting the start between #1 and #10, this bias is eliminated.)

However, systematic sampling is especially vulnerable to periodicities in the list. If periodicity is present and the period is a multiple or factor of the interval used, the sample is especially likely to be *un*representative of the overall population, making the scheme less accurate than simple random sampling.

Example: Consider a street where the odd-numbered houses are all on the north (expensive) side of the road, and the even-numbered houses are all on the south (cheap) side. Under the sampling scheme given above, it is impossible' to get a representative sample; either the houses sampled will all *be from the odd-numbered, expensive side, or they will* all *be from the even-numbered, cheap side.*

Another drawback of systematic sampling is that even in scenarios where it is more accurate than SRS, its theoretical properties make it difficult to *quantify* that accuracy. (In the two examples of systematic sampling that are given above, much of the potential sampling error is due to variation between neighbouring houses-but because this method never selects two neighbouring houses, the sample will not give us any information on that variation.)

As described above, systematic sampling is an EPS method, because all elements have the same probability of selection (in the example given, one in ten). It is *not* 'simple random sampling' because different subsets of the same size have different selection probabilities-e.g. the set {4,14,24,...,994} has a one-in-ten probability of selection, but the set {4,13,24,34,...} has zero probability of selection.

Bibliography

Agrawal, Arvind : *Max Weber and Modern Sociological Theories*, Rawat, 2000.

Arya, R.P. : *Training for Social Work and Rural Development*, Manglam, Delhi, 2007.

Babbie, E.R.: *Survey research methods*. Belmont, CA: Wadsworth, 1973.

Bajpai, R B : *Research Methodology : Data Presentation*, APH, 2007.

Berger, P., & Luckman, T.: *The social construction of reality*. London: Penguin, 1967.

Brannen, J.: *Mixing methods: Qualitative and quantitative research*. London: Avebury, 1992.

Bryman, A.: *Quality and quantity in social research*. London: Unwin Hyman, 1992.

Choudhary, Shanker : *Encyclopaedia of Research Methodology in Social Sciences and Humanities*, Anmol, Delhi, 2009.

Christopher Scott: *The World Fertility Survey: An Assessment*. Oxford: Oxford University Press, 1987.

Dasgupta, Manas: *Research Methodology in Economics : Problems and Issues*, Deep and Deep, 2007.

Denzin, N.: *The research act in sociology*. London: Butterworth, 1970.

Denzin, N.: *The research act: A theoretical introduction to sociological methods*. Chicago: Aldine Press, 1967.

Diwan, Jagmohan: *Fundamentals of Rural Sociology*, Cyber Tech Pub, Delhi, 2009.

Fowler, Floyd J., : *Survey Research Methods* (2nd.). Newbury Park, CA: Sage, 1993.

Fox, J. & Tracy, P.: *Randomized Response: A Method for Sensitive Surveys*. Beverly Hills, CA: Sage, 1986.

Garg, Ajit Lal : *An Introduction to Research Methodology*, RBSA Pub, 2002.

Gupta, Sudhir: *Workshop on Research Methodology*, Centrum Press, 2011.

Iqbal, Azhar : *Principles and Practices of Social Work*, Sublime, Delhi, 2005.

Kalton, Graham: *Introduction to Survey Sampling.* Beverly Hills, CA: Sage, 1983.

Kanti Bagchi: *Research Methodology in Social Sciences: A Practical Guide*, Abhijeet Pub, 2007.

Karthikeyan, C. : *Behavioural Research Methodology*, Classical, 2004.

Kumar, Ajit : *Social Work Concerns and Challenges in the 21 Century*, APH, Delhi, 2009.

Maxwell, J. A.: *Qualitative research design: An interactive approach.* Thousand Oaks, CA: Sage Publishing, 1996.

Mittal, Kapila: *Research Methodology in Social Sciences*, Vista International, 2006.

Mujawar, W.R. : *Research Methodology in Social Work*, Manglam Publications, 2010.

Narender K. Chadha: *Research Methods for Sports Scientists*, Friends, 2001.

Neelam, Sandhya: *Research Methodology in Sociological Research*, Manglam Pub, Delhi, 2008.

Oommen, T.K. : *Knowledge and Society : Situating Sociology and Social Anthropology*, Oxford University Press, London, 2007.

Pearl, Raymond: *The Natural History of Population.* London. Oxford University Press, 1939.

Trochim, W.: *The Research Methods Knowledge Base.* Ithaca, NY: Cornell Custom Publishing, 1999.

Whelpton, Pascal K.: *Social and Psychological Factors Affecting Fertility,* New York: Milbank Memorial Fund, 1946.

Index

O

P

Q

R

S

T

❑❑❑